D0772796

About the Authors

Richard Bolling is a Democratic congressman from Missouri. One of the most powerful and wisest people in Congress, he heads the House Rules Committee.

John Bowles is an investment banker and an astute observer of how things get accomplished in government, business, labor, academia, and the media.

AMERICA'S
COMPETITI
EDGE

AMERICA'S COMPETITIVE EDGE

How to Get Our Country Moving Again

Richard Bolling
Chairman, House Committee on Rules
U.S. Congress

John Bowles
Investment Banker
Kidder, Peabody & Company

McGraw-Hill Book Company
New York   St. Louis   San Francisco   Auckland   Bogotá
Hamburg   Johannesburg   London   Madrid   Mexico
Montreal   New Delhi   Panama   Paris   São Paulo
Singapore   Sydney   Tokyo   Toronto

Library of Congress Cataloging in Publication Data
Bolling, Richard Walker, date
   America's competitive edge.

   Includes bibliographical references and index.
   1. United States—Economic policy—1971–
I. Bowles, John, date. II. Title.
HC106.7.B66   338.973   81–3794
ISBN 0–07–006438–5 AACR2

ISBN 0-07-006438-5

1 2 3 4 5 6 7 8 9 0   DODO   8 9 8 7 6 5 4 3 2

The editors for this book were William A. Sabin, Gail T. Hodges, and Christine M.
Ulwick, the designer was Eliot Epstein, and the production supervisor was Paul A.
Malchow. It was set in Garamond by ComCom.

Printed and bound by R.R. Donnelley & Sons Company.

We dedicate this book to the unborn generation.
May they have an America to inherit.

CONTENTS

FOREWORD

By now the American people are well aware that this nation has plunged itself into an economic mess. They certainly don't need another economist to tell them that or another book purporting to explain how to survive the coming terrible times. What they do need is some precise knowledge about why they're in the mess they're in, and something more than vague phrases about how to get out of it.

Finally, here is a pair of authors, one from the halls of Congress, the other from the world of Wall Street, with no strange new ideology to sell us. What they have produced is a dispassionate and fully documented examination of why things once worked so well in this country and why they don't now.

Their starting point may seem a surprise—the creation of the Marshall Plan and the Hoover Commission and the passage of the Employment Act and the Eisenhower highway program. But if those decisions played a central role in the long economic prosperity that followed, the consensus building that made them possible also holds some important lessons for today's troubled and uncertain policymakers.

Somehow, in the last two decades, that consensus has slipped away. Instead, policymakers appear at times paralyzed by single-issue pressure groups, few of which have any broad general backing. Most people agreed that the country needed a tough energy policy, and some said it didn't matter what program as long as there was one. Yet one group canceled out another, and energy policy remained for too long both uncertain and conflicting.

Somehow in that same period, American business began paying more attention to immediate profit and loss statements, to what it took to keep the stock price high today. In the process, they penalized their future operations, fell behind foreign competitors, and then began screaming to Washington for relief.

How bad will it get before new leadership emerges? To some

pessimists, it is already too late. But Messrs. Bolling and Bowles are not among them. This is not a book to send folks into the bomb shelters. It is on the whole an optimistic book, with the optimism well grounded on the firm policy recommendations with which they conclude. Theirs is an achievable, sustainable program, of the sort this nation has not seen in recent years. It is neither a liberal nor a conservative program; it relies on no unusual assumptions about economic theory. To the contrary, it is a call for coalition building, for bringing back into being the cooperative spirit which led America to its position of leadership—and which, significantly, now so dominates and propels the amazing Japanese economy.

Simply put, this book does not exhort or attempt to frighten. Rather, it focuses the issues better than they've been focused before. Hopefully, the time has come for the nation's political leaders to conduct their politicking in the national interest. Hopefully, American corporate management is on the verge of shaking itself from the infirmities of nearsightedness. This book should be a guide for them and for the American public from which the pressure for change must come.

John F. Lawrence
Assistant Managing Editor for Economic Affairs
Los Angeles Times

INTRODUCTION

In late April 1980, about 150 men and women met at Harvard University to exchange ideas about our declining economic position at home and abroad. The assemblage included members of both houses of Congress, senior business executives, academics, and a very few representatives of labor.

What had happened to bring us together? The answer is: individuals and issues. My colleague, Professor Ezra Vogel, had written a book with the arresting title *Japan As Number One* in which he not only praised Japanese efficiency but also suggested that the time had come for Americans to look beyond our frontiers for ideas and practices. William M. Batten, the chairman of the New York Stock Exchange, read the book and found that it matched many of his concerns. The same was true of Senator Abraham Ribicoff, the chairman of the Subcommittee on International Trade of the Senate.

My own feelings were very similar. As the dean of Harvard's Faculty of Arts and Sciences, responsible for an annual budget of about $150 million, I watched with increasing frustration the erosion of our endowments through inflation, declines in real income for our faculty and staff, and rising tuition costs that placed enormous pressures on parents and students. It was entirely obvious that our position could only be changed by a vast improvement in the general state of health of the American economy. Furthermore, as someone who had lived in Japan for five years in the 1950s and 1960s—as both student and teacher—I also knew how far we had slipped in a variety of crucial areas. And as an economic historian, I had some sense of the long run and its lessons, namely, the dangers of economic decline.

For all of these reasons, then, it seemed appropriate that a meeting be held to consider how our economy might regain its health and its competitive vigor. Here is some of what I said at the opening session at Harvard:

People from different walks of life are assembled here to ask a question that some will consider astonishing and others frightening: Can the United States remain competitive? That this question even has to be asked certainly is regrettable; that it is being asked is a hopeful sign. Becoming less competitive may be the symptom of a serious national disease. If recognized, analyzed, and understood, one can perhaps suggest some remedies.

Just for a moment, look back at the world one century ago—really not such a very long time in historical terms. In the 1880s, Great Britain was, by a considerable margin, the leading industrial power in the world. The Industrial Revolution was born in Britain during the second half of the eighteenth century, and one hundred years later the British Empire was at its zenith.

In the 1880s, very few people realized that Britain's economic decline had already begun—that for a great variety of reasons, Britain would not remain competitive. The principal challengers were the United States and a recently united Germany. Russia also was becoming a factor in the world economy, although that development was effectively halted by the Communist Revolution. Japan had just opened herself to international contact after nearly 200 years of virtually total isolation. No one—except perhaps some Japanese— believed that Japan would ever be a major economic power, least of all the leading industrial power of the world: for that is what Japan is today.

Why this bit of history? Because I wish to stress a number of points.

1. Between the start of the Industrial Revolution in the eighteenth century and today, approximately twenty countries have experienced modern economic growth. New countries are joining the parade all the time, and the early industrializers—primarily Britain, France, and the United States—are continually facing new challengers. At present, the most rapidly growing area of the world is in northeast Asia, and it may be elsewhere in the future. The point is simple: remaining on top or in contention is not a static process.

2. It takes a long time to become aware of decline. Although most economic historians agree that Britain's climacteric occurred about one hundred years ago, this fact did not really become a matter of public concern until after World War I, and forty years of relative decline may have been an insurmountable obstacle.

3. Although a great many reasons have been given for Britain's economic decline, in my opinion the principal factors were internal and human, and therefore avoidable: British entrepreneurship had become flabby; growth and industries and new technology were not pursued with sufficient vigor; technical education and science were lagging; the government-business relationship was not one of mutual support.

When we look at our own country today in the perspective of history, the danger signals seem obvious. Productivity growth is slow; quality frequently is low; capital formation is inadequate; all too often the latest technology is not in use; in many parts of the world our export markets are deteriorating; and the communications gap between business, government, and the public is vast. These are the issues that have brought us together: government, business, labor, and the academy. We have not met, I think, to discuss partisan positions or to praise and blame anybody. We are seeking understanding and guidelines for a national consensus. This meeting may be only a small beginning, but I hope that it will have larger consequences.

There have, in fact, been a variety of consequences. Further meetings have been held in Washington, D.C., sponsored by the L.B.J. School of Public Affairs of the University of Texas and the Joint Economic Committee, and other regional gatherings are planned. The hope is to build a nonpartisan coalition, in and out of government, that will suggest policies for improved productivity and steady growth and press for their adoption.

However, one of the major consequences may be this book in which Messrs. Bolling and Bowles—in and out of government—attempt to trace the sources of our current predicament and to indicate a series of solutions. I do not expect that everyone will agree with all the arguments, but this certainly does not diminish the value of their efforts. This is a provocative book that provides much of the necessary background for all of us to participate intelligently in the national debate that is so badly needed. Let us remember, however, that the purpose of the exercise is not endless debate in which each one of us rigidly defends a narrow constituency. A new road has to be found and, as the authors point out, that will require all of us to compromise so that we can become a part of a strong coalition dedicated to continued social and economic progress.

Henry Rosovsky
Dean of the Faculty of Arts and Sciences
Harvard University

ACKNOWLEDGMENTS

We want to thank the diverse group of individuals who read and critiqued the original manuscript: John M. Albertine, president of the American Business Conference; William M. Batten, chairman of the New York Stock Exchange; Stuart E. Eisenstat, former assistant to President Carter for domestic affairs and policy; Donald F. Ephlin, vice president, United Auto Workers; Governor Averell Harriman; Janet Howard; Lawrence R. Klein, Nobel Laureate in economics; John F. Lawrence, assistant managing editor for economic affairs, the *Los Angeles Times;* Bruce K. MacLaury, president of The Brookings Institution; Henry Rosovsky, dean of the Faculty of Arts and Sciences, Harvard University; Dr. Ezra Vogel, the author of *Japan as Number One—Lessons for America;* and Lewis H. Young, editor in chief, *Business Week.*

We especially thank Richard F. Reynolds IV for his outstanding job of research; Louis C. Krauthoff II, director of the Joint Economic Committee's Special Study on Economic Change; Timothy Roth of the Joint Economic Committee staff; Gladys Uhl and Mary Elizabeth Menk for their detailed involvement with the development of the manuscript; and the many members of the Congressional Research Service who were so helpful to us in this project.

And, of course, we are indebted to our editors William A. Sabin and Gail T. Hodges for their astute ability to help us focus our material in a clear and readable way.

Finally, we thank Michael H. Trotter of the Atlanta law firm of Trotter, Bondurant, Griffin, Miller and Hishon for his help in the structuring of our contract with McGraw-Hill. That contract stipulates that the authors' royalties will go to a charity of McGraw-Hill's selection in order that we will gain no monetary benefits—directly or indirectly—from this joint effort in public policy advocacy.

Richard Bolling
John Bowles

1 FROM STRENGTH TO WEAKNESS TO STRENGTH

It had been a cold and brutal winter in Europe. The Second World War was over. The euphoria that accompanied its end had been replaced by a deeply unsettled peace. Europe was on the brink of economic disaster. Commerce between the cities and the agricultural areas had deteriorated badly. There was serious doubt that Western Europe had the manufacturing capability, the foreign exchange, or the social will to make it through another year. There was a sense of imminent collapse. And there was the specter of Russian communism and Stalin—a former ally—in the East. It was a sober time. A time for action, not reflection.[1]

THE MARSHALL PLAN AND EUROPE By spring a direction for action had crystalized. The Secretary of State went to Harvard to give a commencement speech on June 5, 1947. He was a man of Olympian stature. Even the President of the United States addressed him as "General Marshall." The man and the symbolism of a commencement —a beginning—from the American shore of the Atlantic were well chosen.[2]

General Marshall wore a plain civilian suit and spoke with modest language[3], but his message had profound implications:

The remedy lies in breaking the vicious circle and restoring the confidence of the European people in the economic future of their own countries and of Europe as a whole. . . . It is logical that the United States should do whatever it is able to do to assist in the return of normal economic health in the world, without which there can be no political stability and no assured peace.[4]

Then he stated the premise of the offered relationship. It would be one of assistance coupled with occasional diplomatic persuasion, but

1

it would not be one of forced and compulsory direction: "Any government that is willing to assist in the task of recovery will find full cooperation, I am sure, on the part of the United States government."[5]

The emphasis was to be on self-initiative and cooperation. Europeans themselves, with the assistance of Americans, would do the job of reconstruction. Marshall's speech reflected an obvious, but vital, understanding of human motivation. This understanding would set the tone of the relationship and be the principal reason for the success of the Marshall Plan.

Shortly thereafter, on June 22, the Harriman Committee (more formally known as the President's Committee on Foreign Aid) was established by President Truman. The Harriman Committee was an important step in building the coalition that would be critical to the development of the Marshall Plan, to the passage of enabling legislation on April 3, 1948, and to the revitalization of the Western European economy.

MACARTHUR AND JAPAN During the same period, General MacArthur was directing the reconstruction of Japan. Like Europe, Japan had been devastated by the war. Unlike Europe, it was an integrated nation with a people of common heritage.

With the Russians boxed out by Truman, MacArthur had become Japan's commander. To the surprise of many and the consternation of some, he moved with swift and liberal purpose toward achieving a three-phase objective of the Occupation: demilitarization, political reform, and economic revival. And all of the rebuilding was to be done through Japanese leadership.[6]

By April 1947, the MacArthur Constitution was in place. Among its principal reforms were the reduction of the Emperor to the position of figurehead, the empowering of the Diet as a law-making body, and the renouncing forever of war as a sovereign national right.[7]

At the end of 1945, industrial production in Japan was at 16 percent of its prewar level. With $2 billion in aid, Japan cut its imports from the United States in half within three years; in five years national income passed prewar levels.[8] With the signing of the treaty in San Francisco on September 8, 1951, Japan was on its way to becoming the world power in economics and trade that it is today.[9] As with Western Europe, recovery was to be accomplished by the Japanese themselves.

Thus the vision of two remarkable—though very different—generals set in motion post-World War II economic growth in the free world. Recovery was to be achieved by European and Japanese self-initiative and American aid and assistance.

THE BASIS OF STRENGTH IN POST-WORLD WAR II AMERICA
The Marshall Plan is a guide to the thesis of this book. It is one of several major public policies that should be considered if we are to look at where we had a competitive edge, where and how we went wrong in maintaining that edge, and how we might regain it. We were the strongest nation both militarily and economically immediately after World War II, we coasted into the sixties, we went into decline from 1965 to 1975, and we were economically weak as we entered the eighties. The basis of our strength in the post-World War II period illustrates that we can return to economic strength and regain our competitive edge.

The Marshall Plan   The Marshall Plan is a constructive example of how the United States can regain economic strength and a competitive edge for two reasons. First, it was the result of coalition building based on a spirit of *cooperation, compromise,* and *consensus* in America. Second, it worked because, as in the reconstruction plan for Japan, it was essentially a balanced economic policy that focused on both investment and consumption and was based on self-initiative and cooperation.

The Employment Act and the Hoover Commission   In addition to the Marshall Plan, two other public policies offer constructive examples of why America was strong in the immediate postwar era. The first is the Employment Act of 1946. It was based upon another simple but very powerful idea: jobs for all those willing to work, based on government economic policies to increase production and purchasing power. That idea caught the public interest and led to a postwar boom based primarily on automobile sales and housing expansion. Consumption led to jobs, which led to a rise in the standard of living, which in turn made more consumption possible. There was a continuous upward cycle of economic expansion of jobs and consumption and jobs and consumption.

There was, however, a flaw in the Employment Act of 1946. Because of the circumstances of the times and the legislative process itself, the act did not create a balanced economic policy. Productivity was not mentioned, and with supply constraints not the immediate problem, policymakers were not cautioned to keep a long-term watch on the supply side of the economic equation. Further, investment was not linked to job creation and full employment.

The Hoover Commission is the other public policy that provided a framework for a strong America. The overall major achievement of the first Hoover Commission was the positive establishment of the President as manager of the executive branch. It called for and institutionalized the possibility of strong Presidents. Policy-making decisions were centralized and operating decisions were decentralized, with a more orderly grouping of the functions of government into major departments and agencies.

The Hoover Commission resulted in the Reorganization Act of 1949, which President Truman used to strengthen the Presidency. He established an unbroken line of responsibility from the President to his department heads. This framework of government worked very well until the functional relationships between federal, state, and local governments were drastically altered in the decade 1965–1975.

Economic Strength: Trade, Energy, Productivity As we entered the fifties, America had a strong bipartisan foreign policy, a definite domestic economic policy, and a sound framework of government. We were also the world leaders in *trade, energy,* and *productivity.* These three key economic factors represented a triangle of strength supporting our economy. This strength gave us a competitive edge.

Trade In 1950, we were the major trading nation in the world, and we maintained that position throughout our period of economic strength. During the period 1951–1955, when world trade in exports averaged $85 billion, the United States's share was almost 18 percent. That strength in trade continued into the second half of the fifties. When world exports increased to an average of $113 billion in the period 1955–1960, the United States's share was almost 17 percent. Our merchandise trade balance was comfortably in the black in every year of the fifties. Even in steel—which would become our economic "Achilles heel"—our exports exceeded our imports until 1959.

Energy In 1950, we were the most powerful nation in energy in the world, and we maintained that position throughout our period of economic strength. Under Presidents Truman and Eisenhower, energy in the form of oil was recognized as a powerful factor in our economic life. Oil was clearly understood to be the energy source essential to manufacturing, housing, and consumer goods, particularly the automobile. Likewise, in the context of the Marshall Plan, oil was recognized as an important part of foreign policy.

The multinational oil companies were a surrogate presence of American economic and political power in the Mediterranean and the

Persian Gulf. The wartime government-business relationship of cooperation was enhanced in the postwar confrontation with Russia. It evolved into a government-business oil partnership, which led to American control of the world oil trade. This partnership was determined to assist third world nations to withstand the encroachment of communism by providing financial assistance to stabilize Arab governments. It provided secure supplies and stable prices for the United States and its allies and ensured the availability of raw materials essential for sound economic growth and a strong national defense.

By 1950, the major U.S. international oil companies, with U.S. government support, had exclusive control over Saudi-Arabian oil. By 1951, 98 percent of the world oil market was controlled by Standard Oil of California, Texaco, Exxon, Mobil, Gulf Oil, and two British-based companies, British Petroleum and Royal Dutch Shell.

Productivity In 1950, we were the most productive nation in the world. Productivity—output per worker—in the United States increased 7.9 percent against a consumer price index increase of 1.0 percent. Through both the Marshall Plan and the reconstruction of Japan, the United States—with the participation of U.S. labor in advisory positions—taught the lessons of productive investment. That investment would result in an increasing output. Because Europe and Japan were reconstructing their economies from a war-battered base, their productivity increases outpaced ours in the decade of the fifties. Our trend, however, was decidedly positive. For the entire period of our economic strength, our productivity increases exceeded our rate of inflation. It was not until 1967 that the consumer price index began its chronic increases in excess of productivity increases.

THE DECLINE OF AMERICAN ECONOMIC STRENGTH As the world approached the sixties, recovery in Europe and Japan was vigorously underway. From 1955 to 1960, output in manufacturing increased 35 percent in France, more than 50 percent in West Germany and Italy, and over 100 percent in Japan. Our policies in the world were working. The free world was gathering strength, and the war was becoming a distant memory.

However, the United States began to coast. The steel industry showed the first sign of our domestic and international economic complacency. There was a 116-day steel strike in 1959. Labor and management antagonism surfaced in this industry, imports increased to 4.4 million tons, exports dropped to 1.7 million tons, and steel trade went permanently into a deficit. The basic cost of finished steel from U.S.

mills rose above that of the Japanese and the differential continued, causing a long-term negative trend for the United States.

At the same time, an important change took place in energy. As a result of a world production increase and domestic import constraints, a glut in the supply of oil developed in 1959. The major international oil companies, because of their cooperative relationship with government, had a buyer's cartel position. A subtle shift away from a balance between national and corporate interest to a self-serving interest took place. In the spring of 1959 and again in August 1960, the majors cut the price paid for crude oil without consulting the producer countries. As a result of this unilateral lowering of producer-country revenues, the Organization of Petroleum Exporting Countries (OPEC) was formed in September 1960; when the world oil supply-and-demand situation reversed from glut to tightness, OPEC reversed the cartel power. That, of course, had dire consequences for the energy-dependent U.S. economy.

As the decade of the sixties opened, the forward momentum of the Marshall Plan in Europe and the MacArthur reconstruction in Japan gathered force. The United States, however, became complacent, riding an economic crest. The seeds of trade deterioration sprouted and the noose of energy dependence very slowly began to tighten, but still, little thought was given to productivity and the supply side of the economic equation.

Then came the era of the Great Society and the Vietnam war, the economic and social costs of which hastened our decline. When the Johnson-Nixon years ended in 1974, we had a weak economic triangle in trade, energy, and productivity. Our competitive edge was gone. As a result of the policies of the Johnson-Nixon decade, the strong and stable economic policy of the Truman-Eisenhower years had deteriorated into one of instability and confusion. It had become short-term oriented, with policymakers attempting demand-side trade-offs between the twin evils of inflation and unemployment, with stop-and-go policies to curtail and then expand consumption. Further, the functions of the levels of government within our federal system had become confused and blurred. Government had become ineffective.

When the Johnson-Nixon years ended, the spirit of cooperation, compromise, and consensus that had made the Marshall Plan possible were gone in America. Our post-World War II economic strength was also gone. In twenty-eight years, we had reversed our position. It was time to assess our standing and begin anew. But change is slow. As we entered the eighties, there was still much to be done in order to regain our previous position of strength.

HISTORY AS A GUIDE TO RENEWAL In this book, we will begin with an analysis of the foundations of stable growth in the postwar period by using four examples of public policies—the Marshall Plan, the Employment Act of 1946, the Hoover Commission, and the Eisenhower highway program (a by-product of the thrust of the Employment Act)—that were developed, enacted, and implemented in a period characterized by a spirit of cooperation, compromise, and consensus in America.

Then we will trace that stable growth to its downward turn and examine the deterioration process and the reasons for it. That analysis will set the stage for a detailed look at the economic triangle of trade, energy, and productivity. We will then examine additional components of the basic problems and their solutions—ingenuity, taxation, government regulation, and the steel and agricultural industries.

Finally, we will propose some solutions we believe will lead to a more balanced economic policy, a new rationalization of the federal government in its relationship to state and local governments, and a recharged economic system that will provide the environment in which we can regain our economic strength and competitive edge in the eighties. We will also describe how those solutions might be developed and implemented in an atmosphere of cooperation, compromise, and consensus.

2 OUR PERIOD OF STRENGTH

By 1950, the United States had developed and begun to implement enlightened economic and public policies, both at home and abroad, that continued our leadership position in the free world. The memories of the Great Depression and of World War II destruction were gradually being replaced by hope for stable world economic growth and peace in the major centers of the globe.

In the postwar period, our leadership position in the free world was based on the far-reaching positivism of the Marshall Plan, the strong commitment to job creation embodied in the Employment Act of 1946, and the rationalization and cohesiveness of government that flowed from the Hoover Commission. The foundation that made possible the legislation and implementation of these policies was a spirit of cooperation, compromise, and consensus that created coalitions of the diverse interests in America.

In this chapter, we will analyze the development and the importance of the Marshall Plan, the Employment Act, the Hoover Commission, and the Eisenhower highway program. These four public policies contributed to our competitive edge at a time when our society functioned coherently and when the trade-energy-productivity economic triangle was strong.

THE MARSHALL PLAN The Marshall Plan is a classic example of events, people, politics, policy, and follow-through coming together into a successful governmental policy. It is also a classic example of the building of an American coalition which had a deep and lasting impact on the world economy.

The primary conditions which led to the development of the Marshall Plan were the breakup of the relationship with the Soviet Union, the clear need to reconstruct Western Europe and stop the hostile advance of communism, and the necessity to end the occupation of West Germany in a manner compatible with the economic and political interests of the other Western European nations.

The Postwar Climate in Western Europe   In March 1947, the Big Four Council of Foreign Ministers met in Moscow. Two weeks before the meeting opened, the British had left a power vacuum in the eastern Mediterranean, and President Truman had moved in quickly with aid to Greece and Turkey. This was the first act in effecting the Truman Doctrine, designed to contain Stalin's thrust into Western Europe. The mood of the Moscow meeting was therefore reserved; but it came to a boiling point when Secretary of State Marshall met with Stalin and Foreign Minister Molotov privately. That meeting convinced Marshall that the Russians were not going to cooperate— or do anything else to lessen distress and tension in Europe.[1] He returned to the United States concerned that Europe would disintegrate if the United States failed to act. His concern precipitated action which a number of people—including President Truman—had been considering.

Marshall quickly brought George Kennan into the State Department to activate the Policy Planning Staff.[2] Kennan, Under Secretary of State Dean Acheson,* and Assistant Secretary William Clayton were the principal individuals who analyzed the deeply troubling situation and contributed to Marshall's Harvard speech, which of course had the complete backing of the President.

Breakup of the Relationship with the Soviet Union   The reaction to General Marshall's June 5 speech was quick and positive—principally in England, France, and Italy. On June 13, French Foreign Minister Georges Bidault invited his British counterpart, Ernest Bevin, to Paris to discuss the American proposal. Molotov was invited to join them, and on June 27, a Big Three conference began. According to Averell Harriman, Marshall took considerable risk in allowing the British and French to meet with the Russians without an American presence. He gambled that the Russians would reject cooperation. The Russian position was stated bluntly: "Ask the Americans how much money they want to contribute, and we'll divide it on the basis of those who have suffered the most."[3] The British and French held firm to Marshall's idea of a cooperative approach, and Molotov—after receiving a message, presumably from Stalin—abruptly broke off the talks and left

*Robert Lovett replaced Acheson on this team as Under Secretary in June 1947.

Paris. Now, as in Japan, the West could proceed with reconstruction unfettered by Russian involvement and interference. The breakup of the relationship with the Soviet Union turned out to be the first condition that led to the development of the Marshall Plan.

The Need to Reconstruct Western Europe   On July 3, Bevin and Bidault invited twenty-two other European nations to discuss a recovery plan. The Russians responded on July 6 with the formation of the Cominform and began to negotiate trade agreements with their satellites in Eastern Europe, agreements that became known as the Molotov Plan. The Russians characterized the Marshall Plan as an instrument for "world domination by American imperialism." This heightened the perception of the threat of communism on both sides of the Atlantic. On July 12, France and Britain were joined by Austria, Belgium, Denmark, Greece, Iceland, Ireland, Italy, Luxembourg, the Netherlands, Norway, Portugal, Sweden, Switzerland, and Turkey at the Sixteen-Power Conference in Paris.

The economic situation in Western Europe was dismal in 1947. The consumption of food was at about 80 percent of the prewar level. As a result, the labor force was undernourished. The war had dislocated labor and interrupted the training of skilled workers in new technologies for postwar agricultural and industrial development. The equipment that had escaped destruction was obsolete. There was a scarcity of basic materials—particularly of coal and steel. Inflation was severe: in France wholesale prices increased 80 percent in 1946. Foreign exchange reserves were almost gone.

This economic environment added a sense of urgency to the deliberations at the Sixteen-Power Conference. The participants set up the interim Committee of European Economic Cooperation (CEEC). Clayton headed a group of advisors from the U.S. State Department who were on hand to give what was characterized as "friendly aid and counsel." There was a clear recognition of the second condition which led to the development of the Marshall Plan: the need to reconstruct Western Europe and to stop the advance of communism.

The Need to End the Occupation of West Germany   In addition to these observable activities, there was a third condition which led to the development of the Marshall Plan: the need to end the occupation of West Germany. Behind the scenes in the United States, there were significant differences of opinion on this subject, primarily between the Departments of Defense and State. There was an institutional tug-of-war between the interests of postwar Germany and those of France. As the summer of 1947 unfolded, however, policy was shaped to reconcile the need to help Germany regain self-sufficiency with French demands for coal, security, and economic advantage.[4]

The CEEC Plan   After some tough bargaining and frank talk in August and September, the CEEC issued its European plan, a plan which had been implicitly called for by Secretary Marshall at Harvard. This compromise was a proposal for direct American economic aid to both Germany and those nations which had anticipated using German assets for their own postwar reconstruction.[5] Necessity had vanquished confrontation. Thus, the urgent need for German recovery and for the general reconstruction of Western Europe was addressed in a way that was politically acceptable in both the United States and Europe.

The CEEC plan proposed a four-year recovery program for the sixteen nations and West Germany, based on (1) a strong production effort in agriculture and industry, (2) the development of internal financial stability, (3) the establishment of a continuing organization to coordinate the cooperative effort, and (4) a resolution of the dollar problem through an expansion of trade. With "aid and counsel" from the State Department, the Europeans had done their part. The product of their efforts was now on the American table.

The American Coalition and Legislative Process   Meanwhile, that June, on the domestic side of the Atlantic, President Truman asked three committees to study various aspects of a proposal for European recovery that could win congressional approval. The Council of Economic Advisors, under Chairman Edwin G. Nourse, analyzed the impact of the anticipated program on the U.S. economy. The Krug Committee, chaired by Secretary of the Interior Julius A. Krug, assessed the ability of the United States to provide the resources necessary for the program to work. The President's Committee on Foreign Aid, chaired by Secretary of Commerce W. Averell Harriman and known as the Harriman Committee, analyzed the principles, policies, magnitude of aid, and financing needed for a program for European recovery.[6]

The Harriman Committee   The Harriman Committee was by far the most important of the three committees. It was the substantive and political driving force behind the actual shaping of the American part of the Marshall Plan. And it was an example of effective coalition building.

At the very beginning, Senator Arthur Vandenberg, Republican chairman of the Senate Foreign Relations Committee, was brought into the process. At a small bipartisan meeting at the White House on

June 22, Vandenberg suggested an advisory council, and Acheson took the lead in organizing it. The President readily accepted Vandenberg's suggestion of former Senator Robert M. LaFollette, Jr., of Wisconsin as a member. The process of building a coalition had begun. From this bipartisan meeting would develop a major coalition.[7]

The Harriman Committee consisted of twenty prominent Americans. It had regional diversity. And it had the elements essential for an American coalition: academia, business, government, labor. The composition of the Harriman Committee represented the range of thoughts, viewpoints, and threads of contact to various groups of Americans that would ultimately be brought together in the final stages of the coalition that made the Marshall Plan possible.

THE PRESIDENT'S COMMITTEE ON FOREIGN AID[8]

Academia	Business and Finance	Government	Labor
Robert Earle Buchanan Iowa State College	Hiland Batcheller Allegheny-Ludlum Steel Corp.	W. Averell Harriman Chairman Robert M.	James B. Carey CIO George Meany AFL
Melville F. Coolbaugh Colorado School of Mines	W. Randolph Burgess National City Bank of N.Y.	LaFollette, Jr. Former Senator Harold G.	
Calvin B. Hoover Duke University	John L. Collyer B. F. Goodrich Co.	Moulton The Brookings Institution	
Edward S. Mason Harvard University	Granville Conway Cosmopolitan Shipping Co. Inc.		
William I. Myers Cornell University	Chester C. Davis Federal Reserve Bank, St. Louis		
Robert Gordon Sproul University of California	R. R. Deupree Procter & Gamble Co.		
	Paul G. Hoffman Studebaker Corp.		
	Robert Koenig Ayrshire Collieries Co.		
	Owen D. Young General Electric		

Richard M. Bissell, Jr., executive secretary of the Harriman Committee, analyzed the group this way: "That body itself was the beginning. It was the beginning of a coalition of social groups in the United States that really characterized the whole history of the Marshall Plan."[9] One of the principals was Paul Hoffman, the head of Studebaker, a founder of the Committee for Economic Development, and a Republican business executive with a considerable influence on Vandenberg. Hoffman, as well as LaFollette and James B. Carey of the CIO—who both played major roles in the successful development of the Harriman report—had the capacity for altruism, as well as concern for the national interest. Concern for the interests of others and of the nation itself would be the driving force that would arouse the American people and develop the momentum behind the Marshall Plan.

The report of the Harriman Committee stressed that any aid program was to be cooperative. Among its conclusions were the following:

1. The hope of Western Europe depends primarily on the industry and straight thinking of its own people.

2. The United States has a vital interest—humanitarian, economic, strategic, and political—in helping the participating countries to achieve economic recovery.

3. The extension of such aid calls for . . . a new agency to administer the aid. . . . [10]

Interdepartmental Effort   While the Harriman Committee prepared its report, Under Secretary of State Robert A. Lovett coordinated an interdepartmental effort in the executive branch. This effort was two-pronged: part consisted of supporting the Harriman, Nourse, and Krug committees, and part was directed to converting the general concept of Marshall's speech into a specific program for presentation to Congress.

The Herter Committee   The concurrent activity of the Herter Committee was also crucial to the successful development of the legislation. On July 29, the House created a select committee to study Marshall's proposal. Republican Congressman Christian A. Herter, its vice chairman, was designated to head the group on a fact-finding mission in Europe. The committee included a geographic and political cross section of the House. Its members traveled extensively and studied the plight of Western Europe in depth, both through conversations with individuals from all walks of life and technical information compiled by the committee staff. There developed among the committee members a deep personal interest in and an understanding of the conditions in Europe and the necessity for action. As a result, both the problems and the proposed program were discussed widely by committee members with members of Congress and with the American people at large.

The Legislative Process By early November, separate actions here and in Europe came together in a basic agreement. The CEEC report, the findings of President Truman's three committees, the effort headed by Lovett, and the work of the Herter Committee channeled information into the legislative process that would begin in January 1948. In preparation for those deliberations, President Truman, on December 19, sent to Congress "A Program for United States Support to European Recovery." He made it clear that the program was to be motivated by idealism and basic national interest: "Our deepest concern with the European recovery is that it is essential to the maintenance of the civilization in which the American way of life is rooted."[11]

The year 1948 was a presidential election year. The Republican-controlled Eightieth Congress was clearly gunning for Harry Truman. However, a broad-based coalition had been formed in preparing for the Marshall Plan legislation, and this issue of profound international importance was raised above the campaign's political infighting. Three factors caused isolationists and internationalists to focus together on the stark realities of Europe rather than on domestic divisions: the fear that communism would devour the tenuous fabric of European society from within, the force of economic self-interest, and the vision of a prosperous international peace.

Nothing, however, was left to chance. The American people had become concerned and aroused. As private organizations became increasingly active, Secretary Marshall and other members of the administration met with these groups around the nation. Late in 1947, under the national chairmanship of Henry L. Stimson (former Secretary of War and Secretary of State), the Committee for the Marshall Plan was formed to take the facts and the issues to the American people. Mrs. Wendell L. Willkie chaired a women's division. Dean Acheson and James B. Carey (from the Harriman Committee) and David Dubinsky (a prominent labor leader) joined the executive committee.

With a membership of over 300 prominent citizens from all parts of the country, the Committee for the Marshall Plan mounted a campaign. Regional committees were set up, funds were raised from the public in almost every state, and newspaper and radio editorials and reports developed broad national interest. The committee registered under the Lobbying Act, and petitions were circulated throughout congressional districts. By the time the legislation was headed for its decisive stage, the Committee for Economic Development was joined by the National Planning Association, the National Association of Manufacturers, the Congress of Industrial Organizations, the National Foreign Trade Council, the American Farm Bureau Federation, the American Federation of Labor, the American Legion, the Chamber of Commerce of the United States, the Americans for Democratic Action, the Federal Council of Churches, the National Catholic Welfare Conference, the League of Women Voters, the National Farmers Union, the National Grange, and the Veterans of Foreign Wars. What had begun with a small bipartisan meeting at the White House on June 22, 1947, became a large national groundswell by March 1, 1948, when Arthur Vandenberg rose to address the Senate of the United States and the nation in support of the Marshall Plan.

The Russians also were inadvertently responsible for the sense of urgency that developed. They fostered strikes and riots in France and Italy and turmoil in Greece and Turkey to protest against American capitalism. They characterized the European Recovery Program as a plan to subjugate Europe to America's will. And then, in mid-February 1948, they crystallized their purpose with a ruthless coup in Czechoslovakia. In Senator Vandenberg's words, the Economic Cooperation Act of 1948 would be a "welcome beacon in the world's dark night (and) it had better be lighted before it is too late."[12] And it was. After a vote of 69 to 17 in the Senate and 329 to 74 in the House and a brief conference, the law was passed on April 3.

The ECA and the OEEC President Truman moved quickly to establish the Economic Cooperation Administration (ECA). After consulting with Vandenberg, he selected Paul Hoffman—not one of the President's ardent Republican admirers—to give the enterprise hardnosed business leadership and a continued image of bipartisanship. For the job of special representative in Europe, Hoffman and the President agreed on Averell Harriman, who stepped down as Secretary of Commerce to move into action. Bissell, whom Harriman characterized as "one of the most courageous economists I have ever known," returned to Washington from MIT to play a key role in the ECA.[13] William C. Foster left the Department of Commerce along with Harriman and went with him to Paris as deputy special representative in Europe. The basic team of the ECA was set. The structure consisted of a strong European headquarters with functions in Europe corresponding to those of the equally strong central office in Washington. Harriman and Hoffman provided strong leadership on both sides of the Atlantic.

The basic thrust of the program was to have each country develop its own economic plan and take it to the Organization for European Economic Cooperation (OEEC) for coordination, without the Americans imposing their judgment at either stage. The idea was to generate enthusiastic cooperation by getting those concerned to participate in the planning.

The OEEC was voted into being by the Committee of European Economic Cooperation on April 16, 1948. The sixteen original countries and West Germany agreed to increase production, achieve internal financial stability, and liberalize trade and payments among themselves. More important, they agreed to develop and execute a joint recovery program; all decisions had to be unanimous.

The emphasis of the program was on the productivity of investment. The means would be cooperative planning and decision making —self-initiated—with American aid.

The test of the fundamental idea came quickly. Rhetoric and documents aside, many of the European representatives to OEEC had assumed that they would quietly go to Washington with their individual programs and negotiate their own aid packages. Hoffman and Harriman, however, were tough. In early May, they told the OEEC to recommend the division of aid for the 1948–1949 fiscal year beginning in June. The members of the OEEC had to cooperate or individually be responsible for wrecking the whole plan. There were, of course, tight controls. Hoffman held the final responsibility for authorizing every transaction of any importance. The OEEC divided the funds, and each country drew against its allocation for certain agreed-upon purposes. Those payments were checked in Washington to make sure they fitted into the overall program of the country.

There was a lot of bargaining between the nations. The United States played a diplomatic role in that process, but it rarely laid down the law. This meant that virtual unanimity had to be achieved. And the process worked.

The Participation of Labor   An important element in the functioning of the recovery program was the participation of American labor. This flowed from Hoffman's appointment as administrator. Given his own philosophy, Hoffman insisted that there be labor advisors in the Washington office, in the Paris office, and in most (if not all) of the country missions. He insisted that they be listened to and that the general objectives of the Marshall Plan be consistent with "liberal" labor policies, with emphasis on improving labor relations in Europe. To Hoffman, this was compatible with the development of productive capacity and increased productivity. And it worked.

The Emphasis on Productivity and Investment As the OEEC members started to analyze Europe's economic crisis in order to develop a joint plan of action, they began to recognize that the war had not been the origin of their economic problems. On the contrary, the war was seen as a development that simply accelerated the decay which had begun after 1913, with the decline of Europe's position in the world economy.

A massive rise in output was required to bring Europe out of chaos. That in turn required a fundamental emphasis on investment and productivity. While it was recognized that higher production required expanding markets both within the OEEC and abroad, it was also recognized that each member's market would be determined by its population, accessibility, productivity per worker day, exportable surpluses, and capacity to pay for imports.

Dollar aid for consumption would raise living standards and might relieve internal political stresses temporarily. But when the money was gone and the program ended, living standards would decline sharply. Then decay, strife, and discord would return.

Dollar aid for investment was another matter altogether. It would be the life blood for economic growth that would enable Europe to break out of a condition of stagnation. An ECA investment of $300 million, for example, generated—with capital accumulation and reinvestment—about $6 billion worth of thermogenerating power in six years. That investment came mostly in the form of thermo-equipment which Europe could not manufacture. Overall, as Hoffman said: "For every dollar of our aid to Europe, Europe puts six dollars into capital formation."[14] Investment was necessary in order to rebuild a sound European economy with internal financial stability and much freer trade and payments. Quite simply, as both Hoffman and Harriman recognized, the Marshall Plan had to be an investment operation.

The European Recovery Program: 1948–1952

The first full year of the European Recovery Program, 1948–1949, was a transition from consumption to economic growth, from food and raw materials to tools and machinery. The program had three important components. The first was the use of American aid for mutually agreed-upon recovery objectives. The second was the introduction of a European payments system based on the flow of American aid, but dependent on the interaction among European countries themselves. The third was the development of a commercial policy for future

OEEC relations. The targets of the policy were (1) increased agricultural production based on increased use of fertilizers and farm machinery, extra effort, and better adaptation to weather conditions, (2) higher production of coal, pig iron, crude steel, nonferrous metals, fertilizers, and wood pulp, (3) a rise in the volume of trade between member countries, and (4) a decrease in the dollar deficit of member countries.

The European economy *did* begin to break out of its condition of destruction and stagnation, and the pace of life quickened into recovery. The statistics of the index of industrial production showed that Europe was on the move (see Table 2-1). By 1953 recovery was fully under way.

The cost of the European Recovery Program is shown in Table 2-2. This totaled $13.16 billion—about what it would have cost to make a couple of our steel companies competitive as we moved into the eighties.

Table 2-1 INDEX OF INDUSTRIAL PRODUCTION, EUROPE, 1947 TO 1952 *(Index: 1938 = 100)*

Year	Industrial Production
1947	80
1948	98
1949	110
1950	122
1951	134
1952	135

SOURCE: Data from H. B. Price, *The Marshall Plan and Its Meaning*, Cornell University Press, Ithaca, N.Y., 1947, p. 118.

Table 2-2 THE EUROPEAN RECOVERY PROGRAM FROM 1948 TO 1952 *(In Billions of Dollars)*

Year	Cost
1948–1949	$6.05
1949–1950	3.78
1950–1951	2.31
1051–1952	1.02

SOURCE: Data from H. B. Price, *The Marshall Plan and Its Meaning*, Cornell University Press, Ithaca, N.Y., 1947, p. 118.

Summary   The Marshall Plan is a major historical example of an American coalition built on cooperation, compromise, and consensus. It grew out of three conditions: (1) the breakup of the relationship with the Russians, (2) the recognition of the need to reconstruct Western Europe and stop Russian encroachment, and (3) the need to end the occupation of West Germany. Pragmatism, in a sense, fused fear and altruism into the idea of a cooperative and self-initiated reconstruction with American aid. Cooperation, compromise, and consensus brought life to the idea and gave it legislative form. Cooperation, self-initiative, and investment made the idea work. Europe recovered rapidly.

As illustrated by the Marshall Plan, an idea can be a powerful force. A vision of the possible can mold that force into concrete action. General Marshall gave us both the idea and the vision.

THE EMPLOYMENT ACT OF 1946   The Employment Act of 1946 has constituted the basic economic policy of our nation since the end of World War II. It provided a powerful force for economic growth in the postwar era. It made job creation for all Americans willing to work a goal of American public policy. It established the Council of Economic Advisers to the President and was the forerunner of the Joint Economic Committee. And it required both a Presidential report to Congress on the state of the economy and its prospects, and an annual analysis of that report for Congress by the Joint Committee. As a result, there has been increased public awareness of economic policy.

The act is a fascinating piece of legislation because of the process through which it evolved and its pervasive impact on our lives. As the country moved from war to peace, the Employment Act took form. It preceded the Marshall Plan and was incorporated into it. But the two developed differently. The Marshall Plan was the result of a broad-based, well-developed coalition of government, labor, business, academia, public-interest groups, and Americans in general. The Employment Act was the result of activist efforts by a group of liberal legislators, labor leaders, and enlightened business executives, who came together into a coalition toward the end of the legislative process, when compromise was a necessity.

From start to finish, the passage of the Employment Act was a rocky and tenuous voyage over fourteen months. The act began in the Senate as the Full Employment Bill. It was modified in committee and further adjusted during debate on the floor. In the House, it became almost unrecognizable as the Employment-Production Act. It emerged from the Senate-House conference as a simple and understandable declaration of policy. In its final form, it changed the direction of postwar economic thinking and action.

In 1946, supplies of basic industrial necessities such as oil were considered unlimited. Furthermore, we were the most productive industrial power in the world. The most pressing issue was the very real fear of a return to the conditions of the Depression—especially high unemployment. It was therefore natural to focus economic policy on job creation, consumption, and the demand for more goods and services that, in turn, would create more jobs. Policymakers naturally assumed that supply would be plentiful, that productivity would not slow.

The people who created the Employment Act did their job well at the time.

The concept of job creation fueled our postwar economic expansion. However, the Employment Act encouraged one-sided, demand-oriented economic policy. At first, demand management was used to ensure economic expansion through increased consumption of goods and services. When inflation became a disease in the late sixties, policymakers would turn demand management into stop-and-go policy. They would attempt to curtail demand with monetary and fiscal policy constraints when inflation threatened. Then they would attempt to increase demand by easing monetary and fiscal policies when unemployment threatened. Because the Employment Act did not give balanced attention to supply, investment, and productivity, the country became vulnerable to unstable economic policy.

Background In 1944, it was apparent to many Americans in decision-making positions that the war was going to end. And there was much thought and consternation about the prospects for the postwar economy. In 1933, unemployment affected almost 13 million Americans, 25 percent of the work force. In 1939 it had come down to 17.2 percent, and by 1944 it fell to 1.2 percent. No one knew to what the troops would return, but all remembered the bitter experience of weathering the Depression. In the minds of those who looked ahead, there was a staggering fear that unemployment might balloon to 8 to 10 million after the war.[15]

Senator James E. Murray of Montana was one of the most concerned individuals. So were Paul Hoffman and Ralph Flanders, businessmen who had formed the Committee for Economic Development to work on the development of a national postwar economic policy, because of their concern about returning to the past. Another concerned person was Bertram Gross, a staffer for Murray, who chaired the War Contracts Subcommittee of the Senate.

The activists, Murray and Gross, had been hard at work in anticipation of the problem of revived unemployment. The Committee for Economic Development watched them sympathetically from the sidelines. By December 11, 1944, Gross felt he had the basic features of a full employment bill. Every American should have the right to a job, and Congress should ensure that right. This objective would require an economic plan, and if the private sector couldn't do the job, there should be a federal mechanism of investment to guarantee the program.

The Legislative Process Begins   On December 18, 1944, Senator Murray submitted a year-end report to the Committee on Military Affairs entitled "Legislation for Reconversion and Full Employment." Lamenting the inaction of Congress to prepare for the future, Murray warned that a postwar economic program would not develop out of thin air. He then went on to the core of his argument:

The right to a job is not self-enforceable. It can be translated into reality only through the joint action of the people of our country—business, labor, agriculture, and all other groups—acting through the medium of their duly elected government. In short, the so-called right to a job is a meaningless figure of speech unless our government assumes responsibility for the expansion of our peacetime economy so that it will be capable of assuring full employment.[16]

The Senator's concept of a coalition was good, but his language was incendiary, at least to some. *The New York Times* and *The Wall Street Journal* both condemned the bill as a deficit-financing measure. However, the activists were on the move. Senator Murray introduced the Full Employment Bill on January 22, 1945, and it was referred to the Committee on Banking and Currency, whose chairman was Robert F. Wagner of New York. Gross became Wagner's special assistant and developed the campaign for the legislation.

However, the timing for a national consensus on postwar economic policy development was premature. The war was still in progress, and public attention was focused on military developments, which dominated the news. The strong Presidential leadership required for a consensus was unavailable as President Roosevelt's attention was riveted on the future of the world and the creation of the United Nations. Moreover, the President was ailing and just a few months away from his death.

To make matters worse, the original draft of the bill was not directed to broad appeal. It was replete with technical economic jargon and contained some lightning-rod language that would attract the reactionary forces as the legislative process unfolded. Nonetheless, the activists, dedicated to their own point of view, aimed squarely at winning Senate approval, even though they were aware of national indifference to their issue.

The heart of their bill was Section 2 which, when passed by the Senate, read, in part: ". . . the *Federal Government* shall . . . develop and pursue a consistent and *carefully planned* economic program . . . such programs shall among other things . . . to the extent that continuing *full* employment cannot otherwise be attained, *provide* . . . such volume of *Federal investment* and *expenditure* as needed . . . to achieve the objective of *continuing full* employment."*[17]

The term *full* in association with *employment* has always fostered vigorous debate in the United States—debate that is generally inconclusive and confusing to the public at best, and bitterly divisive at worst. In conjunction with federal planning and investment, those words would arouse the opposition with visions of governmental controls, governmental takeover of business, and destruction of the free-enterprise system. The fire of debate would almost engulf the objective of developing a sound and reasonable economic policy to prevent a repetition of the post-World War I events that led to the Great Depression.

But the course had been set, a strategy had been devised, and the activists moved into battle. Their first two steps were to unify support and develop favorable public opinion. The Wagner staff arranged speaking schedules and worked closely with sympathetic members of the media and with state legislators. They linked up with the Union for Democratic Action, which had a full-time Washington representative. With the active backing of both Wagner and Murray, they organized an informal "continuations group," which included representatives from labor and organizations of religious groups, blacks, women, farmers, and professionals.

They then took a decisive step that would guarantee a vigorous

*Emphasis added.

reaction later. They attempted to split the potential opposition from business, agricultural, and veterans' groups. They worked with two small business organizations and, of course, the CED. The Secretary of Agriculture supported this initiative with his department, and his staff maintained constant contact with the National Farmers Union. Help also came from the Disabled American War Veterans and the American Veterans Committee. The primary purpose of this step was to mute the opposition and convey to Congress and the public the impression that the opposition was regressive and against working people.

Preliminary Senate hearings began in the summer of 1945. The sponsors of the Senate bill tried to convince their colleagues that there was an urgent need for full employment that could only be accomplished by government policy to ensure the right to work. They tried to characterize their opposition as a small minority who were against a stable and expanding economy.

Legislative Interest Intensifies With the sudden cessation of hostilities in Japan on August 15, the pace of events accelerated. President Truman quickly recognized that virtually nothing had been done for demobilization and transition to a peacetime economy. Economists rose to the occasion with dire forecasts of 8 to 10 million unemployed by the first quarter of 1946. The fact that the forecasts proved wrong, by a margin of 6 to 8 million, was of little consequence. The fact that they were widely circulated was. The element of fear was heightened and lent urgency to the Senate's deliberations. Postwar employment had become a major national concern. The President declared a full-employment bill to be "must" legislation.

The original legislation was redrafted as a result of the preliminary Senate hearings in 1945 and considerable public interest at war's end. More attention was given to agriculture, the language was simplified, and the spending provisions of the bill were strengthened. It was then ready for the Committee on Banking and Currency.

When it appeared that the legislation might become a reality, faint stirrings of opposition were heard. To opposition leaders such as Republican Senators Robert Taft, George Radcliffe, and Bourke Hickenlooper, the objectionable aspects of the bill were, predictably, the term *full employment*, the government guarantee of the right to work, and the reliance on federal investment and expenditure to ensure full employment. The opposition leaders agreed, however, that some sort of economic planning entity was probably desirable. Thus, the Senate received a report with the interesting title of "Assuring

Full Employment in a Free Competitive Economy." It offered the best of both worlds.

In the full Senate deliberations, the policy section of the bill was significantly altered, but the substantive program went unscathed. The obligation to ensure full employment was so obscured that Senator Glen Taylor of Idaho objected strenuously that the full-employment bill did not specifically provide jobs for anyone. It was now nothing more than a declaration of principle. Further, in compromise language it said, in effect, that any federal investment and expenditure program would require taxes calculated to prevent an increase in national debt over a "reasonable period of years," but without interfering with the goal of full employment. The opponents of guaranteed full employment were diluting that idea with confusing legislative language.

The final vote in the Senate on September 28 was 71 to 10. The bill was sent to the House, where the forces of reaction began to mobilize their counterattack.

The House Holds Hearings The Senate bill was referred to the Committee on Expenditures in the Executive Departments, chaired by Congressman Carter Manasco of Alabama. Manasco proceeded, in six weeks of hearings, to tear up the Senate bill and discard it.

His principal ally was Donaldson Brown, a director of the National Association of Manufacturers (NAM) and vice chairman of General Motors. Brown brought in James C. Ingebretsen, a Los Angeles lawyer who frequently worked for the Los Angeles Chamber of Commerce. Ingebretsen became to Manasco and the reactionaries what Gross had been to Murray and Wagner in the Senate. He prepared a list of witnesses, a list of "critical comments and analysis," and questions for Manasco to ask of friendly witnesses opposed to the Senate bill.

He also authored a document described as "A Compilation in Excerpt Form of Statements and Expressions of Views Exposing Inherent Fallacies and Contradictions of the So-Called 'Full Employment' Bill, S. 380." It warned that the full-employment bill would mean government controls, destroy private enterprise, increase the powers of the executive branch, lead to socialism, and be unworkable. It further argued that the bill would prove to be impractical, promise too much, and be worthy only of ridicule.

The reactionary forces, of course, went to work with their own mailing and media campaign. The NAM was joined by the Committee for Constitutional Government and the American Farm Bureau Federation.

The Move Toward Compromise The President, however, wanted some form of employment legislation. Recognizing the inevitable with respect to the Senate version, he talked in late October with both Manasco and Congressman William M. Whittington of Mississippi. He extracted from them a commitment to report a bill from the Expenditures Committee, hoping that it could be strengthened in the conference of the House and Senate.

At the same time, the Committee for Economic Development was continuing its work toward an economic policy to prevent a return to the disorder of the Depression. Robert Lenhart, Secretary of the CED, spent most of his time in Washington working quietly in the interest of compromise. Lenhart had been in the Roosevelt White House and had good contacts in Congress and with labor. He covered the developments closely and wrote daily reports for Hoffman and Flanders, who were the public spokesmen for the CED. The CED worked closely with the Machinery and Allied Products Institute, the National Grange, and Eric Johnston, president of the Chamber of Commerce. Johnston, who was not opposed to the Senate bill personally, was prepared to retreat to the high ground in support of a declaration of principle on high employment policies.

The Bill Is Redrafted When the Committee on Expenditures dispatched the Senate bill, a subcommittee consisting of Representatives Manasco, Whittington, Clare Hoffman, George Bender, and John Cochran, was appointed to draft a substitute bill. Whittington, who became the balancing force and assumed the major responsibility for the new draft, wanted a bill that would exclude federal commitments and assurances. But he also wanted one that would provide for some sort of planning mechanism in both the executive and legislative branches. During the hearings, he was particularly receptive to the comments of Dr. George Terborgh of the Machinery and Allied Products Institute, who summarized his view of an employment bill as follows:

1. It is declared to be the responsibility of the Federal Government to foster private enterprise and to promote by means consistent with this and other obligations and objectives, a high and stable level of employment.

2. In light of this responsibility, the Government is admonished to develop and to pursue consistently an appropriate economic program.

3. The task of evolving such a program is laid in the first instance upon the President, who is instructed to submit to Congress quarterly his analysis of economic conditions and trends and his recommendations for policy.

4. There is created a special congressional joint committee to review the President's proposals and report to both Houses thereon.[18]

Terborgh was asked to submit a draft of a bill. Whittington also sought drafts from the CED, the Chamber of Commerce of the United States, and Secretary of the Treasury Frederick M. Vinson. He then sat down to write the substitute bill of the House. His version was titled the "Employment and Production Act of 1946." It eliminated the right to employment, federal responsibility for full employment, and the pledge of all the federal resources.

Despite a lot of symbolic eloquence about free enterprise, private capital, and statism, Whittington's version took the Terborgh, Flanders, Lenhart, and Johnston approach. The result was a compromise that was flexible enough to permit Congress to proceed to the next stage: a Senate-House conference. As the President had requested, a bill had come out of the House. The reactionaries were beaten.

The Senate-House Conference   The conference opened on January 22 in Senator Alben W. Barkley's office in the Capitol. With Barkley as chairman, the primary players were Senators Taft, Abe Murdock, and Charles Tobey, and Congressmen Whittington, Cochran, and Manasco. Bertram Gross was at Barkley's side, and for two days he watched as the senators and congressmen sparred and measured each other in apparent stalemate.

But the impasse had to break. Labor, enlightened business, and the President all wanted a bill. At this point, Senator Barkley, aided by Gross's brilliant improvisation with words, began to mold a compromise. "Full employment" was translated into "conditions under which there will be afforded useful employment . . . for those able, willing . . . and seeking to work."[19] In other words, everyone willing to work would have a job. With this semantic legerdemain, American economic policy closed the doors on the freedom-to-starve philosophy which had preceded the Great Depression. This change ushered in a great new wave of economic expansion.

An economic program carefully planned by the federal government to provide, as needed, investment and expenditure to achieve the objective of continuing full employment, with another wave of a masterly wand, was compromised into: ". . . the continuing policy and responsibility of the Federal Government to use all practicable means . . . to coordinate and utilize all its plans, functions, and resources for the purpose of . . . maintaining . . . conditions under which there will be afforded useful employment opportunities. . . ."[20]

By maintaining conditions to afford jobs to all those willing to work, policy was directed toward demand management of the economy. Economic policymakers took this new economic philosophy and translated it into a great new wave of economic expansion. Ironically, Donaldson Brown's General Motors would, in the fifties and sixties, be one of the principal beneficiaries of the wordsmithing of Gross and the negotiating skills of Barkley.

With the completion of the policy section, the conference came to quick agreement on the rest of the bill. On February 6, the Employment Act of 1946 was passed in the House by a vote of 320 to 84; two days later it went through the Senate without opposition. It was signed into law by President Truman on February 20, 1946.

Summary From the vantage point of America in the eighties, it seems incredible that the declaration of economic philosophy embodied in the Employment Act—everyone willing to work should have a job— should have had such a tortuous birth. It was an idea that was almost hopelessly splintered by the power struggles of competing political, administrative, activist, and reactionary forces. It was finally pieced together only by the most laborious and complicated coalition strategies.

Unlike the Marshall Plan which it preceded, the Employment Act was not the product of a well-conceived, well-thought-out, and well-developed bipartisan coalition. Although it was the product of the same environment of economic fear that brought forth the Marshall Plan, it came into being with difficulty because it was initiated at a time when the attention of the executive branch was understandably focused elsewhere.

Because the Employment Act developed haphazardly—with a coalition based on necessity rather than design—it was not a fully developed and balanced policy. Because the focus was understandably on jobs and the supply of raw materials such as oil were assumed to be unlimited, it resulted in policy directed to the management of demand. Its authors, exhausted from the fight, moved on to other interests.

While the Employment Act would provide a powerful force for stable economic growth in the United States for the next twenty years, its omissions—lack of focus on supply, productivity, and investment— would be revealed by hindsight in the unstable economic climate of the period from the late sixties on to the early eighties. In Japan and West Germany, on the other hand, our reconstruction programs linked the idea of jobs to supply, productivity, and investment. And investment, the economists will tell you, is linked to savings. The demand-management economy created by the Employment Act was a major disincentive to savings in the United States. In 1960, the savings ratios of the United States, West Germany, and Japan were 4.9, 8.5, and 17.4 percent of disposable income, respectively. By 1976, the savings ratios were 7.4, 16.9, and 24.9 percent, respectively. Sound economic policy was only partially formed in the United States in 1946.

THE HOOVER COMMISSION In the summer of 1947, a third element that would contribute to stable postwar economic growth began to develop. While the Marshall Plan coalition was being built and the reorientation from jobs in war to jobs in peace was taking place, the process of rationalizing government was begun. As might be expected, it was not without political overtones.

On July 7, 1947, Congress passed the Lodge-Brown Act, which established the Commission on Organization of the Executive Branch of the Government. Although initially there was some disagreement as to whether the commission's charter included examination of the policies as well as the structure of government, the commission's goals were crystallized following the 1948 election. The result was the first major reorganization of government since 1913.

The Political Overtones of the Hoover Commission The Republicans had not occupied the Oval Office for sixteen years, but in 1948 they had majorities in both houses of Congress. There was clearly a sense of political momentum and a real belief in the opportunity to roll back much of the New Deal. This was reflected in their view of the proposed study of the government.

The report on the proposed Lodge-Brown Act to the Republican-controlled Senate from the Republican majority in the Committee on Expenditures in the Executive Department was issued on June 25. It stated:

Your committee joins with what it believes to be the prevailing sentiment of the country, as a whole, and of the Congress in particular, that the need is patently imperative for a general, thorough, and detailed study of the entire executive branch of our Government. Detailed evidence is unnecessary to support the contention that the time is ripe for a general overhauling, for going through the Government with a fine-tooth comb, and for casting some light into all the many dark places. For the first time in 16 years, this opportunity is at hand. This is a timely moment to undertake this vital project, now that the period of hostilities has ceased and we are struggling up the hard road to peace. This road is certainly made no easier by a top-heavy governmental structure which costs a staggering sum of money, which seems to satisfy nobody, and which makes efficient, farsighted action difficult, if not altogether impossible.[21]

This was to be the political thrust of the commission.

The Substance of the Hoover Commission The commission's other thrust was the substantive one. In the New Deal, the social reformers had been freewheeling and undisciplined. A view held by serious students of government at the time was that examination of the general administrative and organizational structure of government was imperative in order to bring its disorderly nature under control.

In January 1937, Franklin Roosevelt had submitted to Congress the Report of the Committee on Administrative Management (the Brownlow Committee). The President had proposed that some 100 independent agencies, administrations, boards, and commissions be placed within twelve executive departments. The Brownlow Committee report had very fairly stated that: "Any program to restore our constitutional ideal of a fully coordinated executive branch responsible to the President must bring within reach of that responsible control all work done by these independent commissions which is not judicial in nature."[22]

The Committee recommended that the executive branch be reorganized to create an integrated, responsible structure, with the President as active manager. However, the executive reorganization bill of 1938 was rejected by Congress, largely because it would give too much power to the President and further encourage a trend toward "Presidential dictatorship."

The Brownlow initiative did result, however, in the creation of the Executive Office of the President. The Budget Bureau was moved from the Treasury Department to the Executive Office of the President, and the President was given new administrative assistants. This gave the President the necessary tools to directly control money and personnel in government. However, with the proliferation of wartime activities into additional agencies, by 1947 the executive branch was even more fragmented than it was in 1938. There was general agreement that the problem should be attacked. The time for the Brownlow approach had arrived.

Organization of the Hoover Commission   The Lodge-Brown Act established a "nonpartisan" commission of twelve members. Four were to be appointed by the President—two from the executive branch and two from the private sector. Four were to be appointed by the president of the Senate—two senators and two members from the private sector. And four were to be appointed by the Speaker of the House—two representatives and two members from the private sector. The two classes of members—government and private sector—were to represent the two major political parties equally.

President Truman chose Dean Acheson, then in private law practice. Speaker Joseph W. Martin selected former President Herbert Hoover and, at the suggestion of Minority Leader Sam Rayburn, James H. Rowe, Jr., a former administrative assistant to President Roosevelt. These three—Acheson, Hoover, and Rowe—were the principals in the preelection phase of the commission.

The first meeting of the commission took place at the White House on September 29, 1947. President Truman made the suggestion that former President Hoover chair the commission, and Hoover was elected unanimously. Dean Acheson became vice chairman.

There was clear agreement that the Hoover Commission had been established to bring an integrated organizational structure into government. Hoover, always a forceful person, took command at the outset and moved steadily forward on the structural front. He set up twenty-three task forces, each with a given field of inquiry. About 300 individuals served on the commission, many of whom were distinguished in government, business, and the professions—including law, education, engineering, and the social and physical sciences. This phase of organization, inquiry, and study proceeded from the initial meeting in September 1947 through early June 1948.

Hoover personally served as the task force which would deal with the Presidency and write the final report on the "General Management of Executive Branch." As he said, "Who is there who ought to know more about it?"[23] To work with him on this central aspect of the commission's purpose, he brought in Don K. Price as his assistant. Price was a natural choice: he recently had been head of the Government Organization Branch of the Budget Bureau; he was then running the Washington office of the Public Administration Clearing House; and as a former assistant to Louis Brownlow, he had had an important link to the work of the Brownlow committee.

Hoover and the majority of the commission thought they had the power to look into policy. Others did not. There was, however, substantial disagreement as to whether the commission was established to examine the *policy,* as well as the *structure,* of government. The initiators of a rearguard action against Hoover and his followers were Rowe, the aggressive young man who had clerked for Justice Oliver Wendell Holmes before becoming an assistant to Roosevelt, and Acheson, the wise statesman behind him.

Although the constitution of the task forces was widely considered to be heavily loaded against the remnants of New Deal thinking and the Democratic party, accommodation gradually took place. The task forces, presumably chosen to be the executioners of various parts of the government's policy, slowly came around as they worked on the problems. They were not all that partisan; they were, after all, specialists. Substance, at the working level, eroded politics.

The Effect of the 1948 Election   Beginning in October, the commission held sessions every week, usually for two or three days at a time. Because it was widely expected that Dewey would be elected President in 1948, Hoover quietly deputized Price as the point of contact with Charles Breitel, who was the New York governor's advance man, to work out the transition.

Politics aside, an important relationship developed between President Truman and former President Hoover. Roosevelt had never let Hoover into the White House. There was mutual disregard. Truman, however, began calling Hoover to get his advice and use him as a sounding board. Over time, and over lunch, dinner, and even breakfast, they became pretty good friends.

But when the campaign started in full force, with the political stakes high, the President went out campaigning against Hoover—not Dewey—as all Democrats did. To the disbelief of some, the former President was thin-skinned about it. When Truman was out West lambasting him, Hoover asked Rowe: "How can President Truman do this to me?" Rowe, as partisan a Democrat as ever grew up in Montana, responded: "Well, Mr. President, don't get upset by it. You know, this is an election; we're Democrats. We've been attacking you for years."[24]

Then came the surprising results of the election, which settled both the policy and the transition questions. Recognizing that some very constructive work was underway, Truman moved quickly to soothe ruffled feelings and heal political wounds by having Hoover to lunch. Later, on November 12, 1948, he wrote to Hoover, formally encouraging the continuation of the commission and saying, in part: "There seems to be general agreement that the present organization of the executive branch, in many instances, imposes handicaps on effective and economical administration and must be brought up to date. The task, as you and I have seen from our own experience, is to crystallize this general belief into concrete and wise proposals for action."[25]

The Substantive Impact of the Commission   The time for politics was over. It was time for the serious side of government. With a friendship and an alliance firmly reestablished, Herbert Hoover confidently shifted his commission into high gear, developed consensus reports on the restructuring of government, and, with his task force members as a base, developed a vigorous public-spirited organization to sell the results of the Hoover Commission to the American people and to Congress.

A Citizens' Committee on the Hoover Report was formed under the chairmanship of Robert L. Johnson of Temple University. Hundreds of distinguished leaders from a broad range of fields were recruited to join the national committee, and thirty-two state committees were formed to stimulate interest in and pressures for enactment of the recommendations of the Hoover Commission. There was, in turn, a widespread positive reaction by both the public and the media. And the effort worked.

The principal achievement of the Hoover Commission was the establishment of the President as manager of the executive branch. It called for, and made possible, a strong Presidency. With a bipartisan consensus, it brought to fruition many of the ideas originally proposed by the Brownlow Committee in a different political climate. Policymaking decisions were centralized; operating decisions were decentralized. There was a more orderly grouping of the functions of government into major departments and agencies, leading, for example, to the creation of the Department of Defense and the General Services Administration.

The Reorganization Act of 1949 became one of the vehicles for strengthening the management prerogatives of the President. It extended reorganization authority for four years, allowed creation of executive departments, and won the battle of 1939 by eliminating exemptions of independent agencies.

Over time, statutes had greatly fragmented departmental management by putting power at the bureau level or even lower. Bureau chiefs would resist the instructions of a department head by invoking a statute which made *them* responsible for a decision. Under the Reorganization Act, President Truman followed through with a series of reorganization plans that in almost every department transferred statutory authority from the bureau chief back up to the department head. In effect, implementers of the President's policy were managing again. This was a very sweeping change which nobody would have believed possible two years before, when the Hoover Commission was established.

The Executive Office of the President, which came into existence in 1939, was strengthened by bringing the National Security Council and the National Security Resources Board into the Executive Office. The Office of the Budget and its role in administrative management were also strengthened. The President was given unrestricted discretion in the staffing and organizing of the Executive Office.

Summary The importance of the Hoover Commission and Truman's use of it can be seen in the relationship between structure and control. After twenty years of growth and fragmentation, government was reorganized into a workable number of departments, with the consolidation of a number of smaller functions into bigger departments and the creation of an unbroken line of responsibility. Fully 72 percent of the 273 recommendations proposed by Hoover were implemented either by administrative action, direct legislation, or reorganization plans under the 1949 act.

Once the 1948 election settled the question of who would be President, a bipartisan focus on the structure of government took place. What had been a subject of divisiveness and discord under President Roosevelt became the object of national unity under the orchestration of the coalition formed by President Truman and former President Hoover. Truman's successor, General Eisenhower, found a government that could be managed. The President could be in charge.

The reasons for the success of the Hoover Commission were, in retrospect, simple. The timing and the political climate were right. The bipartisan structure of the commission brought the forces of the legislative branch and the executive branch, along with representatives of the public, together into consensus. The prestige of the chairman and his vigorous follow-through created a heightened sense of public awareness. Throughout the process, and especially in the implementation phase, the work of the commission had both the interest and the full support of President Truman. Herbert Hoover was prophetic when, at 73, he characterized this as his last public service. It was a monumental achievement in the organization of government.

THE EISENHOWER HIGHWAY PROGRAM The Eisenhower highway program was a by-product of the demand-management thrust of the Employment Act. It was consistent with the spirit of cooperation, compromise, and consensus of the time. It was an economic program that the American people wanted, and it was legislated by a bipartisan effort of a Republican President and a Democratic Congress. It is an important example of a major domestic policy that flowed from the period of national unity when the Marshall Plan, the Employment Act, and the Hoover Commission formed the basis for coherent government and sound policy development in America.

Construction for Consumption When the war ended, most economists miscalculated the expansionary power of the $44 billion in savings which the people of America had accumulated. In a demand-management economy, consumer-goods sales would benefit. The automobile industry would be a prime beneficiary of an era of construction for consumption.

From a level of 3.8 million cars in 1941, automobile production virtually ceased during the war. In 1945, only 69,000 cars were manufactured in the United States. Production rebounded to 2.1 million in 1946. Auto production and sales increased dramatically; by 1955, almost 8 million cars were made and sold. The total number of automobiles in America increased from 26 million in 1945, to 40 million in 1950, to 52 million in 1955, to 62 million in 1960, and to 80 million in 1967—an increase of over 200 percent.[26]

The era was one of cheap, plentiful oil. During the same period—1945 to 1967—passenger vehicle fuel usage increased from 14 million gallons to 56 million—a 300 percent increase. In 1945, Americans drove their cars 204 million miles. In 1967, they drove them 779 million miles—a 280 percent increase. The people were on the move, for every purpose, in every direction, and in every part of the country.[27]

That required highways. The nation's total expenditures for highways grew from $1.7 billion in 1945, to $4.5 billion in 1950, to $10.8 billion in 1960, and to $20.8 billion in 1970. This rate of growth was 36 percent faster than that of the gross national product.

The Roots of the Highway Program Planning for the highway program had its roots in the Federal-Aid Highway Act of 1944, which established a target of 40,000 miles for a national interstate highway system. The Public Roads Administration was to develop the interstate system in conjunction with the state highway departments. The Public Roads Administration asked the American Association of State Highway Officials (AASHO) to propose standards to control the location and design of the system; the standards were approved in August 1947. By 1950, AASHO released a study that stated that the nation needed a fifteen-year program costing $60 billion to catch up on its highway needs. At approximately the same time, the Joint Committee on the Economic Report of Congress set the immediate needs for a national program at $41 billion.

The states, during this immediate postwar period, embarked on programs of their own. In 1945, for example, New Jersey enacted a program to relieve congestion in the densely populated New York to Philadelphia corridor. The program was started in 1946 but made slow progress until 1949, when the New Jersey Turnpike Authority was established to build the main highway between the George Washington Bridge and the Delaware River and was authorized to issue bonds to finance construction. The 117-mile toll road was completed in less than three years at a cost of $285 million. By 1953, it returned fully six times its operating expenses for a net operating revenue of $18 million a year. It was obviously meeting a need in an increasingly automobile-oriented society. From Maine to Colorado, similar toll roads began to creep across the map of the interstate highway system. They represented a high standard of excellence against which to compare the inadequacies of the rest of the highway system. That contrast increased the public's desire for better highways.

The Eisenhower Legislation   In July 1954, President Eisenhower addressed the annual conference of state governors and asked for cooperation in the development of: ". . . a grand plan for a properly articulated system that solves the problems of speedy, safe, transcontinental travel—inner-city communication—access highways—and farm-to-market movement—metropolitan area congestion—bottlenecks—and parking."[28] The President called for a $50 billion, ten-year program to get the country moving.

After extensive study by a federal interagency committee, Eisenhower sent Congress a highway bill in March 1955. He proposed a Federal Highway Corporation with authority to issue $20 billion in long-term debt, to be paid off over thirty-two years with revenues from federal taxes on fuel and lubricants. Although there was widespread agreement on the highway program, the corporation concept ran into considerable cross fire in Congress. Congress wanted the funding to come out of current highway revenues on a pay-as-you-go basis. An impasse resulted, and at the end of 1955 there was still no legislation.

When Congress returned in 1956, its members had heard from the public, who wanted action. They had, after all, just finished buying almost 8 million cars in a record year for Detroit. The Administration pragmatically jettisoned the federal corporation idea and endorsed the pay-as-you-go concept. And the federal highway legislation was on its way. A bill was approved by the House on April 27, 1956; the Senate version was approved on May 29; the Senate-House conferees developed a compromise bill on June 25; and President Eisenhower signed the bill into law on June 29, 1956. The pattern of construction for consumption was widening across the land.

Summary The Federal-Aid Highway Act and the Highway Revenue Act of 1956 is an important postwar economic example for two reasons: (1) It was a domestic program legislated and implemented by a consensus developed under a Republican President, working with a Democratic Congress. (2) It illustrates the way economic strength was built in the postwar period, with consumption creating the need for construction in a demand-oriented economy.

IN RETROSPECT In the immediate postwar period there was a strong spirit of cooperation, compromise, and consensus in America. This spirit fostered the development of important foreign and domestic policies and programs—the Marshall Plan, the Employment Act of 1946, the Hoover Commission, and the Eisenhower highway program. These policies and programs were the foundation of our postwar strength at a time when government functioned efficiently and our economic policies resulted in noninflationary growth.

The Marshall Plan entailed what was clearly the best organized and broadest coalition. Because of this, it resulted in a balanced reconstruction of Europe that had a deep impact on the world economic order. Even in the presidential election year of 1948, a united spirit of cooperation, compromise, and consensus elevated the goal of foreign policy above partisan politics. The administration, Congress, an array of American groups and individuals, and our European partners all came together to make the Marshall Plan possible. We were truly united then.

The Employment Act did not enjoy the support of a well-organized coalition from the outset, but it did work out in the end. Initially conceived as a technically complicated piece of activist legislation, it did not have Presidential leadership during the last year of the war. However, as it worked its way through the legislative process, the war ended and a new President and a coalition of labor, business, and congressional legislators forged a compromise and a new economic policy.

The first Hoover Commission evolved in a period of political turmoil between a Democratic President and a Republican Congress. Because of the politics of the times, the commission focused only on the structure of government and not on policy. When the campaign of 1948 resulted in Truman's election and a Democratic Congress, Truman and Hoover joined in an effective coalition that made it possible for Congress to substantially rationalize the structure of government.

The Eisenhower highway program was an outgrowth of the basic principles of the Employment Act. In this case, with a clearly united public behind the program, a Republican President and a Democratic Congress formed a coalition which pulled together the needs and interests of society and embryonic state programs and forged them into a totally integrated national program. And it was a program that worked with economic benefit all around. It created jobs in highway construction, housing construction, and the automobile industry.

Ironically, however, the Employment Act resulted in an unbalanced economic policy that ultimately would have important consequences in the turn of economic events in the United States. Built into that policy was a one-sided emphasis on consumption and demand management. A balanced approach with emphasis on both supply and demand was not part of the Employment Act. Furthermore, the resulting economic policy did not give equal emphasis to productivity and investment.

The Eisenhower highway program was the fruition of that one-sided demand-management policy. We built highways and cars, homes to commute from, and consumer durables to put into the homes. By self-directed policy we became a nation of consumers. We slowly forgot how to save and invest. Basic industry suffered as a result. Our steel industry was the first to go in trade competition, after the 1959 strike. It was followed by our first merchandise trade deficit in 1971. Then our economy was further weakened when world supplies tightened and prices shot up in the 1973–1974 embargo. When productivity growth fell behind growth of the consumer price index, our economy was seriously weakened. It is to an understanding of our transition from economic strength to economic weakness that we therefore now turn.

3 THE DEVELOPING STORM

As the decade of the fifties opened, the United States had in place a rationalized and coherent government, a demand-management and job-oriented economic policy, and a position of free world leadership based upon economic strength and an international outlook.

Western Europe and Japan were on the road to recovery. The world economy, based on vigorously growing international trade, began to expand. The United States led world economic growth through the fifties. But slowly our position of leadership began to erode, and by 1975 we were no longer the world economic leader. Japan was. The fundamental economic situation had changed dramatically.

When Truman, Marshall, Acheson, Harriman, Hoffman, Hoover, and Eisenhower forged policy with the support of the American people, it was backed by three elements: idealism, economic and military strength, and the spirit of cooperation, compromise, and consensus. But as we moved through the sixties and into the seventies, changes took place, almost unnoticed. And the spirit of cooperation, compromise, and consensus disappeared.

The disintegration of that spirit was wrought by a combination of events, including the inconsistencies and controversies inherent in the Great Society at home and the Vietnam war abroad. Over time, our nation suffered a series of shocks and traumatic events. The assassination of President Kennedy, the subsequent killing of his brother Bobby while seeking the Presidency, the murder of Martin Luther King, Kent State—the events accumulated until our nation was split apart. The word *crisis*—that turning point in a disease which indicates whether the result is to be recovery or death—lost its meaning. A "me" generation grew and flourished in America. Finally, with the threatened impeachment of a United States President, our nation was seriously weakened.

The Great Society ushered in massive consumption-oriented expenditures that continued during our involvement in Vietnam and went unchecked in the Nixon administration. That massive consumption, insufficiently financed by tax revenues, was an important factor in our economic decline.

Of equal importance was the shattering of a coherent government policy-making process. The Great Society of Lyndon Johnson and the New Federalism of Richard Nixon resulted in a confusion and a blurring of the functions of the different levels of government within our federal system. Our prolonged involvement in the Vietnam war compounded that confusion in government with bitterness and discord in the nation. Then Watergate broke our trust in government.

By 1975, confusion, discord, and lack of trust had combined to create a governmental environment in which it was impossible to develop bipartisan, coherent long-term policies. We needed powerful long-term policies, but we were unable to form the coalitions that had proved essential for their development in the post-World War II period.

In this chapter, we will trace the process of economic decline, examine what went wrong in our economy, and analyze why it went wrong.

FROM STRENGTH TO ECONOMIC DECLINE   On April 2, 1952, the Supreme Allied Commander of Europe, General Dwight D. Eisenhower, prophetically observed:

No man will fight unless . . . he has something worth fighting for. Next . . . is . . . the strength of the . . . economy. Unless the economy can . . . carry the military establishment, whatever [military] force . . . a nation might create is worse than useless in a crisis. Since behind it there is nothing, it will only disintegrate.[1]

As the American people endured the humiliation of the hostage situation in Iran into 1981, public opinion polls showed an increasing awareness on the part of the American people that our impotence in Iran might be directly related to our economic decline. It was.

Manufacturing Output   Manufacturing output—the real base of productive economic strength—is made up of steel, automobiles, semiconductors, consumer electronics, machine tools, and other goods that are the backbone of world trade. In war-torn Japan, Western

Europe, and the United Kingdom, manufacturing output climbed steadily after the war. With 1967 as a base of 100, Table 3-1 illustrates manufacturing output for the period 1950–1975. The indexes show the relative growth in the different countries.

TABLE 3-1 MANUFACTURING OUTPUT (1950–1975)

Year	United States	Japan	France	Germany	Italy	United Kingdom
1950	51.7	8.6	37.6	26.9	26.4	60.9
1955	65.3	19.2	47.7	50.7	40.9	72.2
1960	67.7	42.0	64.5	73.5	60.2	83.4
1965	92.5	73.5	88.4	100.3	83.3	97.6
1967	100.0	100.0	100.0	100.0	100.0	100.0
1970	102.6	152.9	123.7	132.2	125.6	111.4
1975	106.3	168.3	136.7	137.1	139.4	112.9

SOURCE: United States Department of Labor, Bureau of Labor Statistics.
Indexes: 1967 = 100

The countries that were most torn apart by the war—Japan, Germany, and Italy—obviously had to reconstruct their industrial bases. In a sense, they almost had to start all over again. Those countries put their people back to work, and their recoveries were steady and vigorous. Therefore, they grew more rapidly than the United States on a relative basis.

Japan, which is today our toughest trading competitor in steel, machine tools, automobiles, semiconductors, and consumer electronics, recovered and developed the strongest manufacturing base of all. Japan is a relatively small country compared with the United States. It has virtually no natural resources other than its people. But they make a difference. In both manufacturing and trading activities, they are well organized on a national basis.

From 1950 to 1960, the manufacturing output recovery of Japan, Germany, and Italy was dramatic. From 1960 to 1965, the United States with its much larger manufacturing base still had a relatively strong increase in the index of manufacturing output compared with those countries. However, that changed dramatically after 1967. All the countries listed in Table 3-1 had rates of growth in manufacturing output superior to the United States in the period from 1967 to 1975. Japan—fully recovered from the war—increased its manufacturing output 68.3 percent from 1967 to 1975. Our increase was only 6.3 percent in the same period. Table 3-1 clearly traces our relative decline in manufacturing strength.

By 1975, Japan had unquestionably taken over as the most vigorously growing manufacturing nation in the world. The relative decline of the United States set the stage for the developing economic storm that resulted in our weakness in trade, energy, and productivity, which will be discussed in Chapter 4.

Savings and Investment While our manufacturing output was deteriorating on a relative basis, our rates of savings and investment were also much lower than those of our competitors from 1960 to 1975.

TABLE 3-2 SAVINGS AND INVESTMENT

Year	United States	Japan	France	Germany	United Kingdom
Individual Savings as a Percent of Individual Disposable Income					
1960	4.9	17.4	9.8	8.5	7.2
1975	7.4	24.9	12.6*	16.9	14.1
Total Government and Private Investment as a Percent of GNP					
1960	17.6	30.2	20.2	24.3	16.3
1975	16.2	30.8	23.3	20.8	19.7

SOURCE: United States Department of Commerce.
*1974

Our demand-management economic policy, which the Employment Act of 1946 had established, ultimately led to an almost pervasive emphasis on consumption. Supply, it was assumed, would take care of itself. As we consumed, investment and productivity were neglected. As a result, our rate of investment and manufacturing output deteriorated, compared with the rate of other major free world nations. The irony was that during the reconstruction of Western Europe and Japan, those nations—with our help—developed balanced economic policies. They created jobs through a balance of investment in manufacturing facilities; investment in a workable infrastructure of ports, railroads, and other public systems; and consumption. They paid equal attention to both supply and demand. They learned their lessons. We, however, did not follow our own lessons, with the result that not only were our savings and investment weak, but their weakness in turn eroded our strength in trade, energy, and productivity.

Inflation and Economic Policy With the exception of the Korean war period, when inflation shot up to 7.9 percent in 1951, the period from 1950 to 1967 was characterized by relative stability in the rate of inflation. More importantly, in the 1950–1967 period, increases in productivity—output per person—were at or above increases in the consumer price index (except in 1951 and 1956). That meant that from

1950 to 1967 there was room for general increases in the standard of living in America. As Table 3-3 indicates, the index of productivity increased 39 points, from 61.0 in 1950 to 100.0 in 1967, while the consumer price index rose almost 28 points, from 72.1 to 100.0. Inflation was relatively stable and was substantially outpaced by productivity gains in a period when economic policy was long-term oriented and based upon a national spirit of cooperation, compromise, and consensus.

TABLE 3-3   INFLATION AND PRODUCTIVITY 1950–1979

Years	Consumer Price Index	Productivity Index
1950	72.1	61.0
1955	80.2	70.3
1960	88.7	78.7
1965	94.5	95.0
1967	100.0	100.0
1970	116.3	104.2
1975	161.2	112.4
1979	217.4	118.1

SOURCE: Department of Labor, Bureau of Labor Statistics.
Indexes: 1967 = 100

In 1967, however, the consumer price index for the first time rose more than the productivity index. This was the beginning of a period in which inflation became virulent while productivity slowed to a virtual standstill.

Beginning in 1967 inflation became a disease. By 1973, the consumer price index was heading for double-digit increases. There were the explosion of food prices (following disappointing crops and the mammoth wheat sale to the Russians), a large increase in social security tax rates, and the first signs of dramatic oil-price increases. The American economy was beginning to be hit by supply shocks that would spin inflation out of control.

In 1973 and 1974, credit was tightened, with the resulting credit crunch in the summer of 1974. Predictably, the recession of 1974–1975 roared in to become the deepest since the thirties. Unemployment increased from 5 million in 1974 to almost 8 million in 1975. Also predictably, the government reacted swiftly with a tax cut in 1975, accompanied by unprecedented budget deficits of $45 billion in 1975 and $66 billion in 1976. Demand management was beginning to fail as an economic policy.

From a post-recession low of 5.8 percent in 1976, the inflation rate went over 11 percent in 1979. In October 1979, the Federal Reserve

Board moved to tighten credit, and interest rates marched upwards point by point. By the first quarter of 1980, inflation was at a rate of 18 percent.[2] In mid-March, President Carter addressed the nation on the economy and asked for discipline and sacrifice, and the Federal Reserve applied selective credit controls, particularly on credit cards. Consumption had to be dampened.

The automobile industry, already hard-hit by superior competitive products from Japanese manufacturers and Volkswagen, went into a tailspin. The second oil shock hit, and consumers shifted rapidly to fuel-efficient imports. The credit constraints pushed the economy over the cliff into a free fall. The Composite Index of Leading Indicators dropped the greatest amount ever in April 1980.[3] Credit restraints were eased, but inflation appeared headed for chronic double-digit levels. And that was one of the factors that would cost Jimmy Carter the Presidency.

It was clearly time for a rethinking of our demand-management–oriented economic policy. But that was to prove difficult, because the spirit of cooperation, compromise, and consensus that once had made long-term policy possible had been driven from the land. Our manufacturing output was weak, our savings and investments were weak, and our inflation had become epidemic.

THE CONSEQUENCES OF DOMESTIC POLICY The deterioration of a coherent policymaking process on the domestic front was one reason for our economic decline. It began with Lyndon Johnson. He translated the idealism of previous years into compassion. And out of his compassion there spewed forth a deluge of social legislation that overwhelmed our financial strength with massive consumption-oriented spending.

That same social legislation also fractured the coherent government established by the Hoover Commission by severely confusing the functions of the different levels of government—federal, state, and local—within our system. Under Richard Nixon's New Federalism, a bad situation would become worse.

Lyndon Johnson Lyndon Johnson came to the Presidency upon the assassination of John F. Kennedy. The death—sudden and senseless— of the leader of a new generation of Americans stunned the nation, if not the world. And before he was laid to rest and the nation could complete its mourning, his assassin was shot to death right on television. The events were gruesome—and tragic. And they marked the beginning of a decade of turmoil.

To his great credit, President Johnson moved very quickly, but with a measured sense of humility, from the obscurity of the Vice Presidency to take command. Recognizing that action is better than anguish in any period of severe trial, he set in motion a vigorous pace of legislative activity to complete the agenda of our fallen President. He rose symbolically to carry the standard of his predecessor. He invoked his name in the cause of legislative progress. And in five months, he transformed the New Frontier into a grander image of the Great Society. In less than six months, Lyndon Johnson came to dominate the nation in the same way he had dominated the United States Senate as Majority Leader.

Johnson was a passionate advocate of social causes and insatiable in his fight for legislation or programs in which he became interested. Although he was a man of humble background and unquestionably self-made in the tradition of America's Southwest, he could dominate people and events as few other men in American history have done.

In 1928, as a young teacher of Mexican-American children in Cotulla, Texas, he witnessed the impact of dire poverty on the minds and bodies of human beings. That experience gave him a sense of compassion and a belief in education as the way to overcome the misery and injustice in the world. As he later told his biographer:

I was determined to improve the lives of those poor little kids. I saw hunger in their eyes and pain in their bodies. Those little brown bodies had so little and needed so much. I was determined to spark something inside them, to fill their souls with ambition and interest and belief in the future. I was determined to give them what they needed to make it in this world, to help them finish their education. Then the rest would take care of itself.[4]

Compassion was to be central to the thrust of the Great Society programs.

Another theme central to the Great Society grew from Johnson's involvement in the New Deal at a working level. In June 1935, President Roosevelt created the National Youth Administration to provide constructive labor for young people. By this time, Johnson was in Washington as a congressional aide. He saw a new personal opportunity in the National Youth Administration, and moving with characteristic speed, he became its youngest director in the country. Of course, he excelled. Mrs. Roosevelt praised him to reporters as a brilliant young man when she visited his Austin headquarters in 1936.

The success of that program and his personal participation in it strengthened his belief that all Americans have the same essential values; it is only necessary to pass legislation and put a good person in charge to achieve goals built on those values. Later, as the Great

Society rapidly took form, there would be no time to reflect upon the fact that the circumstances of ghetto unemployment in the sixties might be entirely different from those of Americans in the thirties.

Johnson began to rise in national politics, winning a special by-election to the House of Representatives in 1937. He, of course, vigorously supported FDR right down the line, including Roosevelt's plan to pack the Supreme Court, which some thought might be a subversion of the Constitution. In those early days as a congressman, he became aware of the President's waning ability to get a legislative program through Congress. He learned firsthand that timing is important and that political capital can deteriorate very fast.

And so compassion, the liberal belief that legislative programs solve all problems, a fierce, competitive personality, and a recognition that speed and timing are essential to success became the characteristics of Lyndon Johnson as he grew in stature and influence in the Senate. They were honed into sharp readiness while he was eclipsed by the Kennedy brothers during his Vice Presidency.

The Motivation Behind the Great Society   While this Presidential character was being formed, the economic and social necessity for the Great Society was developing. Progress—like a cassette cartridge—frequently has a reverse side on which unheard dissonance is being recorded. Problems may build beneath the surface of progress. The great prosperity of the postwar period was such a time. As consumption of housing, durable goods, and cars sped forward in the fifties, it was accompanied by an acceleration of white migration to the suburbs. The Eisenhower highway program enhanced this migration.

At the same time, there was a migration from the rural poverty areas of the Deep South to the urban centers of the North, the Midwest, and southern California. It was somewhat like the immigration process of the nineteenth century, which had given America the human capital that made it a world power. Once again the poor migrated because of hope and opportunity. But this time there was a difference. Although the slaves had been emancipated 100 years earlier, their descendants had not been freed from social and economic discrimination. Unfortunately, as the blacks migrated into the cities, jobs began to move into suburbia. And with those jobs went hope and opportunity.

In the late fifties and early sixties, an interaction of the races that had been slowly building for decades began to take form as the civil rights movement. It was directed against observable inequalities in the South: on buses, at lunch counters, in separate but equal public toilets and schools. It grew out of a combination of the heritage of idealism in America and the compulsion of liberal activism to march forward. The liberal attack was against the injustices of the South, but the economic problem was diffused throughout urban America. Beneath the observable, there was growing awareness that life was not quite the same for white and black Americans.

It was into this situation that Lyndon Johnson moved. He brought compassion, a fierce competitive desire to outdo President Roosevelt (and certainly his immediate predecessor), a firm belief that with the United States's resources anything was possible, and the political instinct that he had better move fast to exploit the opportunities for change.

The Great Society Programs   On May 22, 1964, in Ann Arbor, President Johnson gave America his vision of the Great Society:

Your imagination, your initiative and your indignation will determine whether we build a society where progress is the servant of our needs, or a society where old values and new visions are buried under unbridled growth.

For in your time we have the opportunity to move not only towards the rich society and the powerful society, but upward to the Great Society. The Great Society rests on abundance and liberty for all. It demands an end to poverty and racial injustice, to which we are totally committed in our time. But that is just the beginning.

The Great Society is a place where every child can find knowledge to enrich his mind and to enlarge his talents. It is a place where leisure is a welcome chance to build and reflect, not a feared cause of boredom and restlessness. It is a place where the city of man serves not only the needs of the body and the demands of commerce, but the desire for beauty and the hunger for community.

It is a place where man can renew contact with nature. It is a place which honors creation for its own sake and for what it adds to the understanding of the race. It is a place where men are more concerned with the quality of their goals than the quantity of their goods. But most of all, the Great Society is not a safe harbor, a resting place, a final objective, a finished work. It is a challenge constantly renewed, beckoning us toward a destiny where the meaning of our lives matches the marvelous products of our labor.[5]

Two months later, in July 1964, the President's vision was answered by reality in New York City. A black youth was shot and killed by an off-duty policeman. Black leaders called for community action to protest police brutality. They organized a demonstration and marched to a Harlem police station. A scuffle ensued, then a riot which flowed into the Brooklyn ghetto of Bedford-Stuyvesant and lasted six days. When it was over, there were 1 dead, 143 injured, and 461 arrested.[6]

But Lyndon Johnson did not pause. Having set his course, he was navigating by his own set of stars.

Unfortunately, Johnson's drive to achieve the Great Society would require a continued emphasis on consumption. This was to prove to be its critical flaw. The President and most of his advisors did not look beyond the immediate to see the long-term consequences of the programs they were legislating. They did not anticipate that consumption, fueled by increasing inflation, would develop such a rapacious appetite that it would devour the new revenues generated by a powerful tax system and nullify the fiscal dividend that had been anticipated in the early sixties by Economic Advisor Walter Heller:

At the federal level, economic growth and a powerful tax system, interacting under modern fiscal management, generate new revenues faster than they generate new demands on the Federal purse. But at the state-local level, the situation is reversed. Under the whiplash of prosperity, responsibilities are outstripping revenues.[7]

Direct spending on attempts to alleviate social problems such as illiteracy, poor health, and poverty would grow without check in the Nixon administration. And the regulatory impact of attempts to address social concerns for safety and the environment would grow to have a very large unbudgeted impact on the economy. In the haste to legislate, the long-term implications of the Great Society, such as the effect on savings and investment, were not adequately considered.

The Right to Vote   The first priority of President Johnson was the right to vote. The Civil Rights Act of 1964 provided for expanded federal powers to protect voting rights, basically through use of the legal system.[8] The Civil Rights Act of 1965 struck down restrictions on voting by eradicating the various registrations, tests, and devices that had been used for discriminatory purposes. It also provided that, if necessary, federal officials could replace state officials in the functions essential to the right to vote.

Social-Concern and Social-Problem Legislation   Then the actual Great Society program began to unfold. Between 1965 and the end of 1968, the incredible number of 500 programs was enacted. At first, applying lessons learned years earlier, the President literally destroyed any opposition to his objective of total victory for the Great Society. But as early as 1966 he began to lose political capital when the voters signaled "slow down" by cutting into his overwhelming majority in Congress.

From 1964 to 1968, spending for major social programs increased 77 percent, from $30.4 billion to $53.7 billion. At the same time, total budget outlays increased only 50 percent, from $118.6 billion to $178.8 billion. The cost of the Great Society expanded at a rate more than 50 percent faster than the budget as a whole.

The Great Society had, in retrospect, two primary thrusts: regulating social concerns and relieving social problems. The social-concern thrust broke down into programs to improve the infrastructure, redress past neglect of the environment, and protect the consumer. The social-problem thrust broke down into programs in the areas of education (general and specific), racial equality, welfare for the disadvantaged, urban renewal, and health.

The programs enacted in the area of social-concern legislation are listed in Table 3-4 on page 50.

Unfortunately, an increasingly important side effect of social-concern legislation was its economic impact on the country in terms of extensive unfunded regulation. As the regulatory impact gathered momentum during the Nixon administration, what started out as lofty ideas about a cleaner and healthier environment—with which no one could disagree—got translated into an expensive regulatory process. No one in government seemed to want to consider or be responsible for the financial consequences of many of these legislative actions.

In fact, President Johnson himself grew testy when congressional leaders suggested that he focus on how the executive branch would implement the legislation. Sensing an approaching limitation of his power to bend Congress to his will, the President threw his administration into high speed on the legislative front. For example, before specifications could be written for the implementation of the Water Quality Act of 1965, the Clean Water Restoration Act of 1966 was passed and a Water for Peace Act was proposed. Before phase one could be addressed intelligently by the bureaucracy, phases two and three came tumbling out of the White House and everyone raced up to the Hill again to pass more legislation.

The programs enacted in the area of social-problem legislation are listed in Table 3-5 on page 51.

These programs resulted in substantial budgeted spending. Furthermore, solutions were frequently legislated and funds designated to be spent before problems were understood. For example, without really defining what he meant by "educational opportunity," the President, a former teacher, rushed major legislation forward that would expand that opportunity. That legislation was translated into buildings

Table 3-4 SOCIAL-CONCERN LEGISLATION[9]

Improved Infrastructure	Protection of Environment	Consumer Protection
Federal Airport Aid (1964)	Clean Air (1963)	Truth-in-Securities (1964)
	Pesticide Controls (1964)	Truth-in-Packaging (1966)
Urban Mass Transit (1964)	Clean Air (1965)	Protection for Savings (1966)
Federal Highway (1964)	Water Pollutions Control (1965)	Wholesome Meat (1967)
Water Resources Research (1964)	Clean Rivers (1966)	Flammable Fabrics (1967)
High-Speed Transit (1965)	Air Pollution Control (1967)	Product Safety Commission (1967)
Water Desalting (1965)	Aircraft Noise Abatement (1968)	Wholesome Poultry (1968)
Traffic Safety (1966)		
Highway Safety (1966)		U.S. Grain Standards (1968)
Tire Safety (1966)		
Water Research (1966)		Truth-in-Lending (1968)
Urban Mass Transit (1966)		
Federal Highway Aid (1966)		
Gas Pipeline Safety (1968)		
Fire Safety (1968)		
Hazardous Radiation Detection (1968)		
National Water Commission (1968)		

and teachers, whether or not pouring substantial funds into poorly conceived systems made sense in the first place. But the race was on, time was of the essence, and forward movement was the key requirement, measured purely in terms of size, number, and scope of programs. Lyndon Johnson attempted to engulf and overpower all obstacles which were in the way of his Ann Arbor dream.

When programs sputtered with little observable progress and the riots continued, the President turned to a comprehensive developmental approach. The ghettos were to be treated like underdeveloped countries. They would, in effect, receive "foreign aid." The programs would be run by local political authorities who would develop a total plan for the complete economic and social complex of the ghetto. The authority would negotiate the "foreign aid" package with the federal, state, and other interested structural entities. That was the Model

TABLE 3-5 SOCIAL-PROBLEM LEGISLATION[10]

Education—General

College Facilities (1963)
Library Services (1964)
Aid to Education (1965)
Aid to Higher Education (1965)
Arts and Humanities Foundation (1965)
International Education (1966)
Scientific Knowledge Exchange (1966)
Cultural Materials Exchange (1966)
Education Professions (1967)
Education Act (1967)
Public Broadcasting (1967)
College Work Study (1967)

Education—Specific

Vocational Education (1963)
Indian Vocational Training (1963)
Manpower Training (1963)
Older Americans (1965)
Vocational Rehabilitation (1965)
Manpower Training (1965)
Teachers Corps (1966)
New G.I. Bill (1966)
Summer Youth Programs (1967)
Guaranteed Student Loans (1968)
Aid to Handicapped Children (1968)
Vocational Education (1968)

Urban Renewal

Housing Act (1964)
Housing Act (1965)
Model Cities (1966)
Rent Supplements (1966)
Urban Research (1967)
Urban Fellowships (1967)
Better Housing (1968)

Racial Equality

Civil Rights Act of 1964
Voting Rights (1965)
Fair Housing (1968)
Fair Federal Juries (1968)

Welfare for the Disadvantaged

War on Poverty (1964)
Food Stamps (1964)
Social Security Increase (1965)
Anti-Poverty Program (1965)
Aid to Appalachia (1965)
Child Nutrition (1966)
Child Safety (1966)
Mine Safety (1966)
Food Stamps (1967)
Indian Bill of Rights (1968)
School Breakfasts (1968)

Health

Nurses' Training (1964)
Medicare (1965)
Heart, Cancer, Stroke Programs (1965)
Mental Health Facilities (1965)
Health Professions (1965)
Medical Libraries (1965)
Child Health (1965)
Community Health Services (1965)
Military Medicare (1966)
Deaf-Blind Center (1967)
Health Manpower (1968)
Heart, Cancer, Stroke Programs (1968)

Cities program, which even Paul Hoffman couldn't have run as originally conceived. It is an important example of how the process of coherent policy formation dissolved. As with most of his programs, President Johnson did not build a national consensus behind the Model Cities program. By ignoring consensus, he fostered the decay of coherent government.

The Demonstration Cities and Metropolitan Development Act of 1966 was substantially modified as it moved from its congressional conception on January 26 to its final enactment on November 3. It was planned as a five-year, $3.2 billion program for fifteen major city ghettos. Each project would be run by a "metropolitan expediter." The federal government would supply 80 percent of the funds in a block grant that would help implement the five-year comprehensive plan and thus break the process of urban decay and improve life in the ghetto.

Fortunately, treating American citizens as underdeveloped people living in enclaves run by an expeditor was never seriously attempted. The number of qualified cities expanded beyond reason, the concept of an expeditor was politically unviable, and agencies in Washington with direct program funding resisted the idea of the block-grant concept. The Model Cities program never really received the required funding. It was a victim of the President's waning power and of antagonistic forces afoot in the country at a time when coherent government and the spirit of cooperation, compromise, and consensus were deteriorating.

The Great Society never materialized, but the effects of the legislation passed in its name would have a long-term economic impact on the country. Though rooted in the compassion of the New Deal, the Great Society was allowed by its creator to die after it had been put on the books in a torrent of legislation and spending. It was finished when Richard Nixon entered office.

Reasons for Failure The Great Society failed because, unlike the Marshall Plan and the Eisenhower highway program, it was not based on a well-developed national consensus. It was the result of the will of one man and conceived in haste. Furthermore the haste with which its legislation was executed destroyed the atmosphere of bipartisan cooperation and compromise that had resulted in coherent long-term policies in the post-World War II period. Finally, its long-term economic consequences were not adequately considered.

The Great Society was a failure administratively because its scope was so gigantic that it led to confusion in the structure and functions of government itself. For example, Title IV of the Civil Rights Act of 1964 barred discriminatory practices—to the extent they existed—in hospitals and in public schools and colleges in all 50 states. The legislation of the Great Society was replete with this kind of provision. As a result, it was difficult to implement and even more impossible to evaluate.

The Economic Opportunity Act is an example of the implementation and evaluation problems of Great Society legislation that contributed to the destruction of coherent government. The training and employment of the hard-core unemployed, as provided for by the act, depended upon the state employment services offices in each state. Set up in the New Deal era, they generally were not located in the heart of the ghetto. Moreover, they used a thirty-year-old employment form, which resulted in placing the least needy and least unemployable.

The Labor Department, in an effort to rectify the situation, developed a new form which required a reporting of only hard-core placements—persons who had been out of work for eighteen months and made less than $3000 a year. With this focus, employment service employees enticed the hard-core unemployed in off the streets with advance payments. The unemployed took the advances and returned to the streets. The forms showed placements, but they did not record whether these placements were in meaningful and productive jobs. An effective system for implementing the purpose of the law simply was not developed.

Throughout the programs, because of a fear that Congress would cut funds if difficulties were admitted, failure was covered with statistics of success. Through this charade, any hope of proper evaluation of programs disappeared. A functioning government was beginning to dissolve.

The President seemed bent on rolling back the work of the Hoover Commission when he said: "Of course I understand the difficulties of bureaucracy. But what you don't understand is that the President's real problem is with the Congress, not the bureaucracy."[11]

Even if he had mandated that workable programs be developed, administered, evaluated, and improved, the President was running out of time. The horrible specter of Vietnam commanded his attention. Combat deaths—1369 in 1965—escalated to 9378 in 1967.[12] Defense spending—$47.5 billion in 1965—increased to $68.3 billion in 1967.[13] Not having prepared the country for a tax increase in 1966, Johnson was now faced with ballooning deficits and increasing inflation. It was obvious that the country could no longer afford both the Vietnam war and the Great Society. One of his priorities had to give.

Lyndon Johnson chose arrogance of power over compassion. In September 1967, he asked Congress for a 6 percent surcharge to pay for the war and he let the Great Society drift. There was such unenlightened self-interest in the country and Congress at the time that the surcharge stayed in the House Ways and Means Committee for over a year.

By the time the war tax was enacted, inflation had broken out of its pattern of postwar stability. The genie was out of the bottle, and it was to get bigger and uglier as time passed. Just as the economists had misforecast in 1945, they misforecast in the mid-sixties. In 1945 they expected a return to the Great Depression. Twenty years later, they expected ever-increasing productive prosperity, which would produce a "fiscal dividend" that could be spent for extras.

The year 1967 was clearly the time for national reappraisal, before our manufacturing capability and output seriously weakened. Yet, hardly a major economist warned the country of the need to look at trade, energy, and productivity (which we will look at in Chapter 4). The President, having let his Great Society go, withdrew to Texas. Richard M. Nixon was elected to the Presidency, and our national focus shifted to plans for peace with honor.

Richard Nixon and the New Federalism Recognizing that the Great Society had failed, the Nixon administration introduced the concept of New Federalism. The application of this concept was to complete the near disintegration of a functioning government. Instead of a concentration of power in the bureaucracies in Washington, decision making would be decentralized and brought down to the state and local levels in a new relationship with the federal government.

In his budget message of 1971, President Nixon proposed a major overhaul in the method of delivering federal aid to state and local governments. Using the block-grant idea of the Model Cities program, he recommended a consolidation of 129 individual categorical grant programs into six block-grant programs that would cover the areas of education, law enforcement, manpower training, rural community development, transportation, and urban community development. Instead of federal control of funds and their application as under categorical grants, there would now be state and local decision making on application of funds.

The idea was to reduce the jungle of administrative and compliance expenses, strengthen state and local flexibility in using federal aid, improve state and local fiscal positions, and, most important, shift the political power from Washington specialists to the elected generalists in state and local governments. Times being what they were, however, the implementation of an old idea in a new form was slow in coming. It wasn't until 1973 that the first Nixon consolidation took place, when seventeen categorical grant programs were put into the Comprehensive Employment and Training Act. That was followed, ultimately, by consolidation of urban aid programs, social services, and public works.[14,15]

It may have made sense. But in a period when the Great Society and the Vietnam war had destroyed the spirit of cooperation, compromise, and consensus, this idea compounded the confusion in government previously created by the Great Society.

General revenue sharing was another Nixon administration initiative which had been discussed in the sixties. Revenue sharing was a no-strings-attached distribution of federal revenues enacted in the

State and Local Fiscal Assistance Act of 1972. It, too, ultimately resulted in further confusion in functions of the levels of government. Revenue sharing was the complete opposite of the categorical-grant approach of the Great Society. The entire decision-making process for the spending of these funds was given over to state and local officials. Moreover, the law had no stated purpose. The goal apparently was to be interpreted by the recipients themselves, according to their needs as they perceived them. Functional government had spun out of the voters' control.[16]

President Nixon, in an effort to streamline the delivery of funds to the poor, also introduced a welfare reform proposal which would have increased cash transfers and put a floor under the incomes of all families with children. In a period when compromise was an impossibility, this proposal also slowly died. The liberals thought it insufficient, and the conservatives thought it overly generous. The President gradually lost interest in it.[17] The death of this proposal was one more sign that the spirit of cooperation, compromise, and consensus was gone from government.

The Consequences of the Johnson-Nixon Years   Nixon's loss of interest did not, however, affect the growth of social spending. As shown in Table 3-6, while defense spending was flat from 1968 to 1974, social-problem spending expanded dramatically. In fact, because of his increased attention to the Vietnam war and then to Watergate, Richard Nixon let the domestic expenditures set in motion by his predecessor grow pretty much unchecked during his six years in office.

As the United States approached the eighties, the total of federal assistance was in excess of $80 billion a year, which represented a

TABLE 3-6   SELECTED BUDGET OUTLAYS 1968 AND 1974 *(In Billions of Dollars)*

Category	1968	1974
National defense	78.7	77.8
Community and regional development	1.4	4.1
Education and social services	7.6	12.3
Health	9.7	22.1
Income security	33.7	84.4
General-purpose fiscal assistance	.3	6.9

SOURCE: "Federal Government Finances," January 1980.

quarter of state and local expenditures.[18] Consequently, we faced a situation of deep budget deficits. The patient was very sick, and the mechanism of government, which might have effected a cure, seemed incapable of coherent action.

At the root of the country's economic ills was the mistaken notion of leading economists that economic growth would generate new tax revenues at the federal level faster than new spending programs would be devised. Rather than saving and investing in the modernization of our steel plants and machine tool facilities, we consumed and spent our resources trying to solve socioeconomic problems that we had difficulty comprehending. By trying to finance the Vietnam war at the same time, we compounded our economic ills.

The domestic policy of the Johnson and Nixon administrations had two important consequences: It resulted in confusion in government, and it led to short-term economic policy with demand-management actions and reactions.

Prior to the sixties, the administrative focus relating to federal programs was on efficient management. As the sixties unfolded, this objective was sidetracked.[19] There was simply no thought given to how the Great Society programs would be managed and its goals fulfilled, or to the potential administrative problems that might arise to thwart their good intentions.

Problems of administration, evaluation, and multiple-goal complexities were further confused by the hodge-podge philosophical approach to grants themselves. As a result, there is now an inherent contradiction in federal aid programs between the spending of money and who decides how to spend it. Categorical grants focus on how the money is spent. They entail coherent national direction with tight controls on the recipients to ensure uniformity of result. Revenue sharing focuses on who gets the money. It takes the responsibility for wisely spending the funds away from the federal government, which raises them from the taxpayer. In between are block grants, which are an attempt to consolidate categorical grants into larger programs with room for state and local decision making.

With categorical grants, the controls have fragmented the programs. With revenue sharing and block grants, no one seems responsible for prudent spending of public funds. That is functional confusion in government.

Perhaps as a result of this confusion, but certainly because of the interaction of the spending on the Vietnam war and the Great Society, economic policy became increasingly short-term oriented with demand-management actions and reactions. By the time the enormous volume of Great Society programs exploded in consumption-oriented spending, the situation was out of control. And the deterioration of the spirit of cooperation, compromise, and consensus that had occurred as we moved through the sixties and into the seventies made it impossible for anyone in government to think through and implement new long-term policies to deal with our economic decline.

THE CONSEQUENCES OF VIETNAM   Looking back, it is apparent that our involvement in Vietnam wrought economic and social destruction that contributed to our economic decline in the decade of the mid-sixties to mid-seventies. Even if the vast social changes of the Great Society could have been coherently planned, implemented, and financed, the cost and discord created by the Vietnam war made successful undertaking of those social changes impossible. The analysis of the discord created by the war is important in understanding why it was impossible for the nation and its policymakers to come to grips with the decline of our economy and our weakness in trade, energy, and productivity.

Background   At Yalta, President Roosevelt had bought us time in Indochina. The French returned and replaced the Japanese.[20] At the time of Yalta, all of French Indochina—Vietnam, Laos, and Cambodia—was of no strategic significance to the United States. We had no meaningful cultural or trade relations there, and there was nothing for us to lose.

Slowly, however, we escalated our interest in, our commitment to, and our involvement in Vietnam. It was a step-by-step process from Truman to Johnson.

The first step toward Vietnam involvement was President Truman's consideration of Southeast Asia as an area of American strategic interest. His National Security Council said: ". . . if Southeast Asia also is swept by communism we shall have suffered a major political rout the repercussions of which will be felt throughout the rest of the world. . . ."[21]

The second step was President Eisenhower's military aid to the French in their war with the Vietminh and his support of Ngo Dinh Diem after the French surrender at Dien Bien Phu on April 16, 1954.

John Kennedy took the third step. He made it a policy of the United States to prevent the Communists from taking over the government of South Vietnam. He sent in special forces for training purposes, and by 1963 our force level was over 16,000 troops and there had been 120 combat deaths. The United States had become a limited partner in Vietnam.

President Kennedy had inherited Diem from the French through Eisenhower. Neither President had been satisfied with Diem's government. It was corrupt and ineffective, and, compared to the Vietcong, it did not have popular support. There was considerable discussion of replacing Diem and considerable controversy about it. But with the encouragement of Ambassador Lodge, the coup took place on November 1, 1963. That was the fourth step in Vietnam. With our nudge, the government of South Vietnam spun into chaos. By month's end both Kennedy and Diem were dead, and Lyndon Johnson was in charge.

Johnson and Escalation   Three Presidents had brought him to the door of full-scale war in Vietnam, but it was Lyndon Johnson's decision to walk through, even though MacArthur—who knew that part of the world better than any of the diplomatic or military advisers—had told him not to go in. With Lyndon Johnson, Vietnam became America's war.

Events moved fast, and so did he. On February 6, 1965, nine U.S. advisers were killed in Pleiku by a raiding party of Vietcong guerillas. Johnson answered with Operation Rolling Thunder, and the bombing campaign of North Vietnam began. With the strikes from Da Nang, security for the air base was necessary, and on March 8, he sent in 3500 marines for that purpose. In April two more marine battalions were sent in. By June there were 75,000 U.S. troops in Vietnam.

On July 28, 1965, Johnson announced that he was increasing our fighting strength to 125,000 men, with a further commitment by November to over 200,000. In doing this, he rejected advice that he ask Congress for war taxes and declare a state of emergency. Instead, he covered his intentions with a request for an additional appropriation of $1.8 billion in the context of a midday press conference that would ensure a small television audience. He attempted to hide the escalation into a full-scale war. That was a crucial mistake. Though it was undefined at the time, there was a sense of strength being transformed into arrogance of power. By attempting to mislead the American people, President Johnson undermined open government and further eroded the spirit of cooperation, compromise, and consensus.

His reasoning for this course of action was threefold. He feared (1) the entry of China and Russia into the war, (2) a right-wing call for the invasion of North Vietnam and the bombing of Hanoi, and (3) the resultant demise of his vision of the Great Society.

On August 6, shortly after this announcement, the Civil Rights Act of 1965 was signed. On August 11, the riots in Watts broke out resulting in six days of domestic destruction. When they were over, there were 34 dead, 4000 arrested, and an estimated $40 million in property damage.[22]

Within that two-week period in mid-summer 1965 it became obvious that the inconsistencies and controversies of the Great Society and the Vietnam war threatened to split the strength of the nation.

Later the President would believe:

We have helped and we will help (the Vietnamese) to stabilize the economy, to increase the production of goods, to spread the light of education and stamp out disease.

He would also say:

I want to leave the footprints of America in Vietnam. I want them to say when the Americans come, this is what they leave—schools, not long cigars. We're going to turn the Mekong into a Tennessee Valley.

And he would add:

I was determined to be a leader of war *and* a leader of peace. I refused to let my critics push me into choosing one or the other. I wanted both, I believed in both, and I believed America had the resources to provide for both. After all, our country was built by pioneers who had a rifle in one hand to kill their enemies and an axe in the other to build their homes and provide for their families.[23]

The President initiated a Christmas Eve bombing pause in 1965 that lasted 37 days, and he sent a cadre of high-level representatives to embassies around the world. The Vietnam revolutionaries, who had been at it for over thirty years, however, were digging in. Hanoi responded that Johnson was putting everything into the basket of peace except peace itself.

Our forces expanded: 184,300 in December 1965; 385,300 in December 1966; 485,600 in December 1967. Americans killed in action mounted: 1369 in 1965; 5008 in 1966; and 9378 in 1967.[24] And all the while, discord spread in the nation.

Tet and the Beginning of the Long End   On January 30, 1968, the Communists broke out in a countrywide offensive during the Tet holiday truce. It rocked the forces of the government of South Vietnam. It was our Dien Bien Phu, not so much because it was militarily successful, but because it unfolded as a drama of chaos, destruction, and death on the television sets in American homes. That brought a reality to the pronouncements coming out of the White House. There were two scenes that most Americans remembered. The first showed a South Vietnam national police chief executing a Vietcong agent on a street in the midst of a battle. The chief summarily blew the agent's brains out and then let him fall to the pavement as he turned away to other action. The second was the comment of an American officer in an assessment of the decimation of a Vietnam village: "It became necessary to destroy the town to save it."[25]

By March 31, 1968, it was all over. At least the beginning of the end had come. In a prime-time address to the nation, the President took the first step toward deescalation. He stopped the bombing in North Vietnam. And with great dignity he finished:

With America's sons in the fields far away, with America's future under challenge right here at home . . . I do not believe that I should devote an hour or a day of my time to any personal partisan causes. . . . Accordingly, I shall not seek, and will not accept, the nomination of my party for another term as your President.[26]

By the time Richard Nixon was elected in November 1968, the United States had put $47.2 billion into Vietnam in five years. From 1969 through 1972, we would throw in another $59.7 billion. That was over $100 billion.[27] It was total consumption. If it had been invested in modernized manufacturing facilities, we might not have lost our competitive edge. Coupled with the consumption of the Great Society, this massive spending ignited the inflation that has been previously described.

Nixon, Vietnamization, and Negotiated Peace Unfortunately, the war did not end with the election of a new President. Nixon and his national security advisor had a foreign policy of larger scope into which peace with honor in Vietnam would fit.[28] Under the policy of Vietnamization—a transfer of the war back to the government of South Vietnam—the President gradually reduced troop strength, beginning in 1969.[29]

The war was winding down, but it would not be over before America was turned violently in upon itself. On April 20, 1970, President Nixon told the nation that another 150,000 troops would be returning home. And then he took an abrupt change of direction that contributed to and characterized the bitter discord of the period. Caught up in the contradiction of intractable secret peace talks in Paris (Le Doc Tho had the whip hand and he knew it) and his own impossible dream of peace with honor, Richard Nixon abruptly widened the war. On May 1, 1970, he unleashed Operation Rock Crusher into the Cambodian sanctuaries. The reaction was swift and simple: His explanation for the necessity of the operation was not believed. The campuses erupted.[30]

On May 4, at Kent State University, the National Guard fired a fusillade of bullets. In thirteen seconds four students were dead, struck down in innocence.[31] Kent State became a tragic symbol of a nation in deep conflict with itself.

The wave of anger rolled once more across the land. Some colleges were closed for the balance of the year. Hard-hat construction workers in New York's financial district fought with protestors. A statement of objection was signed by 250 State Department employees. A group of employees seized the Peace Corps building and flew a Vietcong flag. The HEW auditorium was occupied by department officials in protest. Interior Secretary Walter Hickel spoke out publicly against the action. A crowd of 75,000 to 100,000 came to Washington to protest on the Ellipse, and the White House was surrounded by police and a ring of sixty buses.[32]

And then, in one of the most unusual appearances of his Presidency, Richard Nixon met by chance with a random group of students in the coming dawn on May 9 at the Lincoln Memorial.[33] He was near exhaustion and his purpose was unknown. An opportunity to reach out to the people, as Lincoln might have done in that symbolic setting, was gone. He seemed not to know compassion. His appearance there could be seen later as symbolic of the loss of the spirit of cooperation, compromise, and consensus that had characterized earlier times. Discord reigned throughout the nation.

The slow, grudging, and unadmitted retreat went on, paced by the secret negotiations. In November 1972, the President was reelected by a wide margin. Instead of being elated, he fired his entire staff and Cabinet in a brutal attempt to start again, but the players did not change significantly. He was sick of Vietnam. He wanted out on almost any terms. After the talks blew up again, he initiated one last salvo, in what became known as the Christmas bombings, to get the opposition back to the table. They came, and by January 23, 1973, his national security advisor negotiated peace. We were out with the release of American prisoners; Hanoi's forces could stay in the South.[34] In 1974, Congress would legislate a ban on all future military involvement. In 1975, it would drastically cut the Administration's aid request, and our ambassador would end our decade of involvement with an unceremonious and hasty departure by helicopter from Saigon.[35]

The economic cost of our involvement in Vietnam later could be spelled out in cold statistics. The social cost of a nation divided against itself would be evident in a continuing unwillingness of people to trust their government—and even each other—and work together. Both costs had a long-term detrimental effect on the nation's competitive edge.

THE CONSEQUENCES OF WATERGATE With the signing of the peace treaty by Secretary Rogers, Richard Nixon turned his attention to other matters. His rest was to be short, for latent in the background was the event of June 17, 1972—the break-in at the Watergate headquarters of the Democratic National Committee. By itself, the event was insignificant.

So it might have remained if Richard Nixon had repudiated the charade at once. Our national descent might not have been as deep. Discord might not have turned into a total loss of trust in government. Nixon, however, directed that the CIA be used to halt the FBI investigation six days after it had taken place. That was obstruction of justice. Of equal importance, it was an improper, and, to many observers, sinister use of the CIA for domestic purposes.[36]

John Dean had contained the Watergate problem during the fall campaign, but as the President turned his attention from Vietnam, the cat began to squirm in the bag. On the morning of March 21, 1973, Dean told the President: "We have a cancer within, close to the Presidency, that is growing. It is growing daily. It's compounded, growing geometrically now, because it compounds itself."[37]

Dean was precise in his analysis. Two months later, in a public statement on May 22, the President lied to the American people when he denied using the CIA for domestic political purposes. For the next fifteen months, the impeachment process grew like Dean's cancer, exhausting the nation and consuming the President until the Supreme Court ruled on July 24, 1974, that Richard Nixon would have to relinquish, among others, the June 23, 1972 "smoking-gun" tape on which he could be heard ordering that the CIA be used to halt the FBI investigation of the Democratic National Committee break-in.[38] On the night of August 8, he addressed the nation with his resignation. After taking the nation through a constitutional crisis, the closest he could bring himself to humility and admission of guilt was: "I regret deeply any injuries that may have been done in the course of events that led to this decision. I would say only that if some of my judgments were wrong, and some were wrong, they were made in what I believed at the time to be in the best interest of the Nation."[39]

From the assassination of John Kennedy to the resignation of Richard Nixon, Americans had lived in civil turmoil. For a short interval, the idealism and strength they had had when General Marshall went to Harvard in 1947 was once again demonstrated as the steady hand of Lyndon Johnson led the country through that most difficult transition period following Kennedy's death. That spirit dissipated when Johnson's compassionate leadership turned to domineering arrogance and finally disappeared in the icy, remote, intractability of Richard Nixon.

SUMMARY In less than fifteen years, America went through a transition from economic strength, through decline, into weakness. At the end of World War II, we were the leader in trade, energy, and productivity. Our manufacturing output was the strongest in the world. Recovery took place in Western Europe and Japan, and we were joined in the sixties by revitalized and vigorously competitive nations.

In the mid-sixties, our manufacturing output began to weaken relative to Japan and Western Europe, and our rates of savings and investment were much lower than those of our increasingly strong competitors. Then inflation began to grow with increasing virulence. This happened because we financed social programs and the Vietnam war largely without paying for them by tax revenues. By 1975, it was obvious that our one-sided demand-management economic policy was inadequate to deal with our contemporary economic problems.

At the same time, the coherent government that had been developed in the postwar period was shattered by the domestic policies of the Johnson and Nixon administrations. By 1975, government was on the verge of not functioning. And the people distrusted it.

It is quite important to keep in mind two basic needs that were present in 1975 and are still present as we proceed into the eighties. The first is the need for a new Hoover Commission to develop a consensus for more effective government through bipartisan efforts. The second is the need again to create a bipartisan setting in which to develop a balanced national economic policy. Before we can develop specific economic policies to solve the problems of weakness in trade, energy, and productivity, we must establish a functioning government framework and a sensible long-term economic policy.

4 THE TRIANGLE OF ECONOMIC WEAKNESS

Trade, energy, and productivity are the economic factors in a triangle of support that is vital to the economic strength of both a nation and its business enterprises. The three elements of the triangle are interdependent, and economic strength and weakness are the direct result of the strength or weakness of the elements. This linkage is perhaps easiest to see on the level of an individual enterprise.

The most important economic unit in America is the manufacturing corporation. It brings people together in the process of transforming materials through energy expenditure into the finished goods it sells. If the production process is not efficient and competitive, the company fails because its products cost too much. If the required energy is not available, the company's production process is slowed or closed down. If the company does not have a strategy and an ability to sell its product, it will fail and jobs will be lost. A manufacturing company must have an overall strategy by which it can sell its product, adequate energy for its production, and an efficient production process if its employees are to keep their jobs. If it is to grow, a company must be able to penetrate new markets, keep its energy costs down, and increase its productivity. Sales, energy, and productivity. These elements form the triangle supporting a company's competitive edge. Likewise trade, energy, and productivity support the nation's competitive edge. Equal attention must be paid to all three in both corporations and nations if they are to thrive.

In the decade of the seventies, the combined forces of our one-sided demand-management economic policy, the discord resulting from the Vietnam war, the complete deterioration of political leadership, and the disappearance of the spirit of cooperation, compromise, and consensus from America undermined the nation's economic triangle of trade, energy, and productivity. This blunted our competitive edge.

In 1971, we experienced our first merchandise trade deficit. The

Nixon administration devalued the dollar, set the stage for a currency float, and went on to geopolitical considerations. That was trade.

In 1970, domestic oil production peaked and our dependence on foreign imports began. In 1973 and 1974, the United States was hit with the oil embargo. Prices skyrocketed. But public policymakers were in disarray, and the American people were blinded to those significant signals. America lost control of its energy destiny to OPEC. That was energy.

From 1966 to 1970, our average productivity grew by only 1.2 percent, and it was down to 0.2 percent in 1969 and 0.7 percent in 1970. In 1979, economist Edward F. Denison of the Brookings Institution concluded that something had gone seriously wrong with American productivity. And in that year it declined 0.9 percent. That was productivity.

From the decade of the seventies and through the end of 1980—which included the Presidential campaign—the leadership of neither political party called for competitive American trade policy. Jimmy Carter, in 1977, did begin to focus the country's attention on energy. But productivity was ignored. And most important, no one recognized the interdependence of trade, energy, and productivity or linked them together as a triangle vital to our economic strength.

Further, something clearly had disappeared since the period of the Marshall Plan, the Employment Act, the Hoover Commission, and the Eisenhower highway program. It was the spirit underlying public policy, a spirit consisting of cooperation, compromise, and consensus. That spirit gave origin and foundation to the public-policy process and enabled it to take form and develop. Without the reestablishment of that spirit of cooperation, compromise, and consensus, our triangle of trade, energy, and productivity will further deteriorate. Only by regaining that spirit will we be able to develop the complete and complex set of public policies necessary to reestablish our strength in trade, energy, and productivity.

In this chapter, we will explore how our position in trade, energy, and productivity was weakened, and how it can be strengthened to regain our competitive edge.

TRADE In 1970—just twenty years after the United States was the strongest nation in the world and Japan was beginning its recovery—Japan and the United States both had positive trade balances. By the end of the seventies, the ravages of uncoordinated policies and discord had thrown America into a position of chronic deficit. Japan weathered the Nixon devaluation shock in 1971 and the 1973–1974 embargo, and it gathered strength as America declined. Table 4-1 illustrates the shockingly blunted edge of America's trade competitiveness.

Table 4-1   BALANCE OF TRADE IN BILLIONS OF DOLLARS

Year	U.S. Global	Japan Global	U.S. Exports to Japan	U.S. Imports from Japan	U.S.–Japan Balance
1970	2.6	4.0			
1971	−2.3	7.8			
1972	−6.4	9.0			
1973	.9	3.7	8.4	9.7	−1.3
1974	−5.3	1.4	10.7	12.4	−1.7
1975	9.1	5.0	9.6	11.3	−1.7
1976	−9.3	9.9	10.2	15.5	−5.3
1977	−30.9	17.3	10.6	18.6	−8.0
1978	−33.8	25.7	13.0	24.5	−11.5
1979	−29.5	1.85	17.4	25.9	−8.5

SOURCE: Department of Commerce, Bureau of Economic Analysis, 1979.

The ascendency of Japan in trade between the two nations is particularly striking. Slowly, from the end of the Johnson-Nixon decade, the momentum of the United States's, decline in economic strength and Japanese growth in economic strength widened the trade gap between the two countries to $8.5 billion in 1979.

Table 4-2   EXPORTS AS A PERCENTAGE OF GROSS NATIONAL PRODUCT

Year	United States	Japan
1960–1964 (avg.)	3.9	8.4
1965–1969 (avg.)	3.9	9.3
1970–1973 (avg.)	4.5	9.7
1974	6.9	12.0
1975	7.0	11.1
1976	6.8	11.9
1977	6.4	11.6
1978	6.8	10.0

SOURCE: Congressional Research Service.

Table 4-2 indicates that in the past two decades exports have increased as a factor in U.S. economic activity. However, we are still well behind Japan. If in 1978 we had exported the same percentage of gross national product as Japan did, we would have had a $33 billion merchandise trading surplus rather than a $34 billion deficit. While we do not want to join a mercantile battle by targeting a specific percentage of gross national product for trade, we must recognize the increasing importance of exports to our economy. We must therefore learn to think in terms of trade expansion. Certainly, we cannot retreat into protectionism, for that would be a retreat into disaster. We must create a balanced policy and substantially increase our trading capability. Japan offers an informative example of how to do this.

Japan's Global Trade Strategy Exports are a way of life in Japan. Foreign trade is of such significance that its importance is taught to fifth-grade children. At an early age, the Japanese learn that their country is poorly endowed with natural resources. They must therefore import raw materials and, with human resources and superior technology, reprocess those raw materials into finished goods that are price-competitive in markets around the world.

As a result of national awareness and concentration on foreign trade, the Japanese have developed a global trade strategy. They seek out long-term sources of raw materials in all parts of the world, they look for the latest developments in manufacturing processes and buy them, and then they penetrate markets. In exporting, their strategy is to develop as large a share of the world market as possible. Once they have penetrated world markets with a competitive product, they focus on improving the technology of the manufacturing process itself in order to lower the cost. Relentlessly, the Japanese grind through this circle of trade: develop long-term raw-material sources, lower production costs, develop new markets. All three elements of this global strategy are important to Japan's success.

Underlying the success of this strategy is the interaction between the government and the private sector. Unlike in the United States, in Japan there is both mutual respect and understanding between business and government. Rather than starting from adversarial positions—that government is incompetent and business is greedy—the Japanese start from the position that only by cooperative employment of their joint talents and resources can their nation survive in a competitive world. At the heart of Japan's success in trade is a close working partnership between government and business.

In Japan, the principal government entity responsible for participation in this partnership is the Ministry of International Trade and Industry (MITI). The dual interest in both trade and manufacturing is placed in one ministry, as it should be. As a result, MITI has been a powerful force in the development of Japan's global strategy.

In the early postwar period, Japan's exports consisted of toys, textiles, and other low-quality, labor-intensive consumer merchandise. Gradually, through the process of government and business cooperation, the emphasis was shifted into basic industries such as steel, shipbuilding, automobiles, and chemicals. Because MITI had the responsibility to look broadly at the development of both trade and industry, it could understand the importance of developing a strong national position in basic industries. Then, with the national position established, the industries could move into the implementation of the global strategy. The government organizational structure has been a very important part of Japanese trading success.

In the early postwar years particularly, the Japanese government assisted the key industries targeted for growth with tax concessions, special access to bank loans, easier export financing terms, and protection against lower-priced foreign goods through high-tariff and non-tariff barriers. As the basic industrial structure of Japan was rebuilt and the strength of the global strategy developed, the tax incentives for trade were reduced in 1964, 1971, and 1972. The special industrialization depreciation allowance was terminated for most industries in 1976. Tariffs were reduced substantially in 1970, and by the end of 1977 government-backed financing of exports in bilateral trade with the United States was nonexistent.

The trading power of Japan was transferred into the private sector. While there is substantial cooperative interaction between government and business in Japan, there is also a clear recognition that the private sector, with its own initiative, is the best vehicle for competitive trade.

Japanese Trading Companies One of the primary forces in the success of Japan's global trade strategy is the trading company. Japan has nine major general trading firms. They are worldwide in scope, and consistent with Japanese emphasis on human resources, they believe that one of their principal assets is people. In 1979, the nine trading companies employed 75,000 individuals in all aspects of trade and trade development. Almost 21,000 of these employees worked in foreign offices, and 5800 of these employees working abroad were Japanese nationals. The Japanese trading companies send their own people out to trade in all corners of the world. These nine trading companies account for about 50 percent of total Japanese trade and about 9 percent of total world trade.

One of the leading Japanese general trading companies is Mitsui, with sales of $44.9 billion for the fiscal year which ended in March 1980. Mitsui trades both in Japan's domestic market as an exporter and importer, and in totally overseas transactions. The company provides an integrated set of services for this trade by facilitating transactions, providing financing, and analyzing information on business conditions on a worldwide basis.

Through the combination of these services and its own interrelated activities, Mitsui makes trade happen. It develops new sources of raw materials, organizes industrial projects in many parts of the world, and contributes to the development of industrial activity around the globe. The company has a staff of 13,000 of eighty-nine different nationalities in 193 offices in 142 cities around the world. Of the 3000 employees serving outside of Japan in that worldwide network of offices, over 1000 are Japanese nationals.

During the postwar period, over 700 Mitsui headquarters people have studied in universities abroad. One of the key components of the trading company's continued momentum in a competitive world is its ongoing program of developing people who have a worldwide scope and can anticipate changing economic trends among different societies and countries. Through well-trained people in trading companies like Mitsui, Japan's global strategy is translated into the worldwide activities which have resulted in its increasingly superior competitive performance.

Post War Evolution   The MacArthur reconstruction set in motion the government-business program to reindustrialize Japan and the drive to expand trade. Mitsui's activities were an important factor in that program, and its evolution mirrors the growth of Japan's economic influences in the world. In the early period of reconstruction, Mitsui focused on heavy industry, identified and imported technologies, worked on the creation of demand within its domestic market, and then developed export markets. The company played a leading role in the development of Japan's chemical industry. Mitsui was also a major factor in providing sources of raw materials, such as iron ore and coal, to fuel Japan's industrial growth.

As all industry in Japan modernized and the basic industries developed competitive advantages, Mitsui's trading-company role gradually reversed itself. As Japanese manufacturing companies developed processes of technological superiority, Mitsui shifted to the exportation of technologies developed in Japan to both industrialized and developing nations. The domestic industrial base grew and a sophisticated industrial structure evolved, in which the major manufacturing companies had their own worldwide information systems. With this, Mitsui turned increasing attention to investment and the development of raw material resources, manufacturing plants, and industrialization projects overseas.

Mitsui's primary function today is to link transactions between the supplier and the user of a commodity or finished product, then expedite the flow of goods between them. Through a worldwide information network, an international financing capability, a wide variety of support services, and assistance in commercial development, Mitsui provides a complete linkage between buyers and sellers.

Information Network   The communication of information is one of the central purposes of Mitsui's network of 193 offices around the world. In order to provide client companies with information on available business opportunities, Mitsui has developed a global telecommunications network designed to transmit data and information on a real-time basis.

The company's highly sophisticated computerized system reads messages at a rate of 2000 characters per second, automatically processes them, and sends them to their destinations around the world. The message transmission is coordinated by satellite at three major centers (in London, Tokyo, and New York). This system is one of the most advanced and extensive of any business enterprise in the world. It handles about 20,000 messages a day, with the longest delivery time being five minutes between Rio de Janeiro and Johannesburg, in separate corners of the world.

This system is closely integrated into Mitsui's service to its clients. Almost instantaneously, the company can use the network to search the world for markets for its clients' products. In doing so, it can rapidly take advantage of temporary market imbalances and continually update information that can lead to future opportunities. Very clearly, this vast and rapid information service enables the people of Mitsui to keep their fingers on the pulse of fast-moving developments, and this makes the difference in the competitive edge of foreign trade.

International Financing Capability   Mitsui also has extensive international financial resources and financing ability. In Japan, the banking system's essential function is to provide long-term capital to industrial companies. The Japanese banking system performs the same function as the equity and debt market system does in the United States. Unlike our banks, however, Japanese banks have not traditionally provided the short- and intermediate-term financing which is necessary for trade to take place. The trading companies bridge this gap.

Mitsui itself, therefore, is not a financial institution. It supplements the activities of the banking industry by providing a large volume of trade credits in the domestic market and direct capital investment in new ventures and the expansion of existing business. In providing trade credits, Mitsui essentially transfers the financial backing of the commercial banking institutions to the companies engaged in distribution and processing. Because of long and close relationships with its clients, Mitsui is in an excellent position to assess the credit worthiness of the client and the soundness of the transactions.

The evolution of this financing role relates directly to Mitsui's basic goal of promoting the flow of trade. As a result, the company has developed banking relationships in virtually all parts of the world and therefore has access to its capital markets. This also means that Mitsui's clients do not have to develop their own costly and time-consuming expertise in financial markets and the mechanism of trade financing. This ability to package trade financing with trading ability is a significant reason for Mitsui's achievement.

On this base of information and financing capability, Mitsui has built its trading success. Its import and export businesses are about evenly balanced and consistently represent about 41.6 percent of its total sales and about 21 percent by volume of the iron ore and coking coal used by the Japanese steel industry. In turn, Mitsui exports about 15.7 percent of the steel products manufactured by the Japanese steel companies.

Support Services In importing raw material for the steel industry, Mitsui provides important support services. It purchases the iron ore and coal under maximum long-term contracts, arranges transportation and customs documentation, distributes the raw materials to the customer's plant, and extends credit for the purchase.

In the broad spectrum of its importing activities, Mitsui provides planning and management of market-entry programs, secondary distribution networks, and marketing support and service facilities. The company will also provide joint-venture capital both in Japan and overseas.

On the export side, Mitsui offers an extensive range of worldwide support. Through its information system and on-site force of over 3000 employees in 142 cities around the globe, the company is on top of export opportunities for its clients. It can therefore handle all multinational arrangements related to export transactions. An embassy is not necessary in Istanbul or Baghdad; Mitsui has offices there to get the exports sold and delivered. And, of course, the export financing and necessary foreign exchange can also be provided.

Commercial Development Assistance   When large-scale export transactions develop (such as equipment for power stations or steelmaking or for chemical and other industrial plants) Mitsui provides a complete series of integrated services which facilitate the trade. They begin by putting together information on plant construction opportunities around the world through their communications network. Working with closely affiliated engineering and construction companies, Mitsui assembles extensive background data on local conditions, which enables the plant exporting company to prepare accurate cost estimates. When the project is costed, Mitsui conducts feasibility studies, including market studies of final-product demand in the country of construction and in other overseas markets. When the decision to build is made, the company organizes the construction project and assembles the necessary construction materials and machinery. Then, of course, Mitsui arranges the financing by guaranteeing credit for the construction companies by direct loans, by equity investment in the venture, and by negotiation with financial institutions in Japan and other financial capitals of the world. When the project is completed and on-stream, Mitsui then assists in worldwide product export.

Mitsui, an example of the Japanese general trading company, has taken the Japanese circle of trade—import, process, and export—and expanded it into a worldwide science of trade. The company now has about $1 billion in loans and direct investments in projects in all parts of the world. About half of these loans and investments are in raw material development, which of course feeds right back into the circle of Japanese trade. Mitsui is a prime example of how and why Japan, in the last decade, has moved ahead of the United States in the competitive battle of foreign trade.

The United States Trade Situation   Unlike Japan we do *not* have:

- A national trade consciousness.

- A global trade strategy.

- A spirit of cooperative interaction between government and business. On the contrary, our interaction is frequently hostile and adversarial.

- A structural and interactive government organization such as the Japanese Ministry of International Trade and Industry. Our trade activities are hopelessly splintered, primarily between the office of the Special Trade Representative and the Departments of Commerce, State, Treasury, Interior, Defense, and Labor.

· A vehicle in the private sector for trade specialization, like the Japanese general trading companies. On the contrary, our antitrust policy—which was established in an age before the United States became a world power—is archaic and, in practical terms, has inhibited the formation and development of export trading companies. Furthermore, our antitrust policy and financial regulations prohibit a direct organization for trading.

The U.S. Machine-Tool Industry   There have been numerous adverse trade developments in specific industries—for example, steel, textiles, television, automobiles. One that has not received such widespread attention is the machine-tool industry. The adverse trade developments in this industry are important because they are fairly recent, they represent a loss of competitive strength in one of our most basic industries, and they illustrate how our one-sided demand-management economic policy has contributed to that loss.

Table 4-3   MACHINE-TOOL TRADE *(In Millions of Dollars)*

Year	U.S. Trade with Japan		U.S. World Trade	
	Imports	*Exports*	*Imports*	*Exports*
1972	14.7	31.3	114.0	260.0
1973	22.0	40.2	167.1	350.0
1974	47.4	49.1	270.7	443.8
1975	62.6	38.6	317.6	567.6
1976	67.3	27.0	318.3	546.5
1977	105.7	22.1	400.9	452.1
1978	220.6	38.9	715.3	560.2

SOURCE: U.S. Department of Commerce, Bureau of Economic Analysis, 1979.

In 1975, the United States machine-tool industry suffered a decided negative bilateral balance of trade with Japan. Then, in 1978, we began importing more machine tools than we sold to other countries. Thus another basic industry fell victim to the forces that have caused our decline in international competitiveness.

The machine-tool industry is relatively small compared with other manufacturing industries in the United States. In 1978, for example, the industry's total sales were slightly over $3 billion. However, machine tools—along with steel—represent the basic component of the manufacturing process. For our key industries—those which produce automobiles, aircraft, bearings, energy equipment, farm machinery, appliances, and general equipment—the machine-tool industry supplies the metal-cutting and metal-forming machinery, critical to all those other manufacturing processes.

The four leading machine-tool firms in the United States produce about 30 percent of the output. The balance is supplied by a large number of small firms. The industry employs about 85,000 people. However, only 10 plants employ more than 1000 workers, and over 1000 plants have fewer than 50 employees.

In the sixties, the industry began to shift to the production of more efficient automated equipment after the development of numerically controlled production systems. These systems, with an electronic control unit, perform a complete work cycle. By integrating different functions, the industry has developed numerically controlled machining centers which accomplish a variety of interrelated steps, such as milling, boring, drilling, and automatic tool changing. More recently, these systems have evolved into computerized numerically controlled equipment and machinery centers. About 23 percent of the industry's output is produced this way. The smaller companies, however, are falling behind, partly because they cannot afford the capital investment for the newest equipment.

Cincinnati Milacron is the largest machine-tool manufacturer in the United States. It had sales in excess of $750 million in 1979, 60 percent of which came from machine tools. It has developed its own computer controls and semiconductor materials and is a leader in the next stage of automated manufacturing: industrial robots. This company began exporting to Japan in 1950 through a trading company. Gradually, it established its own sales, distribution, and service system by hiring some of the trading company employees. It set up a Japanese subsidiary with employee benefits similar to those of a Japanese firm. By 1977, Cincinnati Milacron, with its Japanese style of long-term market penetration, supplied over 25 percent of Japan's imports of machine tools from the United States. That was one company working alone, all by itself.

That same year, working closely within its interactive government-business relationship, Japan began a six-year national project. Its goal is to develop a building-block approach into a flexible computer-controlled machining system, the production capability of which can be expanded or reduced to meet the manufacturer's needs. This is a specific example of Japan's trade strategy: import, learn and improve, and export.

Cincinnati Milacron's management now recognizes that, as with other industries, Japan has made high-technology machine tools a priority for development and export. Recognizing the inevitable, the company has shifted its emphasis to exporting its innovative and competitive plastic machinery products to Japan and its machine tools to other export markets.

The Impact of Demand-Management Policies In analyzing America's developing economic storm in Chapter 3, we focused on manufacturing output and noted that by 1975 the United States had fallen far behind Japan, France, Germany, and Italy, and even somewhat behind the United Kingdom. Age of machinery is an important corollary of that decline.

As in the case of manufacturing output, we are dead last. While the years are not precisely comparable, Table 4-4 indicates that the United States has the oldest machine tools in its industrial base. Japan —and this advantage has undoubtedly increased since 1973—has the newest and most efficient machine-tool structure in its industry.

Table 4-4 AGE OF MACHINE TOOLS IN USE

Country	Year	Percent of Total		
		Under 10 Years	*10–20 Years*	*Over 20 Years*
United States	1976–1978	31	35	34
Japan	1973	61	21	18
France	1974	37	33	30
Germany	1977	37	37	26
Italy	1975	42	30	28
United Kingdom	1976	39	37	24

SOURCE: National Machine Tool Builders Association.

Not only is the American machine-tool structural base the most aged among the industrial nations, but the productive equipment used in the machine-tool industry itself is older than the equipment used in manufacturing industries in general in this country. In 1976, the proportion of machine tools over twenty years old in use by the machine-tool industry was 36 percent greater than those used by all manufacturers of machinery in the United States.

As we came out of the ten-year period of national decline described in Chapter 3, our industrial base was in relative decay.

As Figure 4-1 illustrates, net new orders of machine tools dramatically correlate to changes in tax policy. In order to stimulate invest-

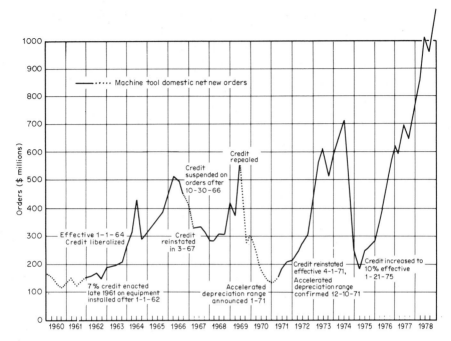

FIGURE 4-1. The machine-tool industry—domestic machine tool net new orders, quarterly. (Courtesy of National Machine Tool Builders' Association.)

ment as a way to increase the growth of gross national product, the Kennedy administration introduced a special investment tax credit of 7 percent on equipment in January 1962. That meant money right off the tax bill for purchases of equipment. It was quite an inducement. The credit was further liberalized in January 1964. Predictably, because of the tax savings, machine-tool orders shot up.

Then, in late 1966, the tax credit was suspended and net new orders went down like a rollercoaster, but they stabilized with the reinstatement of the credit in March 1967 and then began to improve. The investment tax credit was repealed in another stop-and-go policy action in 1969, and net new orders plummeted.

In January 1971, a new range of accelerated depreciation lives for new equipment was proposed. It was designed to allow for a larger initial amount of depreciation and thus result in a reduction in income taxes. The proposal was approved at the end of 1971, with a reinstatement of the investment tax credit in the interim. Net new orders rebounded again.

However, they did not have a positive effect because, for a variety of reasons, the machine-tool industry as a whole lost money in both

1971 and 1972. Losses were 2.7 percent of sales in 1971 and 1.3 percent of sales in 1972.

Then the recession of 1974–1975 brought a collapse in net new orders. The investment tax credit was increased to 10 percent in 1975, and business improved dramatically as the country came out of the recession.

However, the United States manufacturing industry in general— and the machine-tool industry in particular—came out of this ten-year period with an aged equipment base. The total and completely unpredictable stop-and-go, demand-management economic policy practiced in the late sixties and early seventies had taken its toll.

With the severe impact of tax policy added to the normal cyclicality of the industry and the disastrous profit years of 1971 and 1972, the machine-tool industry had neither the capital resources nor the will to embark on a vigorous revitalization program as business began to improve. The industry is a highly fragmented one. Policymakers in both political parties were oblivious to the need to shift economic policies to avoid the consequences of stop-and-go, one-sided demand management. And there certainly was no assurance that disastrous stop-and-go policy would not strike again.

The Trade Consequences   From 1973 to 1978, the Japanese share of U.S. imports of machine tools increased from 13 percent to 31 percent. At the same time, American machine-tool exports to Japan—as a percentage of our total machine-tool exports—decreased from 12 percent to 7 percent. While this was happening, imports as a percentage of Japanese machine-tool consumption declined and imports as a percentage of American machine-tool consumption increased. The result was the marked bilateral deficit with Japan in 1975 and a worldwide deficit in 1978. The long American decline had engulfed the machine-tool industry.

Japanese importers now cite several reasons for the decline of our machine-tool–industry competitiveness. First, they maintain that our prices are not competitive with either their domestic prices or those of Taiwan and Singapore. Second, they maintain that our manufacturers have a poor record of service follow-up, particularly with the numerically controlled machines. Third, they complain of lack of product adaptation to Japanese standards, employee height, and automated characteristics. Fourth, they believe that our manufacturers do not offer discounts that are competitive with those of European manufacturers. Finally, they are concerned about our long delivery times, which are more than twice those of Japanese manufacturers and almost twice those of West German exporters.

High prices, poor service, lack of product adaptation, lack of a volume discount or market-share orientation, stretched-out delivery times—these are all symptoms of an underlying sickness, an economic decline. That they exist is not surprising, considering the wringer through which the industry has passed. Our machine-tool industry has been going one way; that of Japan, another. Down as opposed to up. And this industry is representative of what has happened in the respective countries. We are being outtraded by Japan.

The Need for a National Trade Policy The machine-tool industry in the United States would certainly be helped by:

- A shift to a predictable economic policy, with balanced emphasis on investment to revitalize our industrial base.
- A clearly articulated national trade consciousness and trade strategy, well coordinated and coherently organized to assist basic industries like the machine-tool industry to export.
- An American version of the general trading company which would provide real-time worldwide market information, quick and easy financing, and a strategy of market penetration for a fragmented industry.

Such developments would not only benefit the machine-tool industry, they would be the beginning of a national trade policy that would strengthen one weak side of our economic triangle. A national trade policy would help us start to regain our economic strength and lead to a resharpening of our now very dull competitive edge.

ENERGY In addition to the deterioration of our trade position in such basic industries as machine tools, our rising oil imports with their rising prices came in like a tidal wave in the early seventies to severely upset our merchandise trade balance. Table 4-5 illustrates the link between trade and energy (see p. 80).

The combination of a decaying manufacturing base and increasing oil dependence pushed our trade balance into a series of chronic deficits, which we discussed at the opening of this chapter. From 1965 through 1969, as our policy was focused first on the Great Society and then on the discord of Vietnam, oil imports grew modestly from $2 billion to $2.7 billion. But beneath the surface, the forces of dramatic change were swirling in the United States, Venezuela, and Iran, Libya,

Table 4-5 U.S. OIL IMPORTS AND TRADE
BALANCE *(In Billions of Dollars)*

Year	Oil Imports	Trade Balance
1970	2.9	2.6
1971	3.7	−2.3
1972	4.7	−6.4
1973	8.4	.9
1974	26.6	−5.3
1975	27.0	9.1
1976	34.6	−9.3
1977	45.0	−30.9
1978	42.3	−33.8
1979	60.3	−29.5

SOURCE: "Economic Report of the President," January, 1980.

and the other Arab nations. These forces began to break into the open
sporadically in 1970 and 1971; then, with the 1973–1974 embargo,
they struck with full force.

The United States's production and consumption figures bring the
shift of events into full focus.

Table 4-6 U.S. OIL PRODUCTION AND CONSUMPTION
AND WORLD OIL PRICE

Year	U.S. Production	U.S. Consumption	Price of Saudi Arabian Crude Oil
	(In Millions of Barrels Per Day)		*(In Dollars Per Barrel)*
1965	9.0	11.3	1.80
1966	9.6	11.9	1.80
1967	10.2	12.3	1.80
1968	10.6	13.1	1.80
1969	10.8	13.8	1.80
1970	11.3	14.4	1.80
1971	11.2	14.8	2.29
1972	11.2	16.0	2.48
1973	11.0	16.9	5.04
1974	10.5	16.2	11.25
1975	10.0	15.9	12.38
1976	9.7	17.0	11.51
1977	9.9	17.9	12.70
1978	10.3	18.3	13.34

SOURCE: "Statistical Review of the World Oil Industry," 1968, 1978, The British Petroleum Company.

It was very simple. American production peaked in 1970, our consumption continued to expand relentlessly, world prices increased with the tightened market, and oil power shifted to the OPEC nations. And this was all a part of the developments which took place as our nation went from a period of strength into the developing storm and then to weakness in the economic triangle of trade, energy, and productivity. The energy side of that triangle is inextricably linked to a long series of events which brought about our decline.

Oil Policy Under Truman and Eisenhower Under both Presidents Truman and Eisenhower, oil was recognized as a powerful fact in our economic life. Its role was clearly understood in the framework of our demand-management economic policy as the source of energy in the manufacturing process and in the use of consumer goods, particularly the automobile. In the context of the bipartisan foreign-policy consensus that was responsible for the development of the Marshall Plan, oil was also recognized as a necessary part of foreign policy.

The multinational oil companies were used very carefully by Truman and Eisenhower to implement that foreign policy in the Middle East. They were used to contain the spread of Russian communism in the Mediterranean and the Persian Gulf. They were a surrogate for American economic and political power in that part of the world. These intertwined economic and foreign-policy objectives led to American control of the world oil trade and ensured secure supplies of crude oil and stable prices for the United States and its allies. As part of this policy, financial assistance was provided to stabilize Arab governments.

This policy resulted from the cooperative government-business relationship which developed during the war and was enhanced in the postwar confrontation with Russia. In turn, the relationship evolved into a government-business partnership determined to (1) assist third-world nations against the encroachment of communism and (2) provide the United States with essential raw materials necessary for the sound economic growth that is the foundation of a strong national defense.

This partnership of government and business resulted in a special arrangement that cemented Saudi-American relations and secured American control of the oil market. In 1950, King Ibn Saud wanted more revenues from Aramco—the Arabian American Oil Company—which was jointly owned by Standard Oil of California, Texaco, Exxon, and Mobil. Aramco and the Treasury and State Departments worked out a transfer of tax revenues, previously paid by Aramco to the U.S. government, to King Saud's government. The Saudi government issued a law that taxed 50 percent of Aramco's Saudi Arabian profits. The Treasury, in turn, applied a 1918 tax provision that exempted the income taxes paid to Saudi Arabia by Aramco from U.S. income taxes. The result was a tax wash for Aramco and an undeclared foreign-aid package for King Ibn Saud. It was certainly controversial, but it was the foundation of the special relationship between the Saudi and American governments.

By the early fifties, the major international oil companies, with U.S. government support, had exclusive control of Saudi Arabian oil and exploration rights in the other oil-producing territories. The exception was Iran, whose oil was exclusively controlled by the British-owned Anglo-Iranian Oil Company. But that, too, would change.

As previously mentioned, by 1951, 98 percent of the world oil market was controlled by Aramco, Gulf Oil, and the British-based companies—British Petroleum and Royal Dutch/Shell (60 percent Dutch-owned).[1]

Iran: The First Tremor In 1951, the first tremor of dislocation of foreign companies took place in the Persian Gulf. It was the ominous first wave of a series of developments that would gather momentum in the decade beginning in 1969 and would crash upon the United States and the world economy in 1979. It took place in Iran. Just as it would be Iran in 1979, it was Iran on May 2, 1951. The tremor was the first nationalization of oil.

The British government and the Anglo-Iranian Oil Company were locked in a dispute over revenues with a special oil commission of the Majlis (parliament). The commission was headed by Mohammed Mosaddegh. In the midst of that dispute, Prime Minister Ali Razmara was assassinated, Mosaddegh became prime minister, and oil was nationalized. The Shah later fled the country.[2]

At that time, there was no tight oil supply in the world, and that undermined the Mosaddegh revolution. With the help of the United States, the Shah returned to power and a new production consortium was structured in 1954. The British companies were reduced to a 54 percent share, the major American companies and a few independents got 40 percent, and the balance went to a French company. Thus, the consequences of the first Iranian revolution against the Shah and his subsequent return to power were an American oil presence in Iran and the first nationalization of oil reserves in the Persian Gulf.[3]

The Eisenhower Period of Strength When the Arab-Israeli conflict of 1956 flared up and the Suez Canal was closed, President Eisenhower turned to the oil companies to redirect the flow of oil in the world. A committee of the companies, known as the Middle East Emergency Committee, was formed and given antitrust immunity. Anticipating a transportation problem in what was otherwise a world petroleum surplus situation, this committee was given the task of redistributing tanker schedules to facilitate efficient delivery to meet world oil demand. President Eisenhower recognized the importance of energy in the economic stability of the free world. After the Suez crisis, he was unequivocal about the use of force to prevent an embargo. On July 30, 1957, he wrote: ". . . Should a crisis arise threatening to cut the Western world off from Mid East oil, we would *have* to use force."[4]

Amid growing Arab nationalism and increasing Russian influence in the area, the President recognized the growing dependence on Mideast oil of Western Europe, Japan, and, to a much lesser extent, the United States. As Europe and Japan reconstructed their economies in the fifties, they shifted from coal to oil as an energy source. By 1961, one-third of Western Europe's energy consumption was oil based, and 75 percent of that was imported from the Mideast. Japan relied on the Mideast for 79 percent of its oil imports. Eisenhower, as President, was aware (as he had been as a general) of the importance of a strong economic foundation as the base of a coherent foreign policy and a strong defense. He also recognized the importance of energy in a strong economy.

The Formation of OPEC As a result of an increase in world production and U.S. import constraints, a glut of oil developed in 1959. The major international oil companies, as a result of their cooperative relationship with government, enjoyed a cartel buyer position. But the balance between national interest and corporate interest changed when Big Oil made a major decision that was to prove a short-sighted and devastating mistake. In the spring of 1959, without consulting the producer countries, the majors cut the price paid for crude oil. The posted price for Venezuelan crude was reduced by 5 to 25 cents per barrel and the reduction averaged 18 cents per barrel in the Middle East.[5] Led by Exxon, this action was repeated in August 1960. The reduction in posted prices was unilaterally transferred into lower producer-country revenues by the major oil companies.[6]

This high-handed lack of warning and negotiations understandably resulted in a smoldering rancor in the producer nations and led to the formation of The Organization of the Petroleum Exporting Countries —OPEC. When more militant governments emerged in the third-world countries and the oil glut disappeared, retribution was aimed at both the oil companies and the American nation as a whole. By that time, the partnership between government and business was dead.

OPEC was formed at the first Baghdad conference in September 1960. The original members were the five major exporting countries: Iran, Iraq, Kuwait, Saudi Arabia, and Venezuela. They were ultimately joined by Algeria, Ecuador, Gabon, Indonesia, Libya, Nigeria, Qatar, and the United Arab Emirates. With the exception of Indonesia, oil revenues make up the lion's share of the members' foreign-exchange earnings. At the time of the founding, there was substantial similarity of concession agreements with the majors.[7]

The general arrangement was based on the Aramco-Saudi Arabian formula: 50 percent of the net profit of an operating country calculated on the basis of posted prices. Having opened in 1959 at $2.08 per barrel, the posted price was reduced to $1.80 by the time of the Baghdad meeting in 1960. With the price reduction, each million barrels per day of production led to a revenue drop of about $135,000 a day. It was, therefore, understandable that the producer countries sought to unify their policies in order to restore prices to their previous levels. However, even though the OPEC countries began to unify for pricing purposes, the posted price stayed where it was for the next decade.[8]

The 1967 Mideast War   On June 5, 1967, the third Arab-Israeli war erupted. Both the Suez Canal and the Trans-Arabian Pipeline were shut down. Saudi Arabia, Kuwait, Iraq, Libya, and Algeria boycotted the United States, West Germany, and the United Kingdom. The boycott was ineffective and was over by August.[9] It went largely unnoticed in the United States. Lyndon Johnson was knee-deep in the problems of the Vietnam war and was not inclined to take direct action in another part of the world. The carefully balanced government-business relationship had ended.

The following year, OPEC met in Vienna and issued a Declaratory Statement of Petroleum Policy in Member Countries. That was the first hint of changing supply-and-demand conditions. It stated that changed conditions justified the revision of contract and concession arrangements. Producing countries would have the right to participate in ownership, the right to determine posted prices, and the right to excess profits of the operating companies. Even though we were not watching the forces of production and consumption that were converging from opposite directions, like two trains on the same track, it is very clear that the OPEC nations were.

The Rise of Qaddafi   On September 1, 1969, militant revolutionaries led by Colonel Muammar al-Qaddafi overthrew King Idris of Libya. That was the most significant political development in the turn of events leading to America's energy weakness. The Mediterranean had a revolutionary oil pirate.

Qaddafi moved quickly to escalate his demands in the oil dialogue. In retribution for America's pro-Israel policy, he closed the Wheelus Air Force Base and sent all U.S. military personnel packing. When the U.S. Embassy in Tripoli learned of a countercoup in early 1970, it passed the information on to the Qaddafi government, fearing for the safety of American nationals and not wanting to be associated in any way with an anti-Qaddafi movement.

The Eisenhower administration's understanding of the interrelationship between economic strength and foreign policy and of the strategic importance of Mideast oil had disappeared by the time of the Nixon administration. In the entire 1476 pages of his *White House Years,* President Nixon's national security advisor mentions OPEC only twice, and this event not at all.

Whether or not Qaddafi would have been squashed in the time of Truman or Eisenhower is an immaterial conjecture. A shift away from Eisenhower's policy of protecting America's strategic economic interests in Mideast oil was decidedly underway. The grand design of geopolitics and the escalating war in Vietnam commanded the President's attention.

Supply Tightens   While Qaddafi made more demands and strengthened his bargaining position with production cutbacks, the Texas Independent Producers and Royalty Owners Association warned the nation about its loss of surplus-producing capacity. President Nixon was occupied with planning to extend the Vietnam war into Cambodia. On April 20, 1970, he announced a planned reduction of 150,-000 troops, and then on May 1 he implemented Operation Rock Crusher in Cambodia.[10] The outrage in America was instantaneous and violent: Kent State took place on May 4.

Tucked into this period of heightened turmoil in America was the accidental rupturing of the Trans-Arabian pipeline on May 3. Half a million barrels a day of Arabian oil stopped flowing to the eastern Mediterranean, and Syria refused to allow repairs until the next year.

While American attention was riveted on its own internal discord, supply and demand in the world market collided head-on. Qaddafi had his leverage as tanker rates went spiraling upward, and he used this leverage with a vengeful shrewdness that vindicated the formation of OPEC ten years earlier.[11]

Control of prices was about to shift to OPEC. The Truman-Eisenhower policy on Mideast oil was swept away, almost unnoticed in the violence of domestic events. Even if Nixon had been aware of the importance of what was happening, it would have been impossible at the time to alter the shift in pricing control. Americans would not have tolerated an overt initiative against a third-world nation; our nation would have gone up in flames. Thus, in an area of the world of the most strategic economic importance to the United States, the revolutionaries had the upper hand.

After protracted negotiation, the Occidental Petroleum Company came to terms with Qaddafi in early September 1970 with a 30 cents per barrel increase and a 5 percent increase in the income-tax rate from 50 to 55 percent. The standard Saudi-Aramco arrangement was broken, and the oil pricing mechanism was no longer operational.

The Message to OPEC   On September 25, 1970, the majors and the independents met at the State Department with oil expert James Akins and Under Secretary of State U. Alexis Johnson. There was little sympathy from the government. The State Department took a basic position that our government had little or no influence with the Libyan government and that United States intervention would not be effective. As a result, the companies which had not already done so quickly came to terms. The tenuous thread to previous strength and stability in American oil policy was less than six months from being irrevocably severed.

Kuwait, Iran, and the other producer countries then voiced higher demands, and very quickly the 55 percent tax rate became standard in Iran, Saudi Arabia, Kuwait, Iraq, Nigeria, and the Persian Gulf sheikdoms. Taking advantage of the discord in America, OPEC pressed its demands on the hapless companies.

In early December, Venezuela passed a law raising the tax rate on company profits to 60 percent and giving the president unilateral power to raise posted prices without negotiations with the companies. In a decade, the ability to take action without consultation had passed from Exxon to the Venezuelan president. The vision of the 1960 Baghdad conference was about to materialize.[12]

With the stability of the past unwinding daily, the companies sought to form a joint negotiating front. A proposal for joint negotiations was outlined in an early January 1971 meeting with Under Secretary Johnson at the State Department. It was made very clear that the companies felt that any hope of price stability lay in dealing with the producers on a global basis. With the approval of the Justice Department, a message to OPEC was formulated, which unequivocally put the producers on notice that country-by-country and piecemeal negotiations were unacceptable and out of the question.

After a meeting of the companies with Secretary of State William Rogers, and with the personal authorization of President Nixon, Under Secretary John Irwin II embarked on a mission to the Persian Gulf. His task was to explain why our government had made it possible under our antitrust laws for the companies to negotiate jointly with the Gulf producers and to seek assurances of an uninterrupted supply of oil at reasonable prices. At his first stop in Iran on January 17, Irwin made it clear to the Shah that the United States government was not in the oil business and was not interested in the details of the negotiations with the oil companies. Sensing obvious weakness, the Shah bluntly told Irwin that any attempt by the companies to say that they would not sign the agreement unless other OPEC members signed it would be taken by the Gulf producers and OPEC as a whole as a sign of bad faith.

In a brilliant move, the Shah had characterized the oil companies' collective action and united front to mobilize their strongest bargaining position as an underhanded negotiating strategy. Further, Irwin was cajoled by the Shah into believing that if the companies reached a separate agreement with the Gulf producers, the Gulf countries would not be influenced by the Qaddafi negotiations regardless of their terms. Totally bluffed by the Shah's tough-talk sweet-talk approach, Irwin obtained Secretary Rogers' approval of separate Tehran and Tripoli negotiations. He then left town without consulting the industry negotiators, who learned of the action when they arrived on the 19th. This action—however unintentional or misguided—was pure economic appeasement. Embroiled in the war in Vietnam, the Nixon administration unleashed the OPEC predators to deal with the companies at their leisure. The Truman-Eisenhower oil policy was both dead and buried, and the consequences for the United States would be severe. Our competitive edge was now definitely blunted.

The Tehran and Tripoli Agreements The Tehran agreement, signed on February 14, was to last five years. It provided for an immediate increase in the government take for the Gulf countries of an average of 30 cents per barrel and a 5-cent annual escalation, which would take the total increase to 50 cents by 1975. It was estimated to be an $11.7 billion package. However, the viability of the agreement was put into question by Saudi Arabia's Sheikh Yamani, who observed to one of the company negotiators: "You know the supply situation better than I. You know you cannot take a shutdown."[13] Obviously, the OPEC nations knew what they were about, but the significance of the situation was completely missed by the senior people in American government.

Following the Tehran agreement, Qaddafi threatened to nationalize the companies if they refused to agree to Libya's terms. Predictably, the companies came to heel, and the Tehran agreement was followed by the Tripoli agreement. Libya got another increase of approximately 65 cents per barrel which, when added to the September and October increases, resulted in a posted price increase of 90 cents versus 50 cents for the Shah's group.[14]

The New Economic Policy of 1971 With the then-unrecognized triangle of trade, energy, and productivity severely weakened and the American economy reflecting this weakness, the Nixon administration announced in August 1971 its new economic policy to counterattack increasing inflation. The plan was pure demand management. Domestically, wages and prices were to be frozen. Internationally, there was to be a 10 percent import fee, complete separation of the dollar from gold, and ultimately—with the Smithsonian agreement in December—a 9 percent devaluation of the dollar.[15] Currencies would then float. In demand-management logic, higher-priced foreign goods would be less desirable to Americans, and that would dampen demand for imports in the short run. Over time, of course, those higher prices—particularly that of oil—would get imbedded into the consumer price index.

OPEC was furious. At a Beirut meeting on September 22, they called for an effective participation in the assets of the producing companies and action to avoid the impact of the dollar devaluation. American inflation would not be transferred to the producer nations. The stakes were raised from control of the pricing mechanism to control of the underlying assets themselves.

Predictably, Qaddafi again led in the new game of participation and nationalization. On December 7, 1971, he nationalized British Petroleum's rights and assets in Libya. Six months later, on June 1, 1972, Iraq followed his lead with the nationalization of the Iraq Petroleum

Company. In the fall, the oil companies agreed that the five producing countries of the Persian Gulf could receive an immediate participation of 25 percent of ownership that would rise to 51 percent by 1983. The agreement envisioned compensation on the basis of updated book value and the direct sale of a large part of the government-owned oil to the companies operating the concessions.

In the case of Aramco, the four oil companies would have a preferred right to buy back the Saudi share of Aramco oil, and as the Saudi share increased to 51 percent in 1983, the company partners anticipated that production would increase to 20 million barrels a day. Diminished equity ownership would be offset by substantially increased production. However, by December Yamani demanded an increase in the price terms set in the original agreement for the companies' repurchase of the Saudi share of the oil. In an exploitation of the companies' weakened position, Yamani boldly told them that any deal he made could be altered by deals done elsewhere. While the Saudi style was obviously different from that of Qaddafi, it was clear that a contract was no longer a contract.

Events Build Toward the Embargo   With the lifting of the Mandatory Oil Import Program in April of 1973, the Nixon administration intensified the voracious Western demand for Mideast oil. In May, King Faisal of Saudi Arabia warned his Aramco partners that he would not become isolated in Middle East politics and that, unless U.S. policy in the Mideast were changed, American interests could be completely lost in Saudi Arabia.[16]

On June 11, Qaddafi struck again with the nationalization of the Bunker Hunt assets in Libya, asserting that the United States needed a "good hard slap on its cool and insolent face."[16]

By July, the Shah completed an agreement under which the members of the Iranian consortium turned their assets over to him in return for a long-term supply agreement. Embroiled in Watergate, the Nixon administration was completely passive, without any reaction whatsoever.

In August, Occidental bowed to Libyan demands for a 51 percent participation at new book value compensation,[17] and the other independents fell into line. Then on September 11, Qaddafi nationalized 51 percent of the remaining American companies: Exxon, Mobil, Texaco, Shell, and Arco. Finally, the American government awoke; but its analysis of the situation revealed a complete misunderstanding of reality and an absence of any coherent policy. In a press conference the President said:

The radical elements . . . presently seem to be on ascendency in various countries in the Mideast, like Libya. Those elements, of course, we are not in a position to control, although we may be in a position to influence them, influence them for this reason: oil without a market, as Mr. Mosaddegh learned many, many years ago, does not do a country much good.

We and Europe are the market and I think that the responsible Arab leaders will see to it that if they continue to up the price, if they continue to expropriate, the inevitable result is that they will lose their markets, and other sources will develop.[18]

The stage was set for the Embargo of 1973–1974.

The Embargo The October War broke out on the 6th, with fighting between Egyptian and Israeli forces along the Suez Canal.[19] On the 12th, the four Aramco companies warned the White House that resupplying the Israeli army would result in a production cutback of Mideast oil. The State Department responded on October 15 that the United States had begun to resupply Israel with aircraft and equipment.[20] On the next day, the counteraction was swift. The Gulf Committee of OPEC met in Kuwait and unilaterally raised the posted price of Saudi marker crude from $3.01 to $5.12 per barrel.[21]

On that same day, Melvin Laird, the President's chief domestic affairs advisor, became the first high White House official to publicly discuss possible impeachment proceedings.[22]

On the 17th, the Arab ministers in Kuwait agreed on a mandatory cut in exports and recommended an embargo against unfriendly states.[23] On the 18th, Saudi Arabia cut its production by 10 percent. The cutback would be increased to 25 percent in early November. On the 19th, Libya embargoed the United States. The next day, Saudi Arabia followed suit and shut America off.[24] That evening at an 8:25 P.M. news conference, Press Secretary Ronald Ziegler announced the firing of Archibald Cox and the abolition of the special prosecutor's office, plus the resignation of Attorney General Elliott Richardson and the firing of his deputy William Ruckelshaus for their refusals to dismiss Cox.[25] The American political situation blew up into a firestorm, while the self-assertiveness of the Arab oil powers was growing. The beginning of the Saturday Night Massacre and the Saudi embargo were simultaneous events.

On October 21, Sheikh Yamani informed the Aramco companies that they would implement the embargo and cut back orders or they would be nationalized.[26] By November 2, the Arab producers had embargoed the United States and Holland completely. On November 7, in an announcement that was lost in the Watergate explosions that were erupting around the Presidency, President Nixon said: "Let us pledge that by 1980 under Project Independence we shall be able to meet America's needs from America's own energy resources."[27]

Unreality swept the country on all fronts.

When in a December poll, the American people were asked who was responsible for the energy crisis, two-thirds chose a combination of the oil companies, the federal government, and the Nixon administration. Only 7 percent blamed the Arabs.[28] Perhaps still living with the memory of the strong and consistent foreign and economic policy of Truman and Eisenhower, the American people did not seem to realize that the nation was adrift in a new world of energy uncertainty.

OPEC met again in Tehran on December 22, 1973. The Shah—whom both Henry Kissinger and Jimmy Carter would praise—was impressed by the extraordinary recent oil auction price of $17 per barrel, and he drove for higher prices. King Faisal, less greedy and more concerned about the political goal of the embargo and production cutbacks, spoke for moderation. The result was a compromise of $11.65 per barrel. The embargo continued until March 18 of the next year, but the important decisions were over by the end of 1973. America's dominance over energy economics was dead.

Thus, the energy side of the triangle of trade, energy, and productivity was weakened, and with it America's competitive position was also undermined and weakened. It had taken more than ten years to crumble, but neither the President, his Secretary of State, his energy spokesman William Simon, nor the American people recognized its significance.

Compromise, cooperation, and consensus were gone from the land. In the next six months, as the final chapters of the threatened impeachment spun out, cynicism ruled both Congress and the nation. Americans divided into individual-interest constituencies to fight like a pack of dogs over the differential suddenly created by the explosion of world oil prices against the controlled price of domestic crude reserves. There were billions at stake. Schooled in years of consumption-directed economic policies, America turned inward upon itself, and discord divided the nation.

The Post-Embargo Period Faced with an inevitable impeachment process and therefore leaderless in directing energy policy, the Nixon administration withdrew in the hope that the problem would go away. With the four-fold increase in prices, it was hoped that the cartel would fall apart as supply came on the market. This was a continuation of our erroneous economic policy: manage demand and supply will take care of itself. It didn't. The cartel didn't break. Unfortunately, this unrealistic view of world economic forces was complicated by the price freeze, which had continued with phase IV of the Nixon Wage and Price Control program.

After Nixon's departure in August 1974, President Ford continued the focus on energy with a domestic perspective. From this vantage point, he met the issue head-on in his 1975 State of the Union message and the introduction of his Energy Independence Act of 1975. The heart of the Ford logic was to move to a free market in energy. Higher fuel prices would both foster conservation and stimulate supply. The increased prices created by the free market would be balanced by a windfall profits tax on oil-industry revenues and by energy-oriented tax rebates for consumers.

Unfortunately, there was no national belief in the existence of an energy crisis. If anything, the American people believed the shortages were contrived. This view was complicated by the hangover of price controls, which spawned new layers of controls as world price increases moved through the markets into end products.

Controls were due to expire on August 31, 1975. But it was a hot political issue, and, in December, the Energy Policy and Conservation Act (EPCA) was passed and signed by the President. This increased the two-tier structure of domestic crude-oil prices to three and continued allocation controls. The mandatory controls program would be lifted and altered to a standby basis after forty months, but the President would be required to take positive action to achieve decontrol. Moving into a Presidential election year, the politicians bought time. The assumption that low-cost energy was a consumer right continued to prevail. We were weakened further as contempt for our excessive consumption-oriented policies spread from OPEC to our allies.

Energy Under Carter, 1977-1978   A new President, whose basic campaign theme had been integrity and competence, came to Washington in 1977 from Plains, Georgia. When Jimmy Carter was inaugurated on January 20, 1977, he entered an Oval Office diminished in both power and stature. Two years previously he had been virtually unknown in the nation, and in turn he knew next to nothing about the ways of the nation's capital. In fact, he had campaigned against the Washington establishment. The American people—tired, frustrated, and angry with each other and themselves—had purposely drawn a "wild card" from the middle of the deck.

If he had paused to get to know the folks a bit, he might have survived his first term. He was intelligent enough to understand the underlying problems. He was intelligent enough to understand that in order to build a base to solve those problems he would have to reestablish a spirit of cooperation, compromise, and consensus. But he did not take time to diagnose the interrelationship of the institutions of our government. He rushed in to take command. And in the end he left, as he had come, without an understanding that our greatest need was to revitalize the spirit of cooperation, compromise, and consensus in America.

Very quickly Jimmy Carter recognized that energy was the major economic problem facing the nation, and he developed an energy package. He clearly understood the magnitude of the issue, and although very narrowly elected, he had the political capital and time to spend on getting the energy issue resolved.

But he made two mistakes. The first was to develop his energy program almost exclusively with his energy advisor, James Schlesinger, who would become Secretary of the new Energy Department when it was established in October 1977. There were knowledgeable people to whom he could have turned for counsel and assistance on this complex and important problem. With leadership, a consensus might have been put together.

Right on time, his energy message to Congress was ready for his self-imposed deadline of April 20. Unprecedented in the history of the American Presidency, he addressed the American people on the same subject twice in the same week: from both the Oval Office and in the House of Representatives at a joint session of Congress.

The result of his effort was the exact antithesis of the process that had produced the Marshall Plan. Instead of building consensus, the energy message—as reflected in one poll—was seen by 80 percent of the American people as proposing remedies that were unfair, for a crisis that was not all that bad.

His second mistake flowed from his first. His initial program was an engineer's solution. America was still leaderless and in disarray.

While President Ford had unsuccessfully focused on stimulating supplies from energy producers, Jimmy Carter concentrated on conservation and change in users' demand patterns. It was a direct extension of thirty years of demand-management economic policy. The Carter national energy plan concentrated on conservation of oil imports.

A program to export coal—our most abundant energy resource estimated at 218 trillion tons of recoverable reserves—was not emphasized. Little thought was given to breaking the OPEC stranglehold on the energy pricing mechanism by developing a coal export program.

Although the development of a coal export program was given little emphasis, the Carter proposals did contemplate the use of general tax revenues to stimulate domestic coal production.

The essence of the Carter program was to wean the American people and businesses away from the use of oil and natural gas. In addition to a variety of specific conservation measures and alternative energy initiatives, the core of the program was the crude-oil equalization tax. The tax, to have been paid by crude-oil producers, was intended to close the gap between domestic crude-oil prices and higher world prices. The tax revenues were to be rebated to consumers.

On August 5, 1977, the Carter energy program was passed almost intact by the House. By the time the Senate acted, it had made a number of important changes in favor of markets over regulation. The joint conference began in October, became hopelessly deadlocked, and adjourned in disagreement in December.

Congress came back into session in January and the conference resumed. In May, it made an important breakthrough in the decontrol of natural gas. This included an immediate increase of 44 cents per 1000 cubic feet on newly discovered natural gas, an annual increase of 10 percent, and expiration of controls on new gas in 1984. On November 9, the President signed the National Energy Act of 1978. In addition to the natural gas deregulation, it included a number of conservation grants, tax and loan programs, incentives for utilities to shift to coal, and regulatory changes. The Energy Department was now engaged in research and development in a broad range of areas from coal liquefaction to solar applications. But the tough nut of oil remained uncracked. We were beginning to come out of our total preoccupation with the domestic part of the problem, but the tough battle over oil decontrol was still before us. Before the administration could focus on supply and a world view, that issue had to be resolved.

The Stalemate Breaks, 1979–1980 In the fall of 1978, the focus of events shifted to Iran, at that time second to Saudi Arabia as an exporter of oil. Strikes and the turmoil of a revolution cut production sharply. A normal production level of about 5.5 million barrels per day was cut to a twenty-seven-year low of 500,000 barrels per day, and on December 27 exports were halted. On January 16, 1979, the Shah left Iran to wander rich and homeless until his death on July 27, 1980, and the second oil-supply squeeze was upon the United States and the world.

In early March, Iran began exporting oil again, and by summer production leveled off at 3.6 million barrels per day. By then the average world price was over $21 per barrel, with Saudi marker crude at $15.68 per barrel. On April 5, 1979, as this second energy crisis began building, the President gave his second energy message to the country. Convinced that controls on the price of domestically produced oil encouraged consumption and discouraged production, he made a pragmatic reversal of his 1977 position and announced phased-in decontrol of domestic crude to be accomplished by October 1, 1981.

At the same time, the President took a major gamble, proposed a windfall profits tax, and—with the stick of possible reimposition of controls in his pocket—put the heat on Congress to act on the windfall tax. The Crude Oil Windfall Profit Tax Act of 1980 was eventually passed in late February and signed by the President in April. It was expected to raise $227 billion in cumulative revenues by 1991, then phase out over a thirty-three-month period. The revenues would be allocated as follows: aid to lower-income households—25 percent; income-tax reduction—60 percent; and energy and transportation programs—15 percent. It also included an extensive list of supply-oriented tax incentives to be funded separately. The long ten-year battle to bring American prices up to world oil prices was over.[29]

The gas lines came in the spring and early summer, after the President's April 5 address. Unlike during the 1973–1974 embargo, the Department of Energy had collected its own information. It laid the consumer's plight solely at the door of the Iranian production cutback. This was confirmed by the General Accounting Office study released in early September. The public was beginning to recognize the real roots of the issue: tight supply against increasing demand and the greedy OPEC cartel pricing mechanism.

OPEC met in Geneva from June 26 to June 28. With some split between the moderates like Saudi Arabia and those unfriendly nations like Libya—the price increase averaged 15 percent; the price per barrel ranged from $18 to $23.50. This move crystalized the President's intent. On July 15, after extensive discussion with a varied group of Americans at Camp David, the President again addressed the nation. He proposed an Energy Security Corporation that would finance private development of oil substitutes from coal, oil shale, biomass, and unconventional gas. Its companion bill would establish the Energy Mobilization Board, which would expedite the construction of critical energy facilities. A focus on supply had finally come.

If there was any question of America's understanding of its vulnerability to foreign oil, it was resolved with the seizure of the American Embassy and the hostages in Iran on November 4, 1979. Our economic weakness was beginning to be recognized, at least with respect to energy. Although the Mobilization Board legislation got stuck in conference, on June 30, 1980, the President signed the Energy Security Act. This established the Synthetic Fuels Corporation with funding of $20 billion, and the possibility of up to $68 billion in phase 2. Its goal was to achieve a synthetic-fuel production level of 500,000 barrels per day by 1987 and of at least 2 million barrels per day by 1992.

America was beginning to fight back, to get competitive in energy. The focus on supply was sharpening.

In June 1980, the President also met with our allies at the Venice Economic Summit. He announced the goal of doubling coal production and use by early 1990, the encouragement of long-term producer and consumer commitments, and the improvement of both exporting and importing countries' infrastructures to facilitate increased coal trade.[30]

That was only an idea, but it was the kind of idea and vision that General Marshall took to Harvard. By developing our coal resources, modernizing our transportation system and port facilities, and becoming a reliable long-term supplier of coal, we can break the back of the increasing spiral of OPEC prices, bring stability to world energy prices, and regain our self-respect by becoming a strong, economically competitive leader in the world.

It will not be easy. We will need to develop a new sense of productivity from the mine, to the transportation system, to the embarkation point, to the trading mechanism, and within a framework of enhanced environmental technologies and labor involvement all along the way. The idea and vision of energy competitiveness through coal development can only come with a linkage to the other two sides of the triangle: trade and productivity. A consensus on coal will require substantial cooperation and compromise in our nation. We have not yet regained those characteristics in America, but they will be central to our success or failure.

PRODUCTIVITY In 1979, Edward F. Denison, in *Accounting for Slower Economic Growth,* stood the economics profession on its ear. After analyzing the decline of growth in productivity (output per person) for the period 1973–1976, he bluntly declared that it was a mystery. In a very thoughtful comparison to the period 1948–1973, he found that there had been a drop of over three percentage points to a negative rate of growth—a real decline of productivity. He attributed over two percentage points of the decline to a basket category of "advances in knowledge and not elsewhere classified." In essence, Denison said that two-thirds of the decline came about for mysterious unclassifiable reasons. He then outlined seventeen possible factors that could have contributed to that catch-all category and he concluded that a lot more work should be done to pin down the specific determinants of the decline.[31]

The 1980 Economic Report of the President, noting that productivity had declined by 0.9 in 1979, echoed this puzzle: "Statistical analyses have been able to identify factors responsible for some of the decline, but a significant part remains unexplained."[32] It went on to state: "Since it is difficult to identify a single cause for a slowdown in productivity growth, the immediate prospects for a dramatic improvement in productivity are not good."[33]

The President's report did hint that government regulation, lower research and development expenditures, increased energy costs, and inflation may have had an impact. And it was hinted that some of this impact may have come in ways which were not yet understood.

Without productivity growth, a general increase in the standard of living for Americans is impossible. We will exist in a no-growth environment, with any increase for some coming at a loss for others. This situation, if continued, can only result in social unrest, divisiveness, and real economic decline.

Table 4-7 highlights some very obvious facts. First, for almost thirty years the United States has been last in productivity growth, and Japan has been number one. Second, during the period 1965–1973 United States productivity growth declined precipitously while that of the other nations either increased or fared about as well as in the previous period. Third, while productivity growth of all nations declined in the 1973–1978 period, that of the United States was almost nonexistent.

When General Marshall went to Harvard in 1947, he talked about restoring to Europeans economic confidence in their own future, and

Table 4-7 **AVERAGE ANNUAL PERCENT CHANGE IN PRODUCTIVITY***

Country	1950–1965	1965–1973	1973–1978	1950–1978
United States	2.4	1.6	.4	1.8
Japan	7.2	9.1	3.1	7.0
France	4.7	4.5	2.8	4.3
Germany	5.2	4.3	3.2	4.6
Italy	5.1	5.6	1.3	4.5
United Kingdom	2.2	3.3	.9	2.3

SOURCE: "Joint Economic Report 1980."

*Measured by growth in real domestic product per employed person, using own country's price weights.

he offered the United States's cooperative assistance in that task. When the Harriman Committee rendered its report, one of its major conclusions was that European recovery would depend primarily on the industry and straight thinking of Europeans themselves. When Averell Harriman and Paul Hoffman implemented the Marshall Plan, its primary emphasis was on productive investment.

During the war, when business and labor worked together in this country's war production effort, there was significant attention given to productivity. As a result, Hoffman, among others, required that labor be involved in the implementation of the European recovery program. Somehow, that cooperative spirit in the United States has dwindled away. In some cases, deeply antagonistic adversarial relationships have developed. That is one of the seeds of our productivity problem. Labor-management relationships are overlooked in current productivity analyses. They don't fit easily into complicated statistical compilations.

Another important aspect of the problem is our economic policy itself. Because of its overemphasis on demand management, economists have spent little effort in compiling information on the factors and their interrelationships relating to the supply component of the equation. As the United States headed into the period of decline, policymakers did not see our trade position deteriorating, energy problems developing, regulatory laws becoming costly, research and development slipping, and social spending increasing on unrewarding and unproductive jobs. As a country, we simply were not looking at the larger world around us. It is about time that we do so.

Japan's Example The Japanese not only outtrade us, they also outproduce us. They have had the best growth rate in productivity of the major free-world nations. In Japan, productivity is a major concern at the national, industry, company, and plant levels.

The Japan Productivity Center was organized in 1955 as the focal point of the productivity movement in Japan. On its twenty-fifth anniversary, the center observed:

Technological innovation has brought about drastic changes in the industrial and employment structures as well as in Japanese attitudes generally. Corporations and labor unions have played a central role in dealing with growth and change under these circumstances.

The Productivity Movement, by utilizing information and educational tools intrinsic to a movement of its kind, has sought:

—to foster a climate receptive to change.

—to introduce, develop and disseminate techniques of scientific management.

—to modernize labor-management relations through labor-management cooperation based on the principle of equality.[34]

Government-Industry Planning in Japan Steel is one of the oldest basic industries in the world. Along with machine tools and energy, it is the heart of a nation's manufacturing life. The Japanese recognized this very early in the postwar reconstruction period. They developed the *indicative planning process*—a process in which appropriate government ministries cooperate with industry in developing a consensus on where emphasis will be placed in economic development. When the process was begun by the Ministry of Finance and the Ministry of International Trade and Industry, one of the first industries to be established as a priority in national economic growth and international competitiveness was steel.

It is both interesting and important to note that the indicative planning process is similar in philosophy to the Marshall Plan. It provides guidance and aid, but it is not a dictatorial, government-directed operation, such as the Model Cities program might have been. In this process, the ministries, which have greatest overall knowledge and resources, learn what industry is capable of accomplishing, and business learns in what direction government policies are headed. As a result, consistent long-term policies can be developed which give attention to both supply and demand at the national level and good management at the company level.

This was certainly true of the steel industry immediately after the war. The Ministry of Finance ensured that the industry was properly financed through the second modernization—or "rationalization," as it is frequently termed in Japan—program, which ended in 1960. By that time, the industry was clearly a major world competitor. However, as an important part of the Japanese economic base, the steel industry has not been overlooked since then.

The private banking system in Japan is very much involved in the consensus process. It gets clear signals from the Ministry of Finance and the Bank of Japan. The Ministry of Finance has all of the responsibilities of our Office of Management and Budget, our Treasury Department, and our independent regulatory agencies which affect finance. The Bank of Japan is the equivalent of our Federal Reserve Board. The Ministry of Finance really calls the shots and, in a very subtle way, those in private banking circles understand that the steel industry is to be sustained. This attitude has permitted the creation of a substantial amount of private debt in the capital structure of the industry, which in turn, has fueled the tremendous capacity expansion and modernization programs of the past thirty years.

Immediately after the war, the Minister of International Trade and Industry (MITI) was primarily concerned with the world competitiveness of the steel industry. It used its influence in the consensus process to prevent excessive capacity and inefficient plant size. It also ensured that prices of both raw materials and iron and steel products were subsidized. When the subsidy program ended in 1950, Japan was not yet competitive in the world steel market, but it was well on the way.[35]

In the first modernization program (1951–1955) the industry invested $356 million, with about 13 percent financed by government-backed loans.[36] There were, however, significant tariff, tax, and depreciation incentives. There were exemptions from duties on imported steel-making equipment, tax-free reserves for price changes of inventories and bad debts, a 50 percent increase in the depreciation base on steel-making equipment, and an additional increase of this base by permitting a reevaluation of assets. Export earnings were exempted from income taxes, and an 80 percent increase of depreciation charges was given on export revenues as a percentage of total revenues.[37]

With this assistance, momentum was created; and the Japanese steel industry came within striking distance of a competitive advantage over the United States in 1956, as the second modernization program (1956–1960) began. During this period, investment quadrupled without any government backing. From 1961 to 1976, steelmaking capacity in Japan increased five times to almost equal that of the United States; moreover, the Japanese had a comparative cost advantage that put them in a dominant position.

In the period of recovery from 1957 to 1976, their price competitiveness changed dramatically. In 1956, when U.S. imports of steel from Japan were unimportant, the United States had a comparative advantage in basic cost of $8 dollars a ton. By 1960, this was reversed to a Japanese advantage of $32 dollars a ton. This advantage increased to $54 dollars in 1970 and to $120 in 1976, as will be discussed in detail in Chapter 8.

The amount of capital investment was substantial in both actual amount and growth in each modernization period.

As a result of the close working relationship between government and the steel industry, postwar recovery of the industry was swift, self-sufficiency followed, and the industry grew to a dominant position with substantial capital investment and improved technology.

Table 4-8 JAPANESE STEEL INDUSTRY
INVESTMENT PROGRAM, 1951–1975

Period	Total Invested (In Millions of Dollars)
1951–1955	356
1956–1960	1,737
1961–1965	2,816
1966–1970	6,230
1971–1975	13,210

SOURCE: Federal Trade Commission.

This obviously had an important impact on the productivity of the industry. From 1955 to 1975, production per worker increased ten-fold in the Japanese steel industry.

This growth of labor productivity was the direct result of the increasing of capital expenditures on new plant, equipment, and steel-making technology and the expanded share of world market resulting from the Japanese emphasis on trade. To the Japanese economic policymakers, there was no mystery in this productivity increase. It was an intentional part of their policy to give equal attention to both demand *and* supply management.

The Steel Industry in Japan Education and advances of knowledge are major sources of productivity growth. For the maximum effect, information must be diffused broadly. The steel industry in Japan is especially information oriented. It has both its trade association, the Japan Iron and Steel Foundation, and individual company information networks. The Japanese steel industry, because of its worldwide span of interest, thrives on seeking knowledge and information.

With the turn of the decade in 1980, the world steel industry faced a situation of saturated markets. With major productivity increases from expansion of market share at least temporarily behind it, the Japanese industry emphasized international cooperation, the development of cost-reducing technology, improved efficiency of raw material use, increased modernizing of steel-making facilities, greater energy conservation, improved technology for environmental preservation, better management systems, and enhanced employee productivity through Jishu-Kanri (JK), which are voluntary quality-control activities undertaken by the workers.

The interaction of better management systems and voluntary employee productivity is a fascinating aspect of Japanese management-labor relationships. On the one hand, they have developed extensive and sophisticated computerized management systems; on the other hand, they have recognized the importance of the human factor in the manufacturing process.

Management Information Systems   The management information system in the Japanese steel industry revolves around the use of the computer. Increasingly, top management is relying on integrated computerized information systems. At the senior management level, they have command of the total data base—data relating to information both inside and outside of the company. This is the *strategy level,* where economic forecasts and finance and profit estimates are interwoven into long- and medium-term plans. These plans are periodically reevaluated and updated in light of developing conditions.

From the *administration and planning level* in the middle, information flows in both directions: to the strategy level above and to the operational level below. At this level, the short-term plans are made for materials (both purchasing and distribution to the steelworks), sales and production, budget control, financing, facility planning, and personnel planning. The Japanese steel industry does a lot of planning.

Next in line is the *operational level,* which is split into sales control and production control. Sales control is responsible for order processing, adjustment of sales and production at the facilities, distribution of the end product, and billing. Production control is responsible for control of the steel-making process, inventory, the cost of the production, product quality, and for shipping.

After receiving an order with detailed production specifications from the order center at the head office, the computer system at the steelworks prepares schedules for each production process. These schedules are then transmitted to computers and automatic controllers, which regulate the production processes, monitor the quality of results, and make any necessary control adjustments.

With this complete network of systems covering administration and planning functions, production control at the steelworks, and sales control at the local sales offices, senior management has an integrated computer system with which to plan its strategy and run its business. This is a high-powered, scientific, and potentially dehumanizing organizational approach.

Jishu-Kanri (JK)   While the computer is whirring away, individuals could become depersonalized digits in a random-access memory. This does not happen in the Japanese steel industry. At the top management level, attention is given to the human side of the manufacturing process. As previously mentioned, there is a very real understanding that, because natural resources are relatively scarce in Japan, human resources are Japan's most valuable asset. This attention to people is integrated into the entire planning process, but it is most important in the small, voluntary groups that get together in different parts of each company. Management has recognized that as the industry has become more computerized, work that fully encourages a sense of personal involvement and achievement is all the more vital for each employee.

There is a very real concern with the commonsense idea of what it means to be human. At the core of the JK activities is a concern with individual human worth and quality of the working environment. The JK activities take place in autonomous, self-managed groups of eight or ten employees who work together as a unit. In an effort to stress creativity in the work place, the JK activity is based upon an approach that the participants themselves develop. A major purpose is to create a working environment that—with constructive use of the intellect, the creative power, and all those other faculties that characterize us as human—is permeated with a feeling of human dignity, self-realization, and teamwork.

The members of the group work together to reach their common goal. Just as with nations, individuals must have an optimism about the future; otherwise they will decline. A status quo of suspended animation does not last long. It is, therefore, important for the individuals and the unit as a whole to have forward-looking goals that they can personalize and get excited about. If they are concerned about improvements in their job environment and how they themselves can create these improvements, they go forward, rather than backwards into a fixed routine. In short, they enjoy their work.

The goals of the units, of course, are interrelated with the overall management goals of each plant and each company. The senior management of the company, obviously, provides the overall goals, and these filter down through the levels of organization to the individual units that come together spontaneously. The role of management is to act as the intermediary and coordinator of this process. In this way, all individuals who know their jobs best are encouraged to work together to improve them and, as a result, improve the company's overall productivity performance.

Philosophically, this is an offshoot of the Japanese process of developing policy through national consensus. At the worker level, it is the counterpart of the interaction between the ministries and the industry. Philosophically, it is also very close to what General Marshall said at Harvard with his obvious, but vital, understanding of human motivation: Europeans themselves—with the assistance of Americans— would do the job of the reconstruction. Cooperation. That was the essence of the Marshall Plan, and that is the essence of the JK activities. In the United States we have lost a sense of it; in Japan it permeates right down to the smallest working group.

In understanding cooperation, the Japanese understand that most human beings cannot survive alone. In order to survive, individuals must work with and assist one another. At the corporate level, the Japanese recognize that a company cannot exist without people who come together to perform the manufacturing activities which take raw materials and convert them into products with increased value. People working together can produce more goods more cheaply than people working alone; when these individuals come together to work, the result is a highly effective company. That is the full circle of the cooperation linkage.

The JK activities are at the core of this linkage. The group leaders are elected from among the members, without consideration of their position in the company organization. In some units the leadership role is rotated. The group then chooses a project and sets its quantitative goal, after a thorough discussion among the members. The projects relate to the work environment, including cost savings, consumption of materials, energy conservation, safety, pollution control, and prevention of human error. Targets are set in quantitative terms and in terms of the length of time expected to accomplish them; each member's role in achieving the target is determined in the consensus process. Should company educational or financial assistance be needed, it is generally given if the goal is a sensible one—as it usually is.

When the goal is achieved, there are presentations to report on the process used to solve the problem and its results. These take place at the unit, section, department, and plant levels and at company, regional, and national conventions, where the most outstanding JK activities are recognized for special commendation. Obviously, productivity savings which result directly from JK activities can be passed along to workers in higher compensation—and they are. But of equal importance is the increased morale of the individual employee, unit, and company, which results from successful goal achievement and widespread recognition of that achievement.

Labor is a very important part of the team approach to productivity improvement in Japan.

Nippon Kokan (NKK)   Nippon Kokan is one of the largest industrial corporations in Japan. It is a world leader in steel, shipbuilding, and engineering and construction. It is the second largest steel maker in Japan and the fifth largest in the world in terms of total capacity. It also has the most ultramodern steel-works in the world: Ohgishima.

The thinking, the spirit, and the drive of the people who run NKK in general and Ohgishima in particular are comparable to the best of those qualities which characterize our high-technology companies.

They have, for example, a continuous and vigorous concentration on research and development. They strive to develop technologies that will enable the company to diversify the use of raw materials. They work to develop new steel products of higher quality and varied use in a fast-changing world. NKK has an ongoing R & D program to innovate in the iron- and steel-making processes themselves. In the field of energy, the company constantly seeks to find new petroleum and gas-related technologies to conserve and use energy more efficiently. They have a similar intensity of interest in the development of more productive environment-related technologies. Nippon Kokan also has a comprehensive effort to create new fields of business around the world.

Within this computerized, highly automated, and technologically advanced environment, the employees are an important factor in the production of high-quality steel. The company has about 4000 JK groups, or QC (quality control) circles, which meet within the voluntary framework of that program to discuss and develop goals for productivity improvement. Their discussions range from quality and cost improvement, to workshops on the environment and human relations, and even to labor cost savings.

In 1977 and 1978, NKK saved nearly $15 million by implementing ideas which had originated with the voluntary employee groups. One QC circle, for example, developed a proposal that was translated into a 40 percent savings of fuel consumption in the soaking pit-furnace part of the manufacturing process; the increased energy productivity was achieved without any significant investment in new facilities or alteration of existing equipment. The group of workers which contributed this idea was given a citation by the director of the government's Agency of Natural Resources and Energy.

Nippon Kokan, like other companies in Japan, has fused the potentially conflicting forces of technology and labor. With this program of voluntary involvement, NKK has harnessed technology for the benefit of humanity. Labor involvement in the circle of cooperation has been a potent force in helping the company to maximize the use of the world's most inexhaustible resource: human ingenuity.

Ohgishima: A Model for Strength in Trade, Energy, and Productivity

Ohgishima is the world's most productive steel facility. It is a concrete answer to the economists' confusion about the mystery of productivity. It is also an example of the Japanese working to strengthen their triangle of trade, energy, and productivity. What is a triangle of weakness for us is a citadel of strength in Ohgishima.

Ohgishima grew out of the pervasive planning process that characterizes Japan. Within that process companies are very competitive, each trying to outdo the others. Ohgishima is the most recent result of that healthy competitive drive within the environment of government and business cooperation. Ohgishima was begun in March 1969 with the submission of a construction plan to municipal authorities of the cities of Kawasaki and Yokohama. The facility was finished in July 1979.

There are three significant aspects of this steelmaking complex. First, it has an extraordinarily efficient layout of the most modern production facilities and high-level production control systems in the world. At one end of this largely human-built island, iron ore comes in from Australia, South America, India, South Africa, and Canada, and coal comes in from Australia, Canada, America, South Africa, Russia, Poland, and China. At the other end of the island, finished products are shipped to destinations around the world. That is the Japanese circle of trade: import, process, and export.

Second, there is intense concentration on conservation of energy at every step of the production process with the use of by-product energy rolled back into the production process. This is integrated by a computerized energy center, which is the first of its kind in a steel works anywhere in the world. In the energy center, there is control of every kind of energy generated and used or recycled inside Ohgishima, including the power generation plant which—mostly with recycled energy—generates 90 percent of the electricity consumed in the steel works. This is the largest nonutility-owned power plant in Japan.

Third, with the highest level of computerized automation of steelmaking in the world, Ohgishima is the world's most productive steel facility. On a real-time basis, the central computer center controls seventeen processes from raw-materials handling to product shipment. The proportion of steel produced by continuous casting in 1980 was 88 percent versus 53 percent for Japan as a whole and about 17 percent in the United States. The yield of raw steel into finished steel was 95 percent versus about 71 percent for the average steel mill in the United States. As a result, Ohgishima has set a record productivity figure of 2000 tons per worker per year, considerably higher than any other integrated steelworks in Japan.

There are several interesting aspects of the development of Ohgishima which illustrate the cooperative consensus process between government and business and management and the workers. The Keinhin industrial center is located in the Kanagawa prefecture and is split between the cities of Kawasaki and Yokohama in Tokyo Bay. When NKK conceived the idea of taking a small island and reclaiming additional water area, there was no room in the industrial center for additional steel capacity.

However, the company, in complicated negotiations with the prefecture authorities and the twin municipalities, brought improvement to the industrial area. The project was a refreshingly clean idea. NKK exchanged part of its area—including part of the reclaimed area—to provide for future construction of a Tokyo Bay area expressway and also a scrapped-down area for smaller industries to move into from densely populated areas. The company also agreed to very stringent sulfur oxide, nitrogen oxide, and water purification treatment. Twenty percent of Ohgishima's $4 billion cost—fully $800 million—was willingly spent by NKK on environmental protection technology. There were no adversary lawsuits; there was cooperative agreement.

Another cooperative aspect of the planning of Ohgishima was the reduction of the labor force. About 18,000 workers were employed in the original Keinhin steel-works complex. Of that number, 12,500 were working in jobs involved in the steelmaking processes, which were moved to the reclaimed island. That new facility employs only 3000 working people. As part of the planning process, the new facilities were phased in over a five-year period, as the old facilities were shut down. About 5500 of the jobs reduced were done so by attrition over the ten-year period of the project's development. The other 4000 workers—with their involvement in and understanding of the program—were relocated to the Fukuyama Works in a planned expansion of that area. Human considerations were an integral part of the planning process.

Because of comprehensive, long-range planning and the Japanese cooperative approach of consensus building, the concept of Ohgishima materialized with the harmonious interaction of management, government, and labor. Figure 4-2 is a photograph of the complex.

After a drive from Tokyo through the industrial area of Keinhin—with the harsh ugliness typical of industrial areas around the world—one goes through an underwater tunnel built by Nippon Kokan. On the other side of the tunnel is a different world. It is like coming into an environment of a kind that Lyndon Johnson dreamed of and spoke about in his Great Society speech at Ann Arbor. There are green belts

FIGURE 4-2. The Ohgishima complex. (Courtesy of NKK.)

along the trunk road. The smokestacks have no smoke. Fish swim in a little pool of recycled water. There is little dust and dirt. The people are polite and efficient. There is a sense of quietness and almost timelessness in an automated monument to productivity.

The five basic steps in the steel-making process at Ohgishima are as follows. The first step is the sintering process, which takes fine pieces of iron ore and agglomerates, or bonds, them into uniformly sized lumps called sinter.

The second step is the heating of coal in the absence of air to produce coke for use as a fuel and a source of carbon monoxide in the blast furnace. Ohgishima is the first steel mill in the world to have a single coke battery to supply a 4000-cubic-meter blast furnace.

In the third step, molten iron is made in the blast furnace by the reduction of a combination of iron ore, sinter, and limestone. The larger the blast furnace, the more productive the iron-making process. With increased size of the blast furnace, capital costs, environmental expenditures, and labor costs are spread over the larger output. This results in lower cost per unit of output—the essence of productivity. The size of blast furnaces is measured in what is known as inner volume of cubic meters. There was one blast furnace with inner volume larger than 4000 cubic meters in the United States by the end of 1980. In mid-1980 in Japan there were 15 blast furnaces with inner volume larger than 4000 cubic meters. Two of them are the core of the iron-making process at Ohgishima. They are each capable of producing 9000 tons of hot metal a day.

In the fourth step in a modern integrated steelworks, the hot metal is transferred into the basic oxygen furnace for refining into steel. Nearly pure oxygen is introduced into the molten iron to refine it.

Finally, in a modernized facility the steel is cast on a continuous casting machine into slabs for plates, sheets, and hot-rolled coils or billets for seamless pipes and tubes.

In each step of this process and the materials handling at each end of it, the most advanced technology was introduced at Ohgishima. And it is continuously fine-tuned with JK activities. In 1979, for example, there were 1400 JK groups at the Keinhin Steelworks. They made 84,000 suggestions of which 56,000 were taken up and implemented.

The twin focal points of productivity at Ohgishima are the central computer center and the energy center. The computerized and largely automatic control of iron and steel making was woven into the layout of the facilities. The computer system has two levels, one consisting of two central processing units and one consisting of seventeen process-control computers for the processes of the five basic steps of production. Each of the seventeen production processes is optimally controlled by a process-control computer with input data from the central computer system.

The primary functions of the central system are to work out production, inspection, and shipment schedules based on the data of orders transmitted from the computer system at NKK's head office and the data from the process-control computers. It is the well-planned link between the strategy setters of top management and the production process in the plant itself.

Under the direct and integrated control of the central computers are the operation of the sintering plant, the coke plants, the blast furnace, the basic oxygen furnace, the continuous casting machine, the slabbing and blooming mills, the plate and hot strip mills, and the power station and energy center. In addition, transportation and handling of materials and products at both ends of the process are automated, computerized inspection of test pieces is done in the inspection laboratory, and reports are transmitted by the computer to the main office in written form suitable for the customer. Ohgishima is the closest thing in the world of steel to a completely continuous automated manufacturing process.

The centralized energy control system of Ohgishima regulates the use of generated energy and optimum supply and integrates it with the constantly changing demands of the steel-making process. The central feature of the system is that energy-control operations are directly connected to production-control operations. The most efficient and least expensive combination of energy sources are supplied to precisely equal the requirements of the production lines.

The core of the energy system is the central control of supplies of blast furnace gas, basic oxygen furnace gas, coke oven gas, and other by-product gases which are recycled to fuel the three 125,000 kW on-site power plants. The energy center creates Ohgishima's own energy.

The energy center also controls such innovations as the heat exchangers in the blast furnaces and the boilers which use waste heat at the sintering plant and in the hot reheating furnaces. Every possible attempt is made to translate waste energy into usable energy. In the process, there is a forecasting of the balance of the demand for and supply of energy sources on a 24-hour basis. In addition, the energy center monitors the emission-control process of the pollution-control program. All of this energy control is linked back into the central computer so that energy productivity is completely integrated into the steel-making process.

Productivity at Ohgishima has been increased by a higher rate of fixed capital per worker, economies of scale with the emphasis on market expansion through trade, use of human ingenuity and labor involvement, effective use of research and development in all phases of its company's R & D program, advanced use of technology, a streamlined layout and computerized management system, a cooperative venture with government, planned and integrated use of resources, and a total focus on energy conservation and recycled self-generation.

Ohgishima is a finely sharpened tool for the country of Japan, for Nippon Kokan, and for its employees. It is the product of over thirty years of government and business cooperation in consensus planning with a sharp focus on both the supply and the consumption of goods. It is the product of a labor-management system of cooperation with an emphasis on the coordinated but voluntary use of human ingenuity. It is the product of ten years of planning and building an integrated mixture of the most modern steel-making, computer, pollution-control, and energy technologies. It is, above all, the product of a profound understanding by the Japanese and the management of Nippon Kokan of the important interrelationships of the triangle of trade, energy, and productivity.

The Japanese understand the sharp cutting edge of economic strength. They learned their lessons well during the postwar reconstruction. It is now time for us to learn from them in our post-Vietnam war and Watergate reconstruction period. In Ohgishima is our lesson. The sharp cutting edge of economic strength is honed on a strong triangle of trade, energy, and productivity; and the honing catalyst is the spirit of cooperation, compromise, and consensus.

5 THE PRODUCTIVE POWER OF INGENUITY

From the early experiments in electricity in 1826 by Joseph Henry, to the invention of the electric telegraph in 1832 by Samuel F. B. Morse,[1] to the discovery of the transistor in 1947 at Bell Telephone Laboratories, America has been known throughout the world for its ingenuity. This reputation springs from the very foundation of our nation: the belief that a human being could be free to be an individual and break away from old ideas.

Americans have always possessed a shrewd resourcefulness for devising and designing new ways of doing things more productively. As our nation matured into a world power, we turned that ingenuity toward pure research and became a world leader in the many off-shoots and subcategories of basic science as well. We justifiably have been very proud of the many scientific breakthroughs and Nobel prizes that have come from our universities, our government-sponsored research, and our industrial laboratories. New inventions and new and improved methods of producing them have powered our growth of productivity and, in turn, our economic growth.

Recently, however, our growth of productivity has been both static and relatively unfavorable in comparison with other industrialized countries, particularly Japan. As the steelworks of Ohgishima illustrate, the Japanese—following predictable supply-and-demand economic policies—have put substantial effort, time, and financial resources into research and development designed to improve productivity. While the effect of research and development on productivity may be difficult to measure precisely, particularly in its impact on the overall economy, the existence of an Ohgishima dramatizes the very clear linkage between the two. Human ingenuity has been and should continue to be a highly prized and carefully nurtured American characteristic, as it has been with the Japanese. As a nation, we should make sure we have policies that encourage both the public

113

and private sectors to devote to research and development the material resources necessary to maintain the creative environment for unleashing the full potential of our human ingenuity.

There is a serious question whether or not we have been doing this. While we are still the free world's leader in resources committed to research and development, there are evident disquieting trends which developed during our period of weakness, trends that are dulling our competitive edge and sapping our economic strength.

As the United States moved from a period of strength after World War II into an economic storm, our commitment to research and development as a percentage of gross national product continued to increase. However, as the full brunt of that economic storm hit in 1967 and 1968, our national commitment to spending on research and development began a slow and steady decline. As the decade of the eighties approached, we were committing 18 percent less of our gross national product to research and development than we were when John F. Kennedy inspired the American people with a decade-long commitment to put an American on the moon.

As Table 5-1 illustrates, during the period when our R&D spending was declining by 18 percent, the French and the Germans—with a peak in the middle of the period—increased their R&D spending as a percentage of gross national product 30 percent and 80 percent respectively. The Japanese, with their gradual but relentless competitiveness, have increased their research and development spending by 40 percent. Thus, in another key area of basic national investment, the Japanese were steadily on the move upward, while we were on the decline.

The most important point illustrated in Table 5-1 is that our decline in R&D spending coincided with the Johnson-Nixon period when coherency in government disappeared and economic policy became short-term oriented. In the decade from 1965 to 1974, R&D as a percentage of gross national product declined from 2.91 to 2.32. While our competitors increased their national commitments to R&D, our R&D became a casualty of the discord that grew out of the Johnson-Nixon period. Policymakers were simply not thinking about the important factors underlying our long-term competitive position in the world economy.

PATENTS AND MANPOWER Not all new ideas and inventions are patented. Moreover, patent laws and practices are not always uniform from country to country. Nor do numbers of patents measure the quality or scientific impact of the application of human ingenuity. Nevertheless, patents granted to inventors do give some indication of

Table 5-1 SPENDING ON RESEARCH AND DEVELOPMENT AS A
PERCENTAGE OF GROSS NATIONAL PRODUCT

Year	United States	Japan	France	Germany
1961	2.74	1.39	1.38	NA
1962	2.73	1.47	1.46	1.25
1963	2.87	1.44	1.55	1.41
1964	2.97	1.48	1.81	1.57
1965	2.91	1.54	2.01	1.73
1966	2.90	1.48	2.03	1.81
1967	2.91	1.53	2.13	1.97
1968	2.83	1.61	2.08	1.97
1969	2.74	1.65	1.94	2.05
1970	2.64	1.79	1.91	2.18
1971	2.50	1.84	1.90	2.38
1972	2.43	1.85	1.86	2.33
1973	2.34	1.89	1.77	2.32
1974	2.32	1.95	1.81	2.26
1975	2.31	1.94	1.82	2.38
1976	2.29	1.93	1.78	2.29
1977	2.26	1.92	1.79	2.32
1978	2.27	1.93	NA	2.37

SOURCE: National Science Foundation.

the practical expectations of the potential payoff of a national R&D effort.

Table 5-2 suggests an interesting correlation between the number of patents granted each year and national spending on research and development. The United States invested an increasingly smaller percentage of its gross national product on R&D during the Johnson-Nixon decade of economic decay, and the Japanese did exactly the opposite. The number of patents granted in the United States mirrors that relative activity. Patents granted to Americans were down 15 percent between 1966 and 1975.

The important fact is that during the same period, when Japan increased its spending on research and development, the number of patents granted in Japan to Japanese nationals almost doubled. What is more ominous is that the Japanese have been moving very aggressively in the patent field within the United States itself. During the decade of our developing economic storm, U.S. patents granted to Japanese nationals increased dramatically from 1000 per year to over

Table 5-2. PATENTS GRANTED IN
UNITED STATES AND JAPAN *(In Thousands)*

	United States			Japan		
Year	Total	To Nationals	To Japanese	Total	To Nationals	To Americans
1966	68.4	54.6	1.1	26.3	17.4	4.7
1967	65.7	51.3	1.4	20.8	13.9	3.4
1968	59.1	45.8	1.5	28.0	18.6	4.9
1969	67.6	50.4	2.2	27.7	18.8	4.7
1970	64.4	47.1	2.6	30.8	21.4	4.8
1971	78.3	56.0	4.0	36.4	24.8	5.7
1972	74.8	51.5	5.2	41.5	29.1	5.9
1973	74.1	51.5	4.9	42.3	31.0	5.5
1974	76.3	50.6	5.9	39.6	31.0	4.4
1975	72.0	46.7	6.4	46.7	37.0	4.9
1976	70.2	44.3	6.5	40.3	32.5	4.0

SOURCE: National Science Foundation.

6000 per year. Not surprisingly, the Japanese emphasis was on communications equipment, electronic components, and primary metals.

Underlying the spending of R&D funds and the patents which flow from that spending are the human resources: the scientists and engineers. Here again, the trend is ominous. From 1966 through 1975, the number of scientists and engineers engaged in research and development in the United States rose slightly, from 521,000 to 535,000. In Japan the number almost doubled, from 129,000 to 255,000.

When viewed from the perspective of the labor force as a whole, these numbers suggest an even more startling threat to our technological edge. In 1966, 66 out of every 10,000 individuals in the American labor force were scientists and engineers. By 1975, only 56 out of every 10,000 people were working in research and development. In Japan, these numbers increased from 26 to 48 during that decade. While we focused on consumption, social spending, and a divisive war, Japan brought its percentage of the labor force working in research and development nearer to a par with us. They were again going up while we were going down.

TRADE IN R&D-INTENSIVE INDUSTRIES The active use of ingenuity does not only positively affect productivity by increasing output per worker; it also affects trade, as we described in Chapter 4 with the examples of Mitsui and Ohgishima. In the United States, exports of products from R&D-intensive industries have had an important role in our balance of trade. They have been a very bright spot in our weak trade position, which we also discussed in Chapter 4. Table 5-3 illustrates the importance of R&D-intensive industries in our trading position.

Table 5-3 U.S. TRADE IN
R&D-INTENSIVE INDUSTRIES *(In Billions of Dollars)*

Year	U.S. Balance	U.S. Exports	U.S. Imports	U.S. Exports to Japan	U.S. Imports from Japan	U.S./Japan Balance
1966	8.0	12.2	4.2	.7	.8	−.1
1967	8.8	13.4	4.6	.8	.9	−.1
1968	9.8	15.3	5.5	.9	1.1	−.2
1969	10.5	17.0	6.5	1.2	1.5	−.3
1970	11.7	19.3	7.6	1.5	1.8	−.3
1971	11.7	20.2	8.5	1.5	2.0	−.5
1972	11.0	22.0	11.0	1.6	2.6	−1.0
1973	15.1	29.1	14.0	2.2	3.1	−.9
1974	23.9	41.1	17.2	3.0	3.6	−.6
1975	29.3	46.4	17.1	2.4	3.4	−1.0
1976	29.0	50.8	21.9	2.6	5.4	−2.8
1977	27.6	53.2	25.5	2.8	6.3	−3.5
1978	29.6	63.9	34.3	3.6	8.5	−4.9

SOURCE: National Science Foundation.

R&D-intensive industries are those industries with an average of twenty-five or more scientists and engineers working in R&D per 1000 employees and with total R&D spending of at least 3.5 percent of sales. The industries that fit these characteristics are chemicals, electrical machinery, nonelectrical machinery, aircraft and parts, and professional and scientific instruments.

Table 5-3 highlights three very important developments in our R&D-intensive manufacturing trade picture. First, throughout the entire period of discord and economic decline in this country, American technology affected the trade area in a very positive way. While our command of our own energy destiny was slipping away unnoticed in the late sixties and early seventies and our first trade deficit crept stealthily upon us in 1971, our R&D-intensive trade provided a tough counterpunch in the hard competition of world trade. During the development of our economic weakness, this positive component of our trade balance more than tripled.

Second, from 1972 through 1975, while we lost complete control of our energy destiny, our strength in technology trade intensified. The 166 percent growth during this period came primarily through dramatically increased exports of computers, engines, construction equipment, and mining and well-drilling machinery.

Third, as this expansion subsided following 1975, the Japanese technology trade began flowing in favor of the Japanese. What had begun in the industries of steel, television, and automobiles gradually shifted—with the Japanese system of government-business cooperation and consensus policy development—to our areas of strength. In the United States, widening deficits occurred in electrical machinery products and to a lesser degree in professional and scientific instruments and nonelectrical machinery. The developments in the area of high-technology machine tools (which we explored in Chapter 4) were not an unplanned, random set of events. The years of substantial increases in employment in science and engineering and the steady growth of patents all came to obvious fruition for the Japanese. They experienced an expanded technology trade and a strengthening of their economic triangle; we felt another tremor of weakness in ours.

We are still the major technology power in the Western world, but we were once a dominant force in steel and we once controlled the world's energy-pricing mechanism. At the time of General Marshall's speech at Harvard, our triangle of trade, energy, and productivity was firmly based on sound public policy and its spirit of cooperation, compromise, and consensus.

As that spirit disintegrated and the public policy process fell into disarray, our steel position went first. Then, after a decade of neglect, energy fell under the control of OPEC and the ruthless Qaddafis of the revolutionary movement. And finally our competitive position weakened to the point where we were losing respect from both allies and adversaries around the world. We cannot afford to let our technology edge become blunted as well.

Because research and development has such an obvious impact on productivity and trade and could, in ways perhaps now unseen, have a similar impact on the supply and price of energy, it is important to examine it closely. In order to determine whether we are doing enough, we need to examine how R&D has been funded, how it results in invention and innovation, and how these, in turn, affect our productivity, our trade, and our economy in general.

U.S. SPENDING ON RESEARCH AND DEVELOPMENT As we have indicated, our spending on research and development as a percentage of gross national product declined through the Johnson-Nixon years. In actual dollars, spending increased during that period of time. In real terms, however, R&D spending was flat throughout the entire period. Using the mid-period year of 1972 as a base, Table 5-4 analyzes total R&D spending in constant dollars as well as actual dollars.

Table 5-4 NATIONAL R&D EXPENDITURES *(In Billions of Dollars)*

Year	Total in Actual Dollars	Total in Constant 1972 Dollars	Federal Gov't in Constant 1972 Dollars	Industry in Constant 1972 Dollars	Universities and other Institutions in Constant 1972 Dollars
1965	20.0	27.0	17.5	8.8	.7
1966	21.8	28.5	18.2	9.5	.7
1967	23.1	29.3	18.2	10.3	.7
1968	24.6	29.8	18.1	10.9	.8
1969	25.6	29.6	17.2	11.5	.8
1970	25.9	28.4	16.1	11.4	.9
1971	26.6	27.7	15.5	11.3	.9
1972	28.4	28.4	15.8	11.7	1.0
1973	30.6	29.0	15.4	12.6	1.0
1974	32.7	28.2	14.4	12.8	1.0
1975	32.2	27.8	14.3	12.4	1.0
1976	38.8	29.2	14.7	13.3	1.0
1977	42.9	30.3	15.3	13.9	1.1
1978	48.3	31.8	15.8	14.8	1.2

SOURCE: National Science Foundation.

In terms of constant dollars, spending on research and development in the United States was static from 1966 to 1975. During the entire decade that encompassed our economic deterioration in trade, energy, and productivity, our national attention to R&D went out of focus. Once Neil Armstrong stepped from the lunar module onto the surface of the moon in 1969, the national challenge set by President Kennedy was accomplished and spending on that space program tapered off. R&D spending by the federal government on a constant basis began to decline in 1969 and continued a decline of over 20 percent until a reversal began in 1976.

A decrease in defense spending was a major factor in that decline. Priorities moved away from defense as the quagmire of the war deepened and the American people became increasingly hostile to its continuation. In addition, the mix of defense spending shifted into armaments for Vietnam, as the Nixon administration changed the emphasis from American men to American supplies in the policy of Vietnamization. From 1969 through 1972, military spending in Vietnam came to $60 billion, and research and development suffered the natural consequences. From 1967 to 1974 defense spending for R&D was virtually stationary. There was no significant increase until 1977.

Industrial spending on R&D was also flattened out on a constant basis from 1968 through 1971. When Lyndon Johnson finally shifted his policies to pay for the war, a 10 percent corporate surcharge was levied from January 1, 1968, to December 31, 1969; it was then reduced to a 5 percent rate from January 1, 1970, and phased out entirely June 30, 1970. In addition, the investment tax credit was repealed in 1969 and not reinstated until April 1, 1971. As a consequence, business spending became cautious, and in that environment, investment in the future—R&D—suffered from uncertainty. Here was another result of the combination of short-term reaction to necessities and demand-management economic policies overriding any concern for our long-term economic strength.

However, when our involvement in Vietnam ended in 1975 and the 1974–1975 recession turned into recovery, actual spending on research and development bounced up sharply; led by industry spending, constant expenditures rose to a new high in 1977 for the first time in over a decade of economic decline.

In his 1978 State of the Union message, President Carter, recognizing this long neglect of our nation's ingenuity environment, called for a strengthening of America's research centers and a new surge in industrial innovation and technological developments. As with energy, Jimmy Carter recognized the importance of ingenuity and innovation in world economic competition, and he was intent on heading us in the right direction. The President had looked at the national funding record for research and development, realized its neglect during the decade of discord and decline, and called for an increase in our R&D spending as a percentage of gross national product.

It is important to understand that one State of the Union message is not enough. There must be a national understanding of the need for a long-term commitment to excellence in research and development and to the environment which will make achievement of that excellence a reality. Innovation and technological development are long processes; and it is to an understanding of these processes that we now turn.

THE PHASES OF THE TECHNOLOGICAL PROCESS Research and development falls into three categories and results in four phases of the technological process. Over the past twenty years, we have generally spent approximately 13 percent on basic research, 22 percent on applied research, and 65 percent on development.

Basic research is the first and most elemental phase of the technological process. It is a search for knowledge for its own sake. While many important economic opportunities ultimately flow from basic research, they are not the fundamental purpose in undertaking this type of research. The scientists who engage in basic research typically work in an unstructured environment and are free to think in original terms and explore previously unknown dimensions of the universe. Spending on basic research is the lowest percentage of the three categories because it is human intensive and does not require large amounts of capital equipment.

Once a basic scientific breakthrough is made, it frequently creates unexpected economic opportunities. Thus, in the second phase of the technological process, scientists and engineers work to apply the newly discovered basic knowledge to the solution of some specific problem or need. It is sometimes difficult to draw a fine line between basic and applied research. Scientists who make basic discoveries frequently move right into the phase of applied research.

More funds are spent on applied research than on basic research because the possible applications of a basic discovery can be extensive. In addition, research-intensive companies frequently duplicate efforts in the competitive drive to be first with a new product or process.

Once a new idea is proven in the laboratory, the technological process moves on to the third phase: developmental research. This is the most expensive phase because it requires feasibility studies, prototypes, and pilot plants to bring the innovative idea to the point of commercial reality.

When a company is ready to risk the leap into the real world with its new invention, it must then have the necessary capital, skilled labor, energy, access to raw materials, marketing ability, and management to build a full-scale production plant and sell the product. Commercial development of the new invention is the fourth phase of the technological process.

If the initial sortie into the marketplace is successful, the innovating company will either expand its plant or build new plants in different market segments to meet the increasing demand for the product or process. Frequently, the patented product is licensed to other companies with greater corporate resources. Or it may be modified or improved upon by other companies. The speed of the commercialization phase will depend upon the pace of market demand, the capital and human resources available to expand the supply to meet the demand, and, of course, the general economic climate in which the innovators are working.[2]

The Semiconductor Industry   A good contemporary example of the technological process is the development of our semiconductor industry. It is a recent development and still unfolding. And it is important to our competitive economic future.

It began with the invention of the transistor in December 1947 at Bell Telephone Laboratories. The invention grew out of years of basic research in solid-state physics, chemistry, metallurgy, and electrical engineering. Solid-state physics led to the discovery of the semiconductor materials themselves. The wireless telegraph of Samuel F. B. Morse gave creative Americans a vision of faster communications. And the electron vacuum tube made electronic signal amplification economically practical, giving us the radio.

Semiconductor materials conduct electricity better than insulators (materials without free electrons that are therefore poor electrical conductors), but not as well as commonly recognized conductors such as copper. Semiconductor materials can even be altered from a conductor to a nonconductor state.

They also have unusual characteristics that were discovered in basic research beginning in 1833. Unlike metals, semiconductors become better conductors as their temperature rises. They also have a voltage, (known as the photovoltaic effect) at their junction with an electrolyte. Their conductivity changes when illuminated. They rectify or conduct electricity in only one direction when in contact with a metal wire. Therefore, under certain conditions, semiconductors have asymmetrical conduction properties which permit them to rectify, amplify, and perform a variety of other functions relating to the conduction of electricity. The most widely used semiconductor is silicon, which can be refined from a very available resource—sand.

The electron vacuum tube, which preceded the transistor, was a fairly simple device, consisting of three electrodes. Electrons traveled from the cathode (or hot filament) to the anode (or cold electrode). Because the anode could not emit electrons into the surrounding vacuum, the device rectified, that is, the electrons traveled in one direction only. The third electrode, called the grid, influenced the current flowing between the cathode and the anode. When a small electrical signal was applied to the grid, it produced large changes in the current between the cathode and the anode. Thus, the electron vacuum tube amplified. It made the radio possible.

Unfortunately, the tubes were very inefficient. They had to be heated and energized. This not only used energy, but required that other components be protected from the heat. They were also unreliable. They burned out. Their design and structure limited possibilities for reduction in cost. And the tubes were very fragile and easily damaged. When World War II came, communications became a matter of national necessity. It became imperative for scientists in universities and industrial research facilities to zero in on a device that would overcome the drawbacks of the electron vacuum tube.

Many scientists were working on the problem, but the prize of invention went to the AT&T research subsidiary, Bell Telephone Laboratories, the largest industrial research organization in the world. Bell Labs obviously concentrates on communications research that will serve the parent telephone company in positive ways. However, it also has a highly regarded reputation for doing basic research, which enables it to attract the brightest and most able scientists. Two results of this channeling of American ingenuity into a large research organization were the invention of the transistor shortly after the war and a Nobel Prize to the three physicists who played the leading role in the process. Both are developments of which Bell Labs has been justifiably proud.

In such institutions as this, we have a very important edge over the Japanese. The Japanese have been, and are, very good at applied research. They are, however, still very backward in basic research. The Japanese business system is hierarchical and very conservative. It is also averse to taking risks. In basic research, no one ever knows what —if anything—will be discovered. Those are not the kind of odds with which the Japanese are comfortable.

Nippon Telephone and Telegraph is the government-owned equivalent of AT&T. NT&T operates two major laboratories and some smaller satellite facilities. These are superb facilities, and not a scientist in the world would question their sophisticated nature. Their scientists, however, have never won a Nobel Prize. All their research has been directed toward new methods for transmission of electronic information.[3]

The Japanese did not develop the transistor, and this is an important distinction that must be kept in mind. Basic ingenuity has not been encouraged in Japan, as it has been encouraged in the United States. As a result, we have been first in much basic research that has led to such inventions as the transistor. There is nothing to guarantee that our edge in basic research will be maintained. The environment that has fostered basic research must be treasured.

Basic Research The three physicists who played the leading role in the invention of the transistor were John Bardeen, William Shockley, and Walter Brattain. Bardeen was the theorist of the team, Brattain was the experimentalist, and Shockley fell somewhere in between.

As far back as 1939, Brattain and Shockley were attempting to create a semiconductor amplifier. In 1940, another scientist, working outside of Bell Labs, showed them an experiment in which a flashlight was shone on the junction of n-type silicon and p-type silicon on one slice of silicon with a sharp boundary between them. The effect of the light on the junction produced ten times the expected electromotive force. Brattain and Shockley were fascinated with the implications of this experiment. Unfortunately, before they could work with the ideas which flowed from this phenomenon, the war interrupted them, and they turned to research on radar for submarine detection.

Applied Research At the close of the war in 1945, Bardeen joined the team and they began in earnest the work that would result in the invention of the transistor. They recognized that the most important breakthrough from solid-state research would be a semiconductor amplifier. While exploring the surface of a semiconductor with two closely spaced electron wires, Bardeen and Brattain discovered that a small positive charge on one electrode would create holes in the semiconductor surface and greatly increase its current-carrying capacity. By placing two wire electrodes on a germanium crystal, they created an amplifier, which was the first point-contact transistor. This transistor was first demonstrated on December 23, 1947, after years of painstaking work. The invention was the result of superb interaction between the theorist and the intuitive experimentalist. It was also the culmination of the work of hundreds of scientists in many different fields over many years.

Developmental Research The point-contact transistor was followed in 1951 by Shockley's junction transistor in which the amplifying action resulted from sandwiching an n-type semiconductor between a p-type semiconductor. The junction transistor, in which the action took place within the semiconductor, was the beginning of modern solid-state electronics. The junction transistor had the potential to replace the vacuum tube. It was more efficient because there was no filament to heat up, and it acted instantly. It consumed much less power, and because it would not burn out, it could be much more reliable. It was both rugged and capable of being miniaturized. It was indeed a breakthrough.

Commercial Development   The application and development phases of the transistor were time-consuming. It is one thing to make a breakthrough and build a prototype. But it is quite another to manufacture and sell it. It was not until October 1951 that AT&T's production subsidiary, Western Electric, began to manufacture transistors for use in telephone equipment and hearing aids. Even then, in the early fifties, there were bugs in the process which had to be eliminated. The trick was to produce the device in large quantities at very low prices and in a form that would work with uniform reliability.

The original manufacturing process for the junction transistor was very crude. A crystal was slowly withdrawn from a germanium melt in a hot crucible, while a doping pellet was added to the melt to give p-type conductivity to the crystal. The addition of a second pellet produced a thin layer of n-type conductivity, and the addition of a third pellet produced the second area of p-type. The crystal was then cut into slices across the junctions and, under a microscope, leads were carefully attached to each of the three regions.

This process, developed at Western Electric in 1951, was gradually refined. The next year, General Electric introduced an alloy process for manufacturing an alloy-junction transistor, which could operate at higher frequencies and currents and thus greatly improved the transistor's ability to perform digital or switching operations. This was followed in 1953 by Philco's jet-etching process, which resulted in the surface-barrier transistor with increased frequency range and still faster switching speed.

In May 1954, a small company, Texas Instruments, announced its success in manufacturing silicon transistors. Not only was silicon readily available in large quantities, but it would work at much higher temperatures than the germanium transistor and with an increased frequency range. That was a decided plus to the military and had significant implications for a broadening semiconductor market.

This development was followed by another improvement in the manufacturing process, in which an impurity was diffused into the semiconductor. Using careful regulation of time and temperature and a sophisticated photographic technique, the diffusion process made batch-processing production possible, which both reduced costs and increased the reliability and frequency range of the device.

Five years later, in 1960, another innovation, the planar process, further lowered production costs and improved performance characteristics. It would be of great importance in the efficient production of integrated circuits.

Transistor sales began to spurt in 1955, and by 1957 there were about 600 types of transistors with varying characteristics. What had begun slowly at Bell Labs and Western Electric was beginning to spread to other companies. Initially, other large companies such as General Electric and RCA moved resources into the new technology. These large companies were joined by the hard-hitting, fast-moving entrepreneurs, who with their ingenuity and innovative drive would propel the semiconductor industry into a major position in our scientific and industrial life. In 1953, Texas Instruments was still a small geophysical services company. By 1957, it had 20 percent of the total U.S. semiconductor market, a $150 million market which expanded dramatically to over $550 million by 1961, when TI introduced the integrated circuit.

As use of the transistor moved from hearing aids and telephone equipment to radios, it began to make the computer an increasingly viable product. When the first fully electronic computing machine, ENIAC, was built at the University of Pennsylvania in 1946, it was a monster with 18,000 vacuum tubes. By 1955, IBM was able to introduce a commercially viable computer which used 2200 transistors. Computer size was reduced, the need for cooling was eliminated, and the new computer used 95 percent less power than its predecessor. New and widespread uses of semiconductors were beginning to unfold.

The Role of the Military An important part of the application and development phases of the transistor in particular and the semiconductor industry in general has been the role of the military. Defense spending was important in the original development of the industry and continues to be important in the ongoing innovation of new products and applications. This is a form of government-business partnership that evolved during the Truman-Eisenhower years and continued in the Johnson-Nixon decade.

In the early fifties, the military was not as much concerned with price as it was with performance, reliability, and availability of supply. In 1937, for example, a destroyer used only sixty vacuum tubes. By 1952, it required 3200 to be in continuous working order. At that time, only 60 percent of the electronic equipment in the U.S. fleet worked satisfactorily, and half of all failures were the result of tube problems. There was clearly a defense market for the transistor. By 1955, the U.S.

government accounted for 38 percent of the fledgling semiconductor industry's sales of $40 million. By 1960, defense buying accounted for 48 percent of the $542 million in sales.

For new companies, the government market was a source of revenue growth that enabled them to plow money back into the manufacturing process in order to bring down the cost of existing devices and develop new applications. The government market was also a ready buyer of new products. From 1962 to 1965, when integrated-circuit production began to skyrocket, about 87 percent of the sales were of defense products. During that four-year period, the average unit price dropped from $50 to a little over $8. Without the defense market, our semiconductor industry would certainly not have developed as rapidly, and perhaps not as fully, as it did.

Government acted basically as a source of investment and brought out the best of American ingenuity and innovation. It did this by creating markets for new products. Government also assisted the creation and the growth of the industry by direct funding of R&D projects, by financing production refinement programs for transistors through industrial preparedness studies, and by appropriating funds for new weapons systems that were passed on from the prime contractors to the semiconductor firms and used for research and development.

However, the government's efforts to implement economic programs by itself have not been so successful. Although the government had notable success during the Great Depression years with the Tennessee Valley Authority and the Rural Electric Administration, recent economic experience indicates that the government does not perform this function efficiently. Moreover as we have also learned from the serious decline of our economic strength, government does not function well in managing demand with short-term, stop-and-go policies. But as we have learned from both the Marshall Plan and the development of the semiconductor industry, government does function very well when it directs its resources to enhance private initiative and to foster cooperation. It took ten years from the invention of the transistor for the semiconductor industry to complete the four phases of the technological process. Without government cooperation and R&D aid, the process would have taken a good deal longer.

Texas Instruments One of the small, pioneering firms that grew to be a leader in the semiconductor industry is Texas Instruments (TI). To trace its history is to trace the way in which inventions and innovations resulting from research and development affect productivity, trade, and our economy in general.

In 1950, Texas Instruments was a company working primarily on oil exploration surveys under contract. That was a somewhat "iffy" business. With the development of the transistor, the company realized that its potential lay in electronics. It worked out a licensing arrangement with Bell Labs, and, in early 1953, hired Gordon Teal from Bell Labs to direct the TI research effort.

For a small company, Texas Instruments took a high-risk approach and put a substantial part of its resources into several applied research projects. The first was the silicon junction transistor which, as we have previously described, TI successfully introduced in the spring of 1954. The second was the development, that same year, of a commercial transistor radio for mass consumption. The third was the production of large quantities of silicon by chemical methods in late 1956.

From its earliest foray into the uncertain world of electronics, TI combined an emphasis on specific research goals with innovation in production and a coordinated marketing approach. As a result, this small company brought the silicon transistor into the market way ahead of other, larger companies. With its appeal to the military, sales of the silicon transistor expanded dramatically in the late fifties. This gave TI the profits and the capital resources to plow back into the cycle of research on new products, lower production costs, and marketing, marketing, marketing.

The Japanese did not invent this cycle of developing new products, then lowering their production costs, then driving for market share, and then having resources to expand the cycle worldwide. At the time that the Ministry of Finance and the Ministry of International Trade and Industry were developing the indicative planning process of consensus and cooperation with the Japanese steel industry and Nippon Kokan, little Texas Instruments was embarked on a parallel course.

TI's next step from the silicon transistor in the cycle of expansion was the integrated circuit. It was invented in 1958, introduced in 1959, and, with the development of the planar manufacturing process in 1960, became a viable product in 1961. Sales of this exciting new product doubled in each of the next six years. The military, of course, was an important factor in its fast start and explosive growth.

An integrated circuit is a single piece of semiconductor material within which several discrete electrical functions are performed. The batch planar process and the growing demand for vast quantities of separate components led logically to their integration into complete circuits. The planar process made it very economical to make many identical components on one wafer and then cut the wafer into the individual components. The next step was to take the TI idea of an integrated circuit and combine it with the planar manufacturing process. This resulted in volume production of circuits which contained a selection of separate functions on one wafer.

The integrated circuit resulted in substantial reduction in size, weight, and power consumption. It also had obvious potential for greater reliability. With improvement in these characteristics, it was as interesting and important to the military and the newly developing space program as had been the jump from the vacuum tube to the transistor itself. The development of Texas Instruments, defense research and development programs, and the space program were inextricably interrelated. Government and this particular company complemented each other. Government set stable, long-range defense and space policies, and TI, as part of its long-term strategy to serve industrial, consumer, and government markets, moved aggressively in a competitive market environment.

In 1960, Texas Instruments had sales of $232.7 million and employed 16,881 people. By 1970, sales reached $827.6 million and there were 44,752 employees. At the end of 1979, total sales had grown to $3.2 billion, about $1 billion of which represented international sales through both exports and manufacturing facilities abroad. The company's employment rolls accounted for over 85,000 jobs.

By 1980, TI was a leader in metal-oxide semiconductor (MOS) technology, which had been introduced in the early sixties. That was another step toward reduced power usage and a simplified manufacturing process, which led to large-scale integration of many circuits (or bits) on one silicon chip. It was employed in MOS memory devices such as the 4K (1000) bit random-access memory (RAM), 8K-bit erasable, programmable, read-only memories (EPROMs), 16K-bit RAMs and EPROMs, and 64K-bit RAMs and EPROMs. TI was continuing its relentless cycle of new product research, cost and size reduction with better processing, and market and market-share expansion.

By 1980, this company was also one of the major manufacturers of 4K-bit and 16K-bit single-chip microprocessors. This computer on a chip had been introduced in 1977 by another company. However, TI had moved in fast with its usual cycle of research, process, and sell. It had also phased into the computer business itself with minicomputer products, programmable industrial-process controllers, and home computers.

In the process of cycling the profits of its worldwide market expansion back through research and development, and its productivity increases into increased sales and exports, Texas Instruments has concentrated on three interrelated factors: cost reduction, increased circuit sophistication, and improved reliability. These factors are the essence of applied research and its development.

TI has reduced its manufacturing costs per active element group by 35 percent each time manufacturing volume has doubled. A function that was performed by a $7 transistor in 1960 cost less than a penny to perform in 1980. This, of course, was the result of both product and process research and development that put more and more functions on a single chip of silicon. At the beginning of the sixties, small-scale integration of circuits produced a maximum of twelve transistors on a single chip of silicon. The company is now working toward very large-scale integration with more than 100,000 transistors on that same small chip. That is cost reduction.

Semiconductor architecture has proceeded to the point at which a 4-inch silicon wafer contains about 600 chips. Each of those chips is a complete microprocessor which contains over 8000 bits of memory and 6000 transistors. That is increased circuit sophistication.

In the early days of the transistor, reliability was one of the important goals of the research. With increased reliability came increased ruggedness. In 1962, Texas Instruments' integrated circuits had a failure rate of between 7 and 20 percent per 1000 hours. By 1979, the failure rate of a comparable device was reduced to 0.0012 percent per 1000 hours. A television set containing 100 of these devices could operate twenty-four hours a day for 100 years without a circuit failure. That is reliability.

Underlying a concentration on these interrelated factors of lower costs, increased sophistication, and improved reliability is the TI philosophy of innovation management. That philosophy requires basic, understandable, and coherently communicated management strategies. The cornerstone of TI's philosophy is that the company exists to create, make, and market useful products and services to satisfy the needs of its customers throughout the world. The company's success is measured by its profit. That profit—which is not an inherent right —is both an incentive to and a reward for successfully implementing that philosophy. Texas Instruments's management believes that if they do not meet the genuine needs of society and their global markets, the company's profits will dwindle and the company will disappear. That is a Marshall Plan, self-initiative kind of attitude, which Paul Hoffman and Averell Harriman implemented so successfully. It is not new, but it is certainly well founded in a tradition that has proven successful in America.

As was done when Hoffman and Harriman set up the Economic Cooperation Administration, TI's philosophy has been translated into goals which are defined by the types of businesses they operate, their location, their growth objectives, and the direction of corporate expansion. These goals have been achieved through adequate planning and control systems. Planning permeates the Texas Instruments management process. Long-term goals for the expansion of the business are molded into intermediate strategies for the development of the innovations—as happened with the development of the silicon transistor, the integrated circuit, and the microprocessor—that result in reaching the targets of those long-term goals.

The intermediate strategies are broken into shorter-term tactical action programs. These action programs establish specific quantitative goals in detail, with specific resource allocations for one- or two-year periods. Top management closely watches the development of these interlocking strategies, the most important measurement of which is productivity.

Market share is an important element of productivity. Texas Instruments expands its market by aggressively lowering prices after costs have been reduced by effective deployment of human and capital resources. The key to this pricing aggressiveness is the company's design-to-cost program. By making cost a primary design specification and reduction of cost a continuous goal, management relentlessly develops innovations in both product and manufacturing processes. As it lowers costs, it cuts prices, gains market share, and rolls the profits right back into a new phase of the design-to-cost program. TI managers are tough, alert, hard-hitting competitors. Size has not diminished the intensity and strength of their competitive edge, nor has it reduced their commitment to an environment which enhances ingenuity.

Such an environment obviously requires an understanding of human motivation. TI has company-wide "people effectiveness programs" based on involving workers in planning and controlling their own work. The underlying recognition is that the people who do the jobs understand them best and are therefore best able to improve procedures for greater productivity. Out of this program rises a success-sharing program which ties productivity improvements and growth in net sales and profit to the profit sharing and total estate programs for individual employees. These incentives create a motivation to participate in the achievement of the organization's goals. It is a working example of initiative and cooperation combined at the company level in America.

One American variation of the Japanese JK activities is the Team Improvement Program at Texas Instruments. More than 80 percent of the employees meet in small teams regularly, on a voluntary basis, to discuss (and then implement) ways in which they can do their jobs more productively. The teams set their own goals and are able to tap their own human resources in a way that makes them more effective and their jobs more meaningful. Senior management clearly recognizes that the thousands of small improvements that result from the teams make an enormous and very significant contribution to productivity.

Texas Instruments has also used its own innovations in the technological process in its internal cost-reduction programs. As the cost of memory and logic have been lowered, the complicated phases of the manufacturing process have been increasingly automated. TI thus has put its own technological advances together with its human resources to improve productivity in the manufacturing process.

For example, TI has substantially increased productivity in the testing of calculators with the use of a computer-controlled robot. The robot can simultaneously perform complete tests on a number of different handheld calculator models by pushing the calculator's buttons and reading its display to check for accuracy. The robot takes over a mind-numbing job that has, in the past, made manufacturing a dehumanizing process.

The introduction of these cost-reduction programs has not resulted in a decrease in jobs because of technological obsolescence. Employment increased by over 7000 people, or 9 percent, from 1978 to 1979. Texas Instruments is an unmysterious, hard-hitting, and real-world example of how a company can integrate human, capital, and R&D resources to increase productivity, cut prices, expand business, and increase employment. At TI, the fruits of research and development have been increased productivity, increased sales and exports, and more humanized jobs.

Productivity at Texas Instruments has been increased by a higher rate of fixed assets per worker, economies of scale with the emphasis on market expansion through exports and global sales, use of human ingenuity and labor involvement, effective use of research and development in all phases of its business, aggressive involvement in the technological process, a responsive reaction to properly conceived long-term government policy, and a total focus by management on a planned and integrated use of resources.[4]

If Ohgishima is a finely sharpened competitive tool for the country of Japan, for Nippon Kokan, and for its employees, the very same can be said of Texas Instruments in America.

SUMMARY It is clear that in America some of our economic strength has been derived from our historical national commitment to foster ingenuity for the economic rewards of its application to research and development. Unfortunately, during the period of our developing economic storm from 1966 to 1975, that national commitment was weakened as consumption-oriented domestic policies and the war in Vietnam shifted funding away from R&D as a percentage of gross national product. The Kennedy vision of space exploration lost its national priority, defense R&D got cut back during the war, and stop-and-go demand-management economic policies and the lack of coherent long-term public policy created an uncertainty that made long-term R&D planning difficult for business.

As the development of the transistor and the semiconductor industry clearly indicate, the payoff from research and development results only after a painstaking and lengthy process. At the heart of this technological process is basic research, which by its very nature is impossible to assess in real economic terms until long after it results in breakthrough discoveries. However, basic research is the cornerstone of our technological edge, and government support for it is critical.

Government policy support and spending are particularly crucial in the application and development phases of the technological process. As it was in defense in the fifties and early sixties and in the space program through the mid-sixties, government policy focus should be long range. This will enable larger companies to commit resources— both human and capital—to the long-term R&D programs that are necessary for the technological process to mature into economic payoff. It will also enable new little companies—such as Texas Instruments once was—to take the high risks that have made the private sector flourish. If there is some assurance of policy stability continuing into the future, there will be a growing group of entrepreneurs with capital to back them, ready to bet on the success of their new ideas. We need to reemphasize this understanding, with an increased long-term commitment of resources to R&D in both the public and the private sectors.

When invention and innovation reach the commercial phase of the technological process, they result in industrial applications and new consumer products. R&D-intensive industries have become important contributors to our competitive position in merchandise trade. The application of R&D into improved manufacturing processes has been a significant reason for dramatically improved productivity in companies like Texas Instruments.

Perhaps the greatest strength of the American version of the technological process has been the interaction of human ingenuity with capital resources in R&D activities. From the unstructured environment of basic research through the voluntary programs for improving productivity at Texas Instruments, the ingenuity of American scientists, farsighted management, and involved working people has been a key to success.

Texas Instruments is not the only company that has recognized the advantage of tapping human ingenuity. The United Auto Workers and General Motors began a Quality of Work Life cooperative experiment in the GM Tarrytown plant in the early seventies that shifted that facility from one of the least productive to one of the most productive plants in the GM organization. For success of such programs, both management and labor have to recognize their potential benefits: that these programs can lead to increased productivity that can lead to lower costs, then to deeper market penetration, and then to increased employment and job security.

Because of the long period of national neglect of research and development, it is critical that we give redoubled emphasis to R&D and once again regain a growth of research and development as a percentage of gross national product. This will require several initiatives. It will require more spending on research and development by the federal government. It will also require a targeted investment tax credit for research and development spending by business and an immediate write-off for investment in R&D facilities. In order to reverse our negative trade position with the Japanese, we need to give a clear signal to American business that we intend to create a stable environment for long-term investment in research and development.

Most important, we need to bring government, labor, and business together to support a heightened awareness of programs like Quality of Work Life that will let the workers who best know the job help management create new methods, tools, and techniques to increase productivity. In the spirit of the Marshall Plan, the government function would not be one of tinkering in the process. Rather, it should be to create an environment that emphasizes the successful cooperation of management and the working people of America in order to put technology to work for all of us.

6 ACHIEVING POSITIVE TAX POLICY

The first Roosevelt was a colorful, robust, tough, and thoroughly representative American President. In a time before the development of highly refined polling techniques, the Rough Rider had an unusual sense of where events and public attitudes were headed. He anticipated the introduction of permanent corporate and individual taxation during his second term. Using the occasion of the dedication of a House office building on April 14, 1906, he introduced the concept of individual taxation. The event was vintage Teddy Roosevelt, as described by Champ Clark, a congressman from Missouri:

The President made a flamboyant Fourth of July speech for ten minutes, an uplift speech for fifteen, skinned the muckrakers within an inch of their lives, and delivered a few light taps on Democratic ribs. The mouths of the eminent Republican magnates were spread in smiles reaching from ear to ear. They were having the time of their lives, when suddenly, without any connection whatever with anything he had said, apropos of nothing, he declared vehemently for both a graduated income tax and a graduated inheritance tax. The Democrats were jubilant and applauded hilariously, while the smiles froze on the faces of the Republicans. The President seemed to be delighted with the sensation he had created and the consternation he had wrought among Republican statesmen. Their curses on him for that speech were not only deep, but loud.[1]

Later in the year, in his December message to Congress, he put the issue of a graduated income tax in a more sober context and addressed it in some detail. He emphasized the responsibility that men of wealth owed to government because they derived advantages from the mere existence of that government. He also recognized that the process of enacting workable legislation would be intricate, delicate, and difficult. With those astute perceptions, which would underlie the Sixteenth Amendment, the first Roosevelt went on to other pressing demands of his Presidency.

Roosevelt's concept was pushed by his successors, Presidents Taft (a Republican) and Wilson (a Democrat). Through these three Presidents, our contemporary tax system and its philosophy derived from what is best in both political parties when they are representative of the people: an essential belief in the equality of all citizens.

THE THREE PURPOSES OF TAXATION   However, like all products of the legislative process, American tax and fiscal policy evolved through political trade-offs. As a result, three distinct purposes interact in the push and pull of our contemporary tax and fiscal policy. These purposes evolved in stages, were grafted upon each other, developed some inconsistencies in objective, and ultimately rendered the dream of a simple, completely equitable, and neutral tax system a very remote quest. In order to assess how tax policy can help redirect our economy and strengthen our triangle of trade, energy, and productivity, it is important to recognize these three interacting purposes.

The first of the three purposes was the need *to pay the bills* of government. Based on our constitutional principles of democracy, it was necessary to develop a tax system that would be both practical to administer and considered fair by the majority of Americans. Fairness in paying for government was to be at the roots of the Sixteenth Amendment.

In the mid-thirties, the second purpose—*to provide for social justice*—was grafted onto the bill-paying function by the administration of Franklin Roosevelt. Although there was difficulty in legislating this purpose of taxation, it is clearly embedded in our system today. Adequate retirement, health, and educational programs for all Americans are now assumed to be national goals.

The third purpose of taxation—*to foster long-term economic growth* —was introduced by John Kennedy in 1960. Kennedy correctly sensed the possibility that our existing economic system would be unable to generate the real increased economic growth of revenues to pay the bills. He recognized the need for economic expansion to generate the funds required by the growth of social-justice programs for an expanding population. Kennedy introduced the investment tax credit. His idea was to use tax policy to encourage new and productive investment.

Unfortunately, when the costs of the Great Society and the Vietnam war exploded, the Kennedy investment tax credit was overwhelmed by the policy of demand management. During the Johnson and Nixon administrations, tax policy effectively helped to destabilize our economy in a competitive world environment. Policymakers overlooked the need for increases in long-term investment to enhance productivity and provide increased supplies of goods and services. That this attitude prevails is reflected in the fact that, after sixteen years of stop-and-go tax and monetary policy, the President's Economic Report of 1980 still contained Business Fixed Investment as one of the six Major Sectors of Aggregate Demand.

Long-term competitive manufacturing facilities like Ohgishima and long-term corporate growth from an R&D base like that of Texas Instruments require long-term public policies that create long-term growth of investment and a competitive supply of goods. Texas Instruments got its start during the Truman-Eisenhower period of balanced policy; because of its hard-working people and superior management, TI was able to keep its internal investment growing to sustain its competitive momentum.

The challenge of the eighties will be to learn from our recent erratic tax policy and to reincorporate John Kennedy's vision of a vitally competitive America into a reconstructed, balanced environment, similar to that of the Truman-Eisenhower period. In order to do this, we should fully understand the evolution of three purposes of our tax policy.

THE BEGINNING OF TAXATION The first income-tax law was passed to pay the bills for the Civil War. It was written in 1861, redrafted in 1862 before it went into effect, revised in 1864, amended in 1865 and 1866, drastically rewritten in 1867 and 1870 when revenue needs were not so great, and repealed in 1872. In 1864, it was graduated as follows: 5 percent on income between $600 and $5000, 7.5 percent on income over $5000 and under $10,000, and 10 percent on income over $10,000. By 1870, with the war over for five years and Congress eager to reduce taxes, the maximum rate was reduced to 2.5 percent, and there was a $2000 exemption. Teddy Roosevelt derived some of his ideas from this experience.

After William Howard Taft succeeded Roosevelt in 1909, the Secretary of the Treasury reported the first fiscal deficit since the Civil War. In 1908, there had been a decline of $64 million in revenues from tariffs and internal sources, while expenditures had increased more than $136 million. While microscopic by current standards, the deficit required responsible Presidential and congressional action.

As might be expected, an income tax was introduced in the legislature. Its sponsors articulated its fundamental logic: that the framers of the Constitution had intended that all were to be equal in the Republic and that all were to equally bear the burdens of government.

Reasoning that this tax would be the only one ever devised that would rise or fall with a person's ability to pay it, they recognized the cornerstone of the principle of equity in taxation.

Unfortunately, the urgency of the fiscal problem in 1909 could not await the ideal solution, and politics and the legislative process merged. While the Senate was engaged in lofty debate on the income tax and tariff schedules, President Taft went to work both on and with the Republican chairman of the Senate Committee on Finance, Nelson W. Aldrich of Rhode Island, who wanted the income tax killed.

Taft, who wanted to bind together his splintering party, reviewed one of the basic ideas of politics with the chairman: If you want to gut an idea that is advancing, you have to offer something in its stead. The President offered a corporation excise tax.

The Senator, however, saw the excise tax as an income tax in another form. Moreover, there was a real risk that the idea would be characterized as Democratic. But the President was persistent. He kept pressing on the need for the increased revenues that the tax would provide and played on a mutual concern about the possibility of deficit financing with the issuance of bonds.

Word of the Administration's alternative got around, a head count was taken, and it was apparent that the income tax supporters had the votes to amend the tariff legislation. Aldrich postponed the vote to try to work out a deal on the corporate tax with the White House, Republican insurgents, and leading Democrats. A deal was finally cut, and the President prepared his June 16, 1909 message to the Senate.

When he presented the message, he called attention to the need for funds to pay off the rapidly growing deficit. Then he astonished ally and adversary alike by recommending a constitutional amendment, giving the federal government the power to levy an income tax to firmly obviate any lingering constitutional problems from the Supreme Court's rejection of the Income Tax of 1894.

He also proposed a 2 percent excise tax, either as a substitute for or in addition to an inheritance tax. It would be measured by net income and levied on all companies except national banks, savings banks, and building and loan associations. The excise tax—although on income—skirted the Supreme Court ruling of 1894. (In 1913, the Sixteenth Amendment cleared this up by allowing the taxation of income without apportionment among the several states.)

The proposal was shrewd politics on the part of Taft. The conservative Republicans had an alternative to the income tax, and Aldrich, now standing jowl to jowl with the President, could espouse the cause of party unity. The President, in the same message, also usurped the

Democratic platform of 1908 by making the income-tax issue, in due course, his own.

The reactionaries within his party naturally believed that there were not enough wrongheaded people across the land to muster the states required for an amendment. There wasn't one chance in six dozen that that would happen. But apparently many reasoned—as Taft felt they would—that if government is doomed to grow, then it very well ought to be paid for and paid for fairly. The Tariff Act of 1909 with its corporation excise tax cleared Congress on August 5. The law provided that every corporation would be subject to an excise tax of 1 percent of its entire net income in excess of $5000 received from all sources, except dividends from other corporations subject to the tax.

The nation then moved on to ratification of the Sixteenth Amendment and an equitable paying of the country's bills. Ratification would be a very difficult process, the approval of thirty-six out of forty-eight states being required.

The first step was to pass a resolution for the constitutional amendment. This was done without opposition in the Senate and by an overwhelming majority in the House. The resolution proposed that the Sixteenth Amendment to the Constitution of the United States be ratified by the states so that: "The Congress shall have the power to lay and collect taxes on incomes, from whatever source derived, without apportionment among the several States, and without regard to any census or enumeration."[2]

The only state to ratify in 1909 was Alabama. Progress was slow, with eight additional states coming in the following year. Stuyvesant Fish, a prominent New York banker and railroad executive, wrote the case against the Sixteenth Amendment to his State Assembly. He concluded: "Does not . . . every State in the Union need to husband its own resources and to keep down taxation rather than to vote . . . Congress . . . additional and unlimited power in respect thereto, especially . . . when all classes are suffering from the 'high cost of living.' "[3]

Fish was, however, in a minority. The momentum of the amendment slowly gathered speed in 1911 with ratification by twenty-one states, making the running total thirty. Four more were added in 1912, and by early February of 1913 the Sixteenth Amendment went over the top. Only Connecticut, Rhode Island, Pennsylvania, Virginia, Florida, and Utah failed to take action on it or rejected it outright. Roosevelt and Taft had accurately assessed the American electorate's feeling on this issue. The Secretary of State certified adoption of the amendment on February 25, 1913.

Between 1909 and 1913, however, events did not go well for the

Republican party, further weakening the unity which Taft had tried to restore. The Republicans lost the House in 1910, and with that Taft's power as a leader of the party began to deteriorate rapidly.

Roosevelt by that time was bored with his role as elder statesman and party sage. During the summer of 1910, he had been out West making speeches about something called social justice: the reconstruction of society by political action. To Teddy that meant changing the rules of the game in a way that would allow for substantially greater equality of opportunity and reward for equally good service.

Robert M. La Follette began the Presidential campaign of 1912 in early 1911 when he organized the insurgents into a National Progressive Republican League. By early 1912, Teddy Roosevelt had split with his old friend Taft, and he threw his hat into the ring on February 21: his radical call for social justice had hurt him with the party professionals. The conservatives controlled the Republican convention of 1912. They knocked off La Follette, Taft was renominated, and Roosevelt walked out to form the Progressive Party.[4]

Thrice-defeated Presidential candidate William Jennings Bryan led the Democratic convention fight for the nomination of the Governor of New Jersey, Woodrow Wilson. His side prevailed, and Wilson won the election of 1912 with the help of the divisive split created by Taft and Roosevelt.[5]

The emotion of the election having receded, it was now time for Wilson to finish the job on the federal income tax. The Sixteenth Amendment clearly had bipartisan support. Despite the fact that business had been fairly good and the 1912 fiscal year ended with a surplus of receipts over expenditures of $37 million, the income tax had acquired a life of its own based on its intrinsic merit.

The Democrats proposed a reduction in import duties, particularly on those items which affected the cost of living or were an aid in the development of monopolies. Cordell Hull, a Tennessee Democrat on the Ways and Means Committee, was given the intellectually challenging job of writing the income-tax legislation which would offset lost revenues from lowered tariffs.

Hull favored a flat rate in order to introduce the law into the economic system with as little controversy as possible. Now that they were on the inside developing the policy, the Democrats did not want to jeopardize their opportunity for tariff reform by drafting a law that might become a politically unpopular boomerang. It was one thing to get a majority of the voters to agree on the nobility of the income tax; it might be another thing to face the voters after they had to pay it.

By April, the tariff schedules were fairly firm, and the deficit that would have to be met was estimated at $69 million. This forced the legislators in the House to focus squarely on the issue of a progressively graduated income tax. The nub of the argument, as Hull explained, was that every American citizen was responsible for contributing to the support of the government in proportion to the revenue he or she derived under the protection of that government.

That was sound thinking. The bills had to be paid, and they should be paid fairly. The legislation proceeded through the House, went to the Senate, was resolved in conference committee, and was signed into law by President Wilson on October 3, 1913.

A 1 percent tax was levied on the net income of every American citizen. In addition, there was a surtax of 1 percent beginning at the $20,000 level, and graduating up to 6 percent for an income over $500,-000. The proceeds of life insurance and interest from state and federal bonds were exempt, there were numerous business and tax deductions, and there was a personal exemption of $3000 in income for each taxpayer, plus an additional $1000 for those married and living with a husband or wife. The corporate tax rate was the same as the normal tax on individuals, 1 percent on net income. In 1914, the income tax yielded a bit over $71 million from individuals and corporations.

With the outbreak of the First World War in Europe in August 1914, the economy sagged, and that resulted in lower income-tax revenues. With imports off, tariff revenue dropped. Although the war was not yet America's, forward-thinking people backed the idea of preparedness. Appropriations were certain not to be cut. The result was the Revenue Act of 1916, the first income-tax measure to be considered on its own, apart from tariffs. The normal rate was raised to 2 percent for both individuals and corporations. The upper limit of the surcharge was raised to a maximum of 13 percent on income over $2 million. The bill was signed by the President on September 8, 1916.

That same day, Wilson signed another bill to provide for national defense as well as greatly increased domestic spending. Yet even before the new law had gone into effect, the Treasury estimated a deficit of $280 million for the 1918 fiscal year. That led to an Emergency Revenue Act on March 3, 1917. President Wilson was inaugurated into his second term the next day; and war was declared by a special session of Congress on April 6. The Secretary of the Treasury requested an immediate war appropriation of $3.5 billion, debt financing was authorized, and the legislative work on the War Revenue Act of October 3, 1917 was begun.

That Act amended the 1916 Act and raised the normal tax on individuals and corporations to 4 and 6 percent respectively. For individuals, the personal exemption was reduced to $2000 for heads of families and $1000 for single persons. An additional surtax was placed on top of the existing one, the combination of which graduated the highest bracket to 63 percent on amounts over $1 million. A war excess-profits tax was levied on the difference between "normal" profits of businesses in 1911, 1912, and 1913, and those of 1917. The rates were graduated on the basis of a complicated formula related to invested capital.

Before the end of 1917, Congress had appropriated about $19 billion, including a $7 billion loan to the allies. The amended tax code was expected to finance about $2.5 billion of that. The nation was headed into relatively "enormous" deficit financing. The entire cost of the federal government from 1791 to 1917—including four wars—had been, by comparison, a total of $26 billion. We were throwing the resources of the entire nation behind an intense effort to break as fast as possible the enemy's will to resist. The enemy broke, and after the Armistice on November 11, 1918, there was a new fiscal policy in the United States. In five short years, necessity had managed to embed the philosophy of a progressive income tax into American economic policy. There were plenty of bills to pay by the fairest means possible.

POLICY UNDER THE NEW DEAL   In a surprise tax message to Congress on June 19, 1935, Franklin Delano Roosevelt angered the financial power structure when he bluntly stated his position on tax policy: "Our revenue laws have operated in many ways to the unfair advantage of the few, and they have done little to prevent an unjust concentration of wealth and economic power."[6]

The proposal to use taxation for social justice was not introduced in a vacuum. The thirties were a time of economic depression that ate ravenously at the spirit of the American people. There was one deadly word: unemployment. And across the country there were the stirrings of private social-justice movements.

Senator Huey Long of Louisiana had a substantial following, and he formed an organization called the "Share-Our-Wealth-Club: Every Man a King." Eventually there were some 20,000 of these clubs. Long was considered a real political threat to the President in 1936.

In California, a seventy-year-old physician named Dr. Francis Townsend worked out a pension plan that would relieve the agony of despair that had engulfed many people of his age. He too formed a club. Members registered in the club by sending a petition to Congress asking for the enactment of the plan. Millions of the elderly joined. Congress heard their message.

And in Detroit there was Father Charles E. Coughlin, a Roman Catholic priest known for his Sunday afternoon sermons. He had his own twenty-six–station national radio network. He formed The National League for Social Justice. When he spoke out on an issue and asked his listeners to contact their senators and congressmen, they did. The immensity of their response had the power to reverse a sure vote over the weekend.

The second Roosevelt moved within a framework of strong personal conviction on the issue of social justice. But that framework was set in a fertile political context. There were plenty of Americans to the left of him in the summer of 1935. Five days after the surprise message, he called congressional leaders to a White House conference where he pressed for immediate passage of a bill to redress the "unjust concentration of wealth." After a whirlwind of summer activity, the bill was passed and signed on August 30.

The normal tax was unchanged; the surtax rates were changed in the brackets above $50,000. The maximum tax was raised from 59 percent on income over $1 million to 75 percent on income over $500,000. The four-stage graduated corporate tax had an upper limit of 15 percent on income above $40,000. These were not such revolutionary changes after all.

The real impact came in the companion legislation on social security. That law provided for grants-in-aid to the states for programs of unemployment compensation, old-age assistance, aid to dependent children, work with crippled children, vocational rehabilitation, and public health research. Its major innovation, however, was a direct old-age benefits program. The benefits were measured by wages earned and payable to those who reached the age of sixty-five, without respect to need. It was a simple program for people who, after years of productive work, came to the time for retirement. The retirement program funds were to be raised through a payroll tax shared equally by the employer and employee.

From the vantage point of contemporary America, where most modern corporations have substantial add-on packages of employee benefits of their own, it is almost impossible to understand how the redistribution of national wealth by this form of social justice could have been controversial. The results of this legislation are now accepted as a common part of broader programs of corporate responsibility practiced by many companies.

Philosophy can sometimes be overdone, however. The pendulum can swing too far, with unbalancing reverberations that swing back through the economic system with negative results. The Revenue Act of 1936, in contrast to the Act of 1935, took philosophy too far. It clashed with economic reality and the economic consequences were severe.

On March 3, 1936, FDR sent a special tax message to Congress. Among other recommendations, he suggested a tax on undistributed corporate profits to replace the corporate income tax, the capital-stock tax, and the excess-profits tax:

The accumulation of surplus in corporations controlled by taxpayers with large incomes is encouraged by the present freedom of undistributed corporate income from surtaxes. Since stockholders are the beneficial owners of both distributed and undistributed corporate income, the aim . . . should be to seek equality of tax burden on all corporate income whether distributed or withheld from the beneficial owners.[7]

The President recommended a corporate tax rate that would yield revenues equivalent to taxes that would have been paid by individual stockholders if the profits had been distributed to them. Ultimate fairness. Equality of taxation. A piercing of the corporate structure.

Like all proposals to simplify the tax system, the idea emerged from the legislative process not entirely intact. The principal of fairness, however, was sufficiently recognizable.

The graduated ranges of the normal 1935 tax were modified, but the top rate remained 15 percent on income in excess of $40,000. The new surtax on undistributed profits was added to that. It too was graduated, in five steps, from 7 percent up to a maximum of 27 percent. The top corporate rate was therefore 42 percent, a real incentive to pay out earnings.

The most important economic unit in the United States is the corporation. In order to provide viable productive growth of sales and jobs, it must have financing. One obvious source is the internal one of retained earnings. Texas Instruments powered its growth primarily with substantial reinvestment of its earnings into new products and processes. It is easy to envision how that growth would have been thrown off balance if TI management had been operating in an environment with a tax on undistributed profits that encouraged them to pay out earnings rather than reinvest them in productive growth.

And that is what happened after the passage of the 1936 law. The additional progressive tax on retained earnings encouraged a significant increase in dividends. In the two years in which the law operated, dividend distributions increased by an estimated one-third. Manufacturing payout was up 40 percent, while the construction, forestry, fisheries, and agriculture industries increased their payouts by 75 percent. The surtax stimulated greater compensation to corporate employees and outlays for maintenance. Bigger executive salaries and bonuses enabled small businesses to avoid the surtax.[8] The effect of the law was to cut against the grain of long-term competitive economic growth.

At the time, there was an outpouring of complaints from business about the disastrous economic impact of the tax. These complaints began to affect Congress in the summer of 1937, when the House asked the Committee on Ways and Means to study the problem. As the study got underway in the fall, it was obvious that the economy was again declining, perhaps into a serious depression.

Bernard M. Baruch, an advisor to presidents and a prominent Democrat, while agreeing with the attempt to use tax policy as a means of preventing unproductive accumulations of surplus, testified that: "The combined influence of high and unreasonable capital gains and unwise undistributed-profits taxes has almost stopped the development of new enterprise."[9]

The President dug in his heels on principle; but despite a greatly emasculated undistributed profits tax, he neither signed nor vetoed the Revenue Act of 1938, which ultimately repealed the undistributed profits tax. The tax would apply only for the calendar years 1938 and 1939, and the maximum rate was cut sharply from 27 percent to 2.5 percent. The issue, in effect, was decided. An experiment in the extension of the doctrine of fairness had been attempted, it had clashed with economic reality, and policy was returned to equilibrium.

As the Second World War approached in 1941, the maximum corporate tax on income over $38,461 was 31 percent. It had increased steadily from 1 percent when first levied in 1909. The individual tax was at a maximum of 75 percent. It had opened at a maximum rate of 6 percent in 1913, increased to a high marginal rate of 65 percent at the peak of the First World War, been cut back in the mid-twenties to 20 percent, and then reincreased dramatically to 55 percent in 1932.

POLICY UNDER TRUMAN AND EISENHOWER By the end of the Second World War in 1945, individual income taxes ranged from 11.5 percent on net incomes of $1000 to 88.9 percent on those over $500,-000. The forecast for converting from a wartime to a peacetime economy was gloomy, with unemployment expected to skyrocket and a substantial deficit of $30 billion projected for fiscal 1946. President Truman, a tough balanced budgeteer to the core, saw only limited room for tax reduction. In the Revenue Act of 1945 the corporate rate was cut from 40 percent to 38 percent at the $50,000 bracket. It stayed there until the Korean war required its increase. Individual surtax rates were lowered by a modest 3 percentage points.

At the beginning of 1949, Harry Truman told the Eighty-first Congress: "Our prosperity is threatened by inflationary pressures at a number of critical points. . . . [it is necessary] not only that the federal budget be balanced, but also that there be a substantial surplus to reduce inflationary pressures and permit a sizable reduction in the national debt, which now stands at 252 billion dollars."[10]

The next year, when submitting his fiscal 1951 budget, the President said: "Our general objective should be a tax system which will yield sufficient revenue in times of high employment, production, and national income to meet the necessary expenditures of the government and leave some surplus for debt reduction."[11]

He was echoed by President Eisenhower in 1956:

It is essential . . . that we be mindful of our enormous national debt and of the obligation we have toward future Americans to reduce that debt whenever we can appropriately do so. Under conditions of high peacetime prosperity, such as now exist, we can never justify going further into debt to give ourselves a tax cut at the expense of our children. So . . . I earnestly believe that a tax cut can be deemed justifiable only when it will not unbalance the budget, a budget that makes provision for some reduction, even though modest, in our national debt.[12]

The positions of Truman and Eisenhower were interchangeable with respect to the interaction of fiscal and economic policy. Throughout the period of stability during their administrations, broad policy objectives were consistent. The usual disputes arose over whether the tax structure should favor low-income groups or high-income groups, earned income or unearned income, and consumption or investment. The disputes were partisan, sometimes acerbic, but they never ruptured the basic bipartisan accord of dependable, long-term consistency of policy.

There were no major upheavals in over fifteen years. There were a few angry vetoes—with election-year pressures prevailing in the tax cut of 1948. There was the substantial corporate rate increase to 52 percent at the time of the Korean war,[13] and the introduction of special accelerated depreciation of new plants and equipment and first-year expensing of R&D in 1954.

There was even bipartisan unity of purpose between the Republican President and Democratic leadership of Congress in 1958. By the end of 1957, the economy had declined into the third postwar recession. Inflation was beginning to pick up; and it finished the year at a 3.6 percent rate—more than twice that of the previous year.[14] Eisenhower was concerned that a deficit induced by tax cuts would spark increased inflation when the recovery came.

A group of Democrats led by Illinois Senator Paul Douglas, a highly regarded authority on economics, moved for a sizable antirecession tax cut. It was, of course, a congressional election year, and as unemployment hit 5 percent in March 1958, Republican support for a tax cut began to develop. The President, however, stood firm. He got the support of Speaker Sam Rayburn, who brought Lyndon Johnson and the Senate along. Together they prevailed. They beat back the tax cutters. In 1959, the gross national product rose 8.4 percent, employment was up by almost a million, and inflation fell to less than 1 percent. That was the result of a bipartisan and stable economic policy.

The Truman-Eisenhower period of strength was a time of predictable tax policy.

POLICY UNDER KENNEDY   The third purpose of taxation—fostering long-term economic growth—was defined in the early sixties. Having begun as a means of paying the bills fairly, the tax system had been directed to social-justice objectives by President Roosevelt. Now it was time to fine-tune tax policy as a way to get better economic performance. This was the first stirring of the concept of supply-side economics.

President Eisenhower, in his final budget message on January 16, 1961, said: ". . . A better system of capital recovery allowances would foster long-range economic growth and strengthen the competitive position of American producers."[15]

When John Kennedy assumed the Presidency in 1961, he recognized this need to get America moving again. He saw a balance-of-payments problem develop as the United States spent more for imports, travel, investments, and government outlays abroad than our trading partners were spending or investing here. The problem then was primarily a financial one. The real deterioration in merchandise trade was ten years away. But President Kennedy sensed the need for new policies. He proposed to balance the budget over the years of the business cycle and, in a special April 20 tax message, offered a new concept that featured a 15 percent tax credit on all new plant and equipment investment.

The nation, then beginning to coast in its economic prosperity, did not share Kennedy's sense of urgency, and it certainly was not ready for a new role for taxation. His investment tax credit proposal went nowhere in 1961; it languished in committee after controversial hearings.

The President, however, was relentless, and he came back again in 1962. Because of changing economic conditions, the tax bill made progress, and it was passed for a preelection signing on October 16. The investment tax credit—which was not quite the same as the one Kennedy called for—made business investment in new or old equipment after December 31, 1961, eligible for a 7 percent credit. Buildings were excluded, the credit was limited to $25,000 plus 25 percent of any tax liability above that amount, and the depreciation basis of any asset would be reduced by the amount of the tax credit taken. This latter provision reduced the impact of the credit and would later be eliminated in a liberalization of the credit. At the same time, the Treasury Department substantially consolidated depreciation categories and cut the average depreciable life of manufacturing assets from 19 to 12 years. This not only simplified the process, it provided a business tax cut estimated at $1.5 billion in the first year.

This was a beginning, but it was not sufficient for the President. He came back with a major address in New York on December 14 to lay the foundation for his 1963 program. The key problem, he said, was that:

. . . our present tax system exerts too heavy a drag on growth—that it siphons out of the private economy too large a share of personal and business purchasing power—that it reduces the financial incentives for personal effort, investment and risktaking.

In [order] to increase demand and lift the economy, the Federal Government's most useful role is not to rush into a program of excessive increases in public expenditures, but to expand the incentives and opportunities for private expenditures.[16]

That was a new purpose of taxation. Another President was clearly innovating. He seemed to have a clear understanding of the delicate balance of supply and demand: that personal and business purchasing power (consumption) must be balanced by the personal effort and the investment and risktaking (savings and investment) necessary to efficiently produce at stable prices the goods to equal that personal and business purchasing power. Kennedy proposed balanced economic policy for a competitive world.

· There was to be a net tax cut of $10.3 billion.

· Individual brackets were to be reduced from a range of 20 to 91 percent to a range of 14 to 65 percent.

- The corporate rate would be reduced 5 points to 47 percent.
- The maximum capital gains rate would be reduced from 25 percent to 19.5 percent.
- Tax deductions for expenditures for machinery and equipment used directly in research or development activities would be introduced.

Although President Kennedy did achieve widespread understanding and support for the concept of tax reduction to help promote economic growth, the specifics became embroiled in dispute. John Kennedy had the same kind of problem that Jimmy Carter would later face with energy. The policy issues were complex, and there was a complacency about the need for action. President Kennedy was assassinated before his tenacity and understanding of the problem could be rewarded with the results of a balanced policy.

POLICY SINCE 1963 Lyndon Johnson wanted action. As with the Great Society, he did not have the time to think through the implications of what he did in tax policy. The important thing was to get going, get the legislation passed, and get a tax bill signed. Congress finished the omnibus tax reduction and reform bill on February 26, 1964, and Lyndon Johnson called it "the single most important step that we have taken to strengthen our economy since World War II."

The Johnson initiative had the following results:

- Individual rates were reduced to a range of 14 to 70 percent.
- The corporate tax rate was reduced to 48 percent.
- The 7 percent investment tax credit was liberalized so that the depreciation base of assets was not required to be reduced by the amount of the credit. This was a congressional initiative, unopposed by the administration.
- Nothing was done on the capital gains rate.
- R&D remained in a status quo.

This was far from a total victory for President Kennedy's carefully balanced program for a revitalized America. But Lyndon Johnson had his own priorities, which were to result in intensifying our economic problems as he moved the nation into the Great Society and the Vietnam war.

By 1966, as economists Robert Hall of Harvard and Dale Jorgenson of MIT later verified, the investment tax credit was working with powerful effect.[17] This caused internal disagreement within the administration. Inflation was pushing against productive capacity. However, the President's Council of Economic Advisers urged the suspension of the investment incentives of the tax credit and the faster depreciation. The Treasury Department, on the other hand, maintained that the investment incentives should not be altered to influence economic trends of a temporary nature. The important consideration was to increase modernized capacity over the long run. By late summer, the Council prevailed with the President, and John Kennedy's vision of a delicately balanced economic policy was dead.

This decision was a crucial one. Investment became a tool of demand-management policy. Instead of being perceived as the means of creating modernized manufacturing capacity, investment was viewed only as a demander of funds in competition with other engines of consumption. Because it was put on the demand side, investment became an equivalent of consumption.

Henceforth, it would be tinkered with, as economic policymakers sought to push up and then pull down demand in policy reversals directed toward first fighting unemployment and then fighting inflation.

Demand-Management Stabilization Policy   In the first use of demand-management stabilization policy, both the accelerated depreciation of the Eisenhower 1954 law and the Kennedy investment tax credit were suspended on October 10, 1966. Their suspension had been scheduled to last through December 31, 1967. However, they were restored by Congress effective March 9, 1967, when Lyndon Johnson, early in 1967, found that suspension had done its job and that excessive demand pressure on the machine-tool industry had dramatically eased.

At the same time, the increased cost of the Vietnam war was creating inflationary pressures. On August 3, 1967, Johnson asked for a 10 percent surcharge on both individual and corporate incomes. By that time, the policy process was in complete disorder. Voters felt pressured by increases in state and local taxes, the inconsistencies of the Great Society and the Vietnam war lent weight to arguments for drastically reduced government spending, and economists disagreed about the nature of inflation and the economic outlook itself. As a result, there was a complete impasse, and the war tax took almost a year to enact. The President finally signed the Revenue and Expenditure Control Act of 1968 on June 28, all by himself, without the usual bill-signing ceremony, as the country prepared to elect a new President.

Policy under President Nixon did not alter the demand-management treatment of the investment tax credit. It was fully embedded in demand-management policy. Stop-and-go policy had become bipartisan.[18] With the economy heating up again, the Tax Reform Act of 1969 was enacted on December 30, repealing the investment tax credit, retroactive to April. However, fiscal and monetary overkill in 1969 and 1970 resulted in a need to expand the economy again. The Revenue Act of 1971 restored the investment tax credit retroactive to April 1, and introduced the possibility of tax savings through use of a new, flexible, asset-depreciation system for new investment.[19]

This was done against the background of the wage and price controls introduced in August 1971. Economic policymakers were increasing demand with the investment tax credit and depreciation allowances and they were curtailing demand with wage and price controls. The result was conflict and confusion, all in the name of stabilization.

By the time the investment tax credit was increased to 10 percent with the Tax Reduction Act of 1975 and made permanent in 1978, confusion and a severe earnings depression had stifled the competitiveness of our machine-tool industry. As we noted in Chapter 4, the equipment of our industrial base was more decrepit than that of our trading competitors, and the machinery used by the machine-tool industry itself was older than the equipment of American industry in general. The economic policymakers of both political parties had given a new definition to the word "stability."

Capital Gains Taxes   In addition to reversing the investment tax credit, the Tax Reform Act of 1969 affected capital gains taxes for the first time since 1942. Contrary to their treatment in Kennedy's revitalization program, capital gains taxes were increased in 1969. The Tax Reform Act of 1976 increased the capital gains tax rate to a high of 49.125 percent, which was almost equivalent to the 50 percent maximum tax on earned income.

In contrast to these disincentives to investment in productive businesses, the tax code encouraged investment in homes. Any individual could roll over the capital gains on the sale of a home, as long as the gain was applied to the purchase of a new home. With inflation a fact of economic life, the prices of homes would only go up. A $50,000 home was likely to be worth $100,000 in only a few years; then the increased equity at sale could be rolled over into a replacement home of equal or greater value without paying any capital gains tax. If a $50,000 investment in a job-creating productive business were to appreciate to the same amount, capital gains tax would be due if the investment were sold. On an after-tax basis, homes became relatively attractive investments compared to productive businesses.

These factors, combined with the general instability of economic policy, had a significant impact on investment in new and more risky businesses. In the early fifties, our capital markets had fostered the development of enterprises like Texas Instruments. An investment cycle had been developed. First, professional venture capitalists—backed by corporations, financial institutions, and wealthy investors—supplied the venture capital for a new idea or new product. The professionals took the high risk. Then, if the idea worked and a growing business developed, the company could go to the public equity market, where individuals and institutions oriented to smaller risks would buy some of the stock of the venture investors and provide new capital for the expanding business. All investors along the line hoped that the company would become another Texas Instruments. This investment cycle was broken in our period of decline.

In 1978 Congress reduced the maximum capital gains rate to 28 percent, effective October 31. President Carter signed the Revenue Act of 1978 and, as Table 6-1 indicates, investment in new companies soared. After a period of starvation, venture capital increased dramatically from $39 million in 1977 to $570 million in 1978, when the rate on capital gains was lowered. While there has also been a noticeable pickup in the number of new companies that have raised money in the public equity market, public investor financing will probably not return to its 1969 level for some time.

However, progress has been made. If we can strengthen the climate for long-term investment, this progress can gather momentum. When capital markets strengthen, a balance will return to those financial markets. In recent years, the financial markets have learned to look only to Washington, waiting with abject fear for the next signal from the monetary authority or the administration concerning the next stop-and-go shift in demand-management policy. Financial markets have lurched up and down in reaction to America's short-term, action-and-reaction policy process. If the 1978 reduction of capital gains taxes is followed by additional tax incentives to encourage savings and investment, investors once again will seek out sound, long-term investment opportunities. An emphasis on real long-term economic growth will be accompanied by investor emphasis on long-term equity invest-

Table 6-1 VENTURE CAPITAL AND PUBLIC-MARKET FINANCING

Year	New Private Capital Committed to Venture Investment (in Millions of Dollars)	Equity Capital Raised by Companies With Net Worth Less than $5 Million	
		Number of Offerings	Funds Raised (in Millions of Dollars)
1969	$171	698	$1,366.9
1970	97	198	375.0
1971	95	248	550.0
1972	62	409	896.0
1973	56	69	159.7
1974	57	9	16.1
1975	10	4	16.2
1976	50	29	144.8
1977	39	13	42.6
1978	570	21	89.3
1979	319	46	182.9
1980	900	135	821.5

SOURCE: Venture Capital Journal.

ments. The cycle for investment in new and more risky ventures will be restored to health. And that will lead to an increase in productive jobs.

Siltec Corporation   Siltec Corporation is an example of a company that has already benefited from this improved market environment for small companies. It is also an example of a company that has the potential to provide productive new jobs and contribute exports to help reverse our trade problem.

On March 11, 1980, Siltec offered 750,000 shares to public investors at $20 a share. The company raised $7.8 million for the expansion of its business, with the balance of the proceeds going to the selling stockholders. If it had not been for the lowered capital gains tax rate and the resultant improved markets for small companies, this would not have been possible.

In 1975, Siltec was a small company in the silicon business with $5.7 million in sales and $212,000 in earnings. By 1979—in only five years —its sales increased to $43.6 million. Earnings were up more than ten times to $2.6 million. Employment increased from 188 to 900. The company was now ready for the public investor market. Though somewhat seasoned, it was still a risky investment. However, its silicon business was in a high-growth area; as long as a better semiconductor material was not discovered it might turn out to be a good investment and produce capital gains. With the lowered capital gains tax rate, individuals and financial institutions were willing to invest in the firm.

The company's Silicon Division manufactures basic silicon materials. As the remarkable growth of the semiconductor industry continues, Siltec is in an excellent position to participate in that growth. Because of access to improving capital markets and reinvested earnings, Siltec has the financial resources to do fundamental research on the intrinsic properties of silicon. The intent of this research is to develop increasingly sophisticated production equipment for high-volume manufacturing. If this research pays off in improved processing, there will be additional productivity.

The company's Instrument Division works on the development of products external to its own needs. Its mission is to participate in what the company believes will be a revolution in semiconductor processing equipment by increasing automation. If it is successful, it will further contribute to productivity in the semiconductor industry in general.

Although it is still a very small company, Siltec has a global view of its market potential. The Instrument Division has developed business for its automation and wafer-handling products in China, Korea, and India, as well as in Europe and Japan. This business is a drop in the bucket of our merchandise trade balance. But it is business developed by the market-share approach, and if the company continues to grow, the results could make a positive contribution to the country's trade picture.[20]

Siltec and other small companies have begun to benefit from the capital available because of lower capital gains tax rates. As these companies mature, they will help America strengthen its triangle of trade, energy, and productivity. The process will take many years and will require continued access to financial resources in stable capital markets. But we have to begin on all fronts with our revitalization, with small firms as well as large ones. Just as Texas Instruments' people-effectiveness program results in significant productivity increases from the sum of small gains in productivity, so also can many small Siltecs add up to make a difference, particularly in trade and productivity. In the process, some small companies may develop into major companies like Texas Instruments and have a major effect on trade and productivity.

SUMMARY If the tax system is to be used to help reconstruct America's economic strength, the interrelationship of the three purposes of taxation must be considered.

We must pay the bills of government. The experimental attempt to balance the budget over the business cycle has failed. Balance was achieved only once in the last twenty years, whereas the cycle went up and down four times. The result has been ever-widening inflation and unemployment and a cumulative budget deficit of more than $990 billion by 1981. For this reason, we need to reestablish the discipline of the Truman-Eisenhower period and focus on the bill-paying aspect of taxation that contributed so much to our period of strength.

At the same time, we should not retrogress in our commitment to social justice. Poverty, sickness, illiteracy, and unemployment are still with us, particularly in our urban areas. For this reason, in giving priority to reestablishing a competitive, stable, and growing economy, we must treat our urban areas as an integral part of reconstruction and revitalization.

Finally, we must return to the vision of a tax-supported program of long-term growth that we viewed briefly with John F. Kennedy. The single most important national policy we need is a readjustment of the Employment Act to provide for full employment through creation of productive jobs. The President should be required to report annually to Congress on both aggregate supply and demand. The Council of Economic Advisers would then have to give equal attention to both supply and demand in a long-term context.

In order to encourage savings, we should legislate an investment tax credit for individuals. This could, for example, be a tax credit of $1000 per taxpayer to be deducted from total federal income tax. In order to be eligible for this credit, the taxpayer would have to put the tax credit into an individual long-term savings and investment account. That account should provide for complete investment rollover of both income and capital gains, with those returns taxable at regular rates only when they are taken out of the account and consumed. For fairness and to encourage all taxpayers to save and invest, the maximum investment consisting of individual investment tax credits and other capital allowed any one individual should be capped at $50,000; but any income and any capital gains would be allowed to accumulate as long as the funds are rolled into new investment.

This long-term rollover investment account for all American taxpayers would initiate an important shift in economic policy. It would emphasize savings and the long-term balance between supply and demand. It would be an incentive to make personal savings a positive contribution to long-term economic growth. Rather than restricting consumers—as with the 1980 credit-card controls—in order to dampen demand with another stop-and-go policy rebuke, we would begin to gradually increase the supply of capital for long-term growth. The investment tax credit for business has worked to increase business investment. An individual investment tax credit would work to increase savings. Coupled with a rollover investment account, it would increase investment further. The individual investment tax credit would provide all Americans and our trading partners and adversaries around the world with a clear signal that our nation is determined to spur investment in order to sharpen our competitive edge and regain economic strength.

In seeking to revive balanced economic policy, we must carefully review the need to follow up with additional tax incentives such as investment tax credits and depreciation allowances for investment in energy research and conservation, for high-risk investment in small but promising companies, and for increasing research and development.

As we reestablish balanced economic policy, we must expand the economic research on the supply side of the equation by such eminent economists as Lawrence Klein, Otto Eckstein, and Martin Feldstein. We should recognize that because short-term policies have led only to destabilization, we have to focus on our long-term convictions. In doing so, we should vastly improve our return to a competitive rate of long-term economic growth.

Japanese economic growth has been driven by cooperation, compromise, and consensus in the development of consistent long-term policies. We once knew how to develop policy that way. It is time for our nation to return to a spirit of cooperation, compromise, and consensus and to forge the three purposes of taxation into a balanced policy for real, long-term economic growth.

7 BALANCING REGULATORY POLICY

In 1980, three developments took place which characterized the discord that was still present in America six years after the end of the Johnson-Nixon period. They were commonplace in the America of our time.

SIGNS OF DISCORD   In Utah, there was a dispute between U.S. Steel and the Environmental Protection Agency. In New Jersey and Connecticut, state environmental protection commissioners prepared to sue Douglas M. Costle, national administrator of the EPA. And Lester C. Thurow, the MIT economist, explored reasons for our lack of real economic growth in a book entitled *The Zero-Sum Society.*

A Business Versus the EPA   In Provo, Utah, the federal government built the Geneva Steelworks to supply steel plates for West Coast shipyards in World War II. By 1980, the facilities—no longer youthful —were owned by U.S. Steel, employed 5000 persons, and were the underpinning of the economy of the local area.

In fulfilling its national mandate, the EPA had given U.S. Steel until July 1984 to meet the agency's standards for clean air and water around the mill. The steel company had agreed to spend $78 million to meet the air standards, but it claimed that the EPA was so unreasonable on the water standards that the plant might have to be shut down. The company claimed that the water coming out of its plant tested cleaner than the water that it was flowing into. The company further accused the EPA of trying to force it to outdo Mother Nature and, in the process, spend many millions of dollars that would not result in a materially cleaner lake.

The EPA's regional director of enforcement was unmoved. He took the position that when the agency imposes standards on industry, it simply provides the standards to be met and does not dictate how much to spend to meet them.

Since the economic stakes for 5000 employees and their families were very high, the state's political leaders announced support for legislation which would give governors the power to overrule the EPA and keep a plant open by extending clean-up deadlines and relaxing pollution requirements when plants are being modernized.[1]

Ten years after the formation of the EPA, in the summer of 1980, there was little to celebrate in Provo, Utah. There was discord between government and business, and there was friction between levels of government within our federal system. Most important, the EPA's regional director articulated one of the great flaws of the social-concern legislation which began in the Great Society: there was absolutely no consideration of cost. There was no concern about what the costs would be, who would pay them, and what impact they might have on the supply of goods and services and on inflation itself.

A State Versus the EPA At about the same time, New Jersey's Department of Environmental Protection was considering joining with Connecticut's environmental protection commissioner, Stanley J. Pac, in a lawsuit against Costle of the EPA. The EPA had approved an experiment with Consolidated Edison Company (Con Ed) of New York which would permit three of Con Ed's plants, on a one-year test basis, to burn oil with a sulfur content of up to 1.5 percent, rather than the 0.3 percent sulfur oil it had been burning. The utility contended that the lower price of the higher-sulfur fuel would mean substantial savings for its customers.

Pac, on the other hand, contended that the EPA's action would grievously harm the state of Connecticut. New Jersey officials shared his concern. Because of the direction of the winds, the two states sometimes share New York's air. If Con Ed were allowed to burn higher-sulfur oil, the additional wind-driven air pollution in the contiguous states of New Jersey and Connecticut would bring them closer to the maximum level of pollution—the level at which the federal government would prohibit future industrial growth.[2] Savings for New York utility consumers could thus result in economic stagnation in New Jersey and Connecticut.

This incident represented another unintentional side effect of the social-concern legislation of the Great Society: an environmental protection administrator at one level of government can become the adversary of an environmental protection administrator at another level of government. If the average citizen wonders whether government is working right in the area of environmental protection, no one should be surprised. After all, lawsuits are the action of last resort, when the absence of reason renders compromise impossible.

The Zero-Sum Society   In *The Zero-Sum Society*, Lester Thurow described a major environmental group that had learned to use our legal system with nihilistic intent. The group had developed a strategy called "analysis paralysis," the thrust of which is to delay a program until it is killed. The idea is to get laws passed that require both government and business to undertake complicated analyses prior to moving forward with new projects. Then environmentalists go to court to challenge the analyses. When delays and uncertainties build up and costs mount, both government and industry decide that it just is not worth it to continue. The costs exceed the returns. Projects that might favorably affect our productive economic growth are thus stillborn.[3]

It is unquestionable that the diverse group of concerned Americans who worked so hard for the better part of a decade for environmental legislation and who celebrated the formation of the EPA in 1970 could neither have intended nor envisioned that ten years later their dream would degenerate into "analysis paralysis." That it did is a tragic reality of the eighties.

These three random events illustrate the fact that national discord is still present in America. They illustrate an assault—sometimes unintentional and sometimes intentional—on the ability of society to function. That assault is the exact opposite of the spirit of cooperation, compromise, and consensus. While we have been fighting among ourselves about World War II-vintage steel plants, the Japanese have been building a highly productive, pollution-controlled, efficient steelworks at Ohgishima, with a planned reduction of the labor force to soften the impact of technological improvement.

Our challenge in the eighties will be to reexamine the goals of social-concern legislation, extricate them from the adversarial framework that permits "analysis paralysis," and merge them with the goal of productive economic growth. In order to meet that challenge, we will have to rethink the process by which we make the hard trade-offs between real economic growth resulting in jobs, and our quality of life both at and away from those jobs.

THE ROOTS OF REGULATION   In this chapter, we will discuss both economic and social-concern regulation, the processes by which they have been evaluated, the reversal of economic regulation, and the need for policymakers to come to grips with the tough trade-offs required by the effect of social regulation on our economy. The principal areas affected by economic regulation have been transportation, energy, and communications. The principal areas affected by social-concern regulation have been environmental protection, highway safety, occupational safety, consumer-product safety, and mining.

Before treating economic and social-concern regulation separately, it is important to put regulation in perspective in terms of its effect on our economy and the regulatory process itself.

In just fifteen years—from the beginning of the Great Society's social-concern legislation intended to improve the infrastructure, overcome the neglect of the environment, and promote protection for the consumer, to 1980—the regulated share of the economy expanded from one-tenth to almost one-fourth of the gross national product. In 1965, $69 billion worth of goods and services were produced by regulated industry. By the end of 1979, goods and services totaling $592 billion were produced under varying degrees of regulation.[4] Adjusted for inflation, that was almost a fourfold increase in the size of the regulated economy. This dramatic surge in regulation was accompanied by a dramatic growth in the number of regulatory agencies. By 1980, there were fifty-eight regulatory agencies, eighteen of which were independent commissions. In 1980, these agencies issued about 7000 rules and policy statements, including some 2000 legally binding rules that had a significant impact on government or the private sector. About 130 had major economic effects with compliance costs estimated at over $100 million for each regulation.[5]

The impact of these regulations on inflation, productivity, and our worldwide competitive position has been immeasurable—immeasurable because no one thought to require cost-impact statements at the beginning.

In 1960, President-elect Kennedy asked James M. Landis, a Dean of the Harvard Law School, to survey the state of our federal regulation. Landis had been one of the bright young men of the New Deal era who had drafted and then administered significant reform legislation. He had served as a commissioner of three major agencies: the Federal Trade Commission, the Securities and Exchange Commission, and the Civil Aeronautics Board. He was one of the individuals most knowledgeable about federal regulation.[6]

When his report was rendered, it contained harsh indictments of agency after agency. It detailed the inefficiencies that had crept into almost all of the commissions in the previous twenty years. He found, for example, that even with a tripled staff, the Federal Power Commission could not dispose of its current case load until the year 2043. He characterized the regulatory situation as one of interminable delay.[7] Unwritten in his report was the clear implication that some of the agencies, such as the Civil Aeronautics Board, were engaged in economic regulation of a dubious and perhaps even inappropriate nature. Through pricing and entry controls, they set the terms of competitive behavior and perhaps, through the regulatory process itself, created inefficiencies and higher costs for the consumer.

As important as this report was, it was put aside while we went about creating our affluent economic environment in the pre-Vietnam days of the early sixties. The report was a prophetic forerunner of the deregulation movement.

Although the Landis report documented the fact that there was a serious question about the effectiveness of the economic regulatory process, policymakers did not follow through to prove that the regulatory process was ineffective. Thus, as the Great Society programs became law, they fed into an out-of-date and adversarial regulatory process for their implementation.

As the decade beginning in 1965 unfolded, two divergent trends in the regulatory field emerged. Economic regulation came under increasing scrutiny and reassessment. Social-concern regulation, however, expanded with unmeasured economic effect.

ECONOMIC REGULATION Eight principal industries have been subject to economic regulation by four regulatory agencies. Among the best known is the Civil Aeronautics Board, founded under the Civil Aeronautics Act of 1938, with the power to promote and regulate the airlines industry, grant licenses, and regulate routes and fares. The Airline Deregulation Act of 1978, as we will discuss, significantly altered the regulatory climate of the airline industry. It was the first successful target of the move toward economic deregulation.

As every consumer knows, the generation of electricity is widely regulated on both a national and state level. On an interstate basis, the Federal Energy Regulatory Commission (FERC) oversees the electric utility industry. The FERC also regulates the interstate transmission and wholesale production of natural gas. This is the old Federal Power Commission, which was given its electric utility oversight in the original Federal Water Power Act of 1920 and its natural gas oversight under the Natural Gas Act of 1938.

Highway freight services and railroad transportation are regulated by the Interstate Commerce Commission (ICC). The granddaddy of the regulatory agencies, the ICC was organized under the Interstate Commerce Act of 1887. The ICC is responsible for granting carriers the right to operate, regulating their rates, and approving all construction or abandonment of railroads.

The Federal Communications Commission (FCC), set up after the passage of the Communications Act of 1934, serves along with 50 state agencies to set rates and entry and service conditions for telephone companies. The FCC also licenses broadcasting stations and has influence over the newly developing telecommunications industry.

The original reason for regulating these industries was to protect consumers from monopoly pricing while ensuring quality of service. The principal mechanisms were price and entry controls. Price controls protected consumers from the rapacious greed so characteristic of monopolies. Entry controls, in some industries, prevented too many companies from going into business (so that none could make sufficient profits) and ensured the continuation of a stable industry structure that would be capable of providing a desirable level of service to the consumer.

The regulatory process was embodied in the Administrative Procedures Act of 1946, which set requirements for open hearings, presentation of evidence, and judicial review in the courts. The regulatory process that developed resembled a courtlike proceeding under which issues on pricing and entry were decided on a case-by-case basis. When a company requested a change in the regulations, the agencies sought testimony and evidence from a wide range of interests in order to ensure a fair decision. Physical and financial accounting measures of previous activities (historical costs) formed the basis of regulatory decision on price and entry. Rate increases became justified by changes in historical cost because that is what the accounting systems measured.

The result of the Administrative Procedures Act was an emphasis on past data and existing conditions. Litigious and time-consuming, this process gradually led to the delays and inefficiencies that James Landis so carefully documented and denounced. The regulatory process also tended to work against consideration of new developments, innovation, and future opportunities.

The Airlines and Regulatory Reversal   Gradually, the message of the Landis report began to reach policymakers. The most striking example of deregulation—the reversal of the regulatory process—was in the airline industry. From 1938 to 1978 the regulatory process went full circle.

The Civil Aeronautics Act of 1938 was passed to rescue the airlines industry from impending chaos. During this period of deflation and depression, industry analysts and lawmakers thought the existing level of competition was higher than was considered healthy. Thus, the 1938 legislation was intended to prevent excessive air fares while discouraging competing carriers from engaging in rate wars (which ● would undermine the financial stability of the industry and thus prevent adequate investment funds from flowing into the industry on an orderly basis). In short, the CAB was set up to ensure price stability and adequate service.

By the sixties, the airline industry was characterized by a fairly rigid national route system dominated by a handful of large airlines, several of which flew internationally. On one hand, analysts were beginning to question whether or not the regulatory process had pushed air fares above levels that might prevail in a more competitive structure. On the other hand, the higher air fares subsidized expansion and quality of consumer services, and these subsidies were believed by other analysts to be consistent with the intent of the act. The high fares permitted expansion of capacity with improved technology, and successive generations of new jets were introduced.

The Civil Aeronautics Board set its rates on the basis of average industry costs to prevent excess profits on an industrywide basis. Some of the better-managed airlines with more lucrative routes were more profitable than the average. Others were less so. The CAB also structured the rates so that the profit margin on long-distance fares was about 25 percent higher than that on short-haul flights. This higher profit margin on long-haul fares was an intentional subsidy program for sometimes unprofitable service to small communities.

The average annual fare increase from 1958 to 1961 was 4.5 percent for the industry. It actually decreased by 0.7 percent from 1961 through 1965. It then stabilized to a 0.1 rate of increase from 1965 to 1969. In 1965, however, inflation began to rise sharply. The airline industry began to experience the price-cost squeeze. Against the 0.1 percentage increase in fares, the industry's average annual increase in labor and capital costs were 3.1 percent and 5.1 percent, respectively, from 1965 to 1969. Investment in new jets increased by 16 percent during that period.

However, as the cost increases of inflation outpaced the fare increases because of regulatory lag, the domestic airlines reduced capital investment by 5 percent between 1969 and 1973, and then by 25 percent between 1973 and 1977. Capacity was tightened and the quality of service began to deteriorate. While traffic grew, the number of flights decreased, and the flying public experienced inconvenient scheduling between medium-sized cities, crowded flights, and the occasional frustration of being victimized by overbooking.

The twin goals of the 1938 legislation—stability of rates and stable service—were in conflict. Regulation had ceased to work in the airline industry. In the late seventies, policymakers turned vehemently against the regulatory process in general and the CAB specifically.

By 1978, Congress was told that inflexible pricing and entry regulations had created serious inefficiencies within the airline industry. On the basis of lower intrastate flight fares in California and Texas, prices were estimated to be excessive by 30 percent.[8] Alfred E. Kahn, chairman of the CAB, led the attack on the regulatory process. After an expanded range of discount fares and liberalized rules on charter-flight eligibility were introduced in 1977, the CAB approved an across-the-board reduction in normal fares in March 1978. In May 1978, the CAB proposed the opening of routes to competition on a broad scale. Chairman Kahn envisioned "a structure that offers the maximum possible assurance of the continuation of competitive spur, and that offers exciting new opportunities for managerial enterprise."[9]

By the end of 1978, the Airline Deregulation Act was passed, and the CAB was scheduled to be phased out completely by 1985. The prophetic Landis report had come of age. In forty years, public policy with respect to regulation had come full circle. After lengthy experience, the verdict was that it didn't work.

Economic Deregulation at the End of 1980   As Ronald Reagan prepared to assume the Presidency, this was the assessment of the Carter administration:

- *Airlines.* President Carter estimated that, in the first year of the Deregulation Act, consumers had saved $2.5 billion. With plane departures up in small cities as well as large, airline productivity had surged, with fares rising much more slowly than costs.

- *Energy.* He also estimated that phased-in oil decontrol would reduce imports by 2 million barrels a day by 1990, with price-induced lower demand and increased supply. With the 1978 Energy Act, natural gas was also under phased-in deregulation.

- *Trucking.* The President noted that Congress had passed the Motor Carrier Act of 1980. By removing costly restrictions on the routes truckers may drive and the goods they may carry, the law intended that entry would be increased and pricing would become more flexible. The Congressional Budget Office estimated that this law would save between $5 and $8 billion a year, cut the inflation rate by almost one-half of 1 percent because of increased competition, and result in greater efficiency.

· *Railroads.* In October 1980, Carter also signed legislation that would give railroads more freedom to set rates, enter contracts, and serve new markets. Characterizing overregulation as a major reason for the deep trouble in which we find our railroad system, he stressed that passage of this legislation would allow the railroad industry to make the independent business decisions needed to restore its financial health.

· *Communications.* Under its own charter, the FCC has made telephone equipment manufacturing and long-distance service more competitive and further promoted competition and deregulation in the telecommunications and broadcasting industries.[10]

As we moved into the eighties, only in the electric utilities industry were price and entry mechanisms untouched in the sweeping wave of deregulation. Set in motion by ideas in the Landis report, deregulation gathered momentum in the late sixties and early seventies as economists closely analyzed and tested the consequences of economic regulation. In the late seventies, this kind of analysis and testing produced the legislation needed to reverse the policies of the previous forty years. Competition became a respectable word in legislation once again. Having done a reversal from economic regulation to economic deregulation, we now have a detailed data base that will permit us to determine the real effectiveness of economic competition as a servant of social good.

SOCIAL-CONCERN REGULATION While the movement toward economic deregulation was building beneath the surface, the social-concern legislation of the sixties gathered momentum. This movement toward increased social regulation evolved at a time when our economic machine was considered to be so powerful that it would generate new revenues faster than we could think of good uses for them. It received impetus from Lyndon Johnson, who pressured Congress to pass the legislation without giving thought to its future consequences. No sensible person in the nation was against cleaner rivers, lakes, oceans, and air. No thoughtful person was against improved safety on the job or in the car. No intelligent person was against requiring businesses to deal honestly and truthfully with consumers. Given these compelling objectives, a whole body of legislation·was passed, with two serious flaws.

Basic Flaws   The first flaw was that no one considered the costs of the legislation. Achieving the objectives was the important thing; the fact that those objectives resulted in substantial unbudgeted costs was not important at the time.

The second flaw flowed from the first. Because the intents were general, the legislation was general. However, it was implemented through the litigious and adversarial regulatory process, which at that very time was being reevaluated in its economic form.

While the nation tore itself apart during the Vietnam war and Watergate, all that were needed to push regulatory legislation through were a computer printout, some stamps and envelopes, the absolute belief in the importance of a single issue, and zeal. The intent was not wrong, for the goals were laudable and shared by most thinking Americans. It was the implementation of the legislation through the regulatory process that was wrong, for that led to a situation in which the pursuit of the ideal degenerated into the pursuit of individual social-concern goals. The attainment of each goal was of such over-powering importance to its advocates that even the slightest compromise became too great. That unwillingness to compromise, in turn, degenerated into "analysis paralysis" within the adversarial process. Eventually it was to affect the economic fabric of our nation and all of us individually.

Congress laid out broad goals in the social-concern legislation for improving the conditions of health, safety, and the environment. As it had with the earlier economic regulatory legislation, it gave the agencies broad authority to set the standards by which to achieve these ends. The agencies, using the example of their forerunners in the economic fields, developed uniformly mechanistic standards of design which entailed detailed specifications for the conditions of production and the actual characteristics of equipment.[11]

The Clean Air Act Amendments of 1970, for example, authorized the setting of national air-quality standards reflecting acceptable levels of exposure to specific pollutants. It also set performance standards for electric power plants and automobiles. The regulatory standards were set in terms of emission per unit of production and were based on use of specific control methods. Those air-quality performance standards were translated into regulations for very specific kinds of equipment. Just as the old economic regulatory agencies developed cost-data procedures that enabled them to handle their case loads in a way that would withstand judicial review, the new agencies found that equipment standards provided a fairly objective basis for setting and enforcing health, safety, and environmental regulations.

That was in 1970, when the Environmental Protection Agency

(EPA) was formed in a reorganization of the Nixon administration. While our steelworks—already old and uncompetitive against the Japanese—were adding specified pollution-control equipment to relatively unproductive facilities, Nippon Kokan was negotiating with three political entities on standards that were performance-oriented and that allowed the development of new technologies that cycled some of the emissions back into a new, self-generating energy system.

Areas of Regulation As previously mentioned, the social-concern legislation of the sixties led to regulation in five principal areas: environmental protection, highway safety, occupational safety, consumer product safety, and mining.

The Environmental Protection Agency was established in 1970 to protect and enhance the physical environment of America. It is supposed to cooperate with state and local governments in the control of pollution through regulation, surveillance, and enforcement of standards for air, water, solid waste, pesticides, toxic substances, drinking water, radiation, and noise. It had an annual budget of over a billion dollars and a staff of over 10,000 in 1979. Its responsibilities have been updated and expanded by each session of Congress since its inception.[12]

The National Highway Traffic Safety Administration (NHTSA), also established in 1970, was charged with setting standards for motor vehicle safety and fuel economy, and federal standards for various state highway safety programs. This covers mandatory average fuel-economy standards for new motor vehicles and equipment (including tires), investigation of auto safety defects not covered by standards and the remedy of those defects, auto ratings for crashes, and diagnostic auto inspections. NHTSA's responsibilities have also been updated by legislation since 1970. In 1979, its budget was $114 million dollars and its employment was slightly less than 900 persons.[13]

The Occupational Safety and Health Administration (OSHA) was formed as a result of the Occupational Safety and Health Act of 1970 to develop and enforce worker safety and health regulations. It is responsible for setting standards to protect workers against safety and health hazards, conducts inspections to enforce its standards, issues citations and proposes financial penalties for violations, oversees half the funding for state-administered programs, and requires employers to report fatalities, injuries, and illnesses related to the workplace. OSHA had a budget of $155 million and employed about 2900 people in 1979.[14]

Mining regulation is a two-pronged responsibility carried out by the

Mine Safety and Health Administration (MSHA) in the Department of Labor and the Office of Surface Mining Reclamation and Enforcement in the Department of Interior. Both groups were established in 1977. MSHA is responsible for protecting the health and safety of U.S. miners. The Office of Surface Mining Reclamation and Enforcement regulates both the use of new land for strip mining and the reclamation of land. This is done by requiring strip-mine operators to obtain permits for their mining, to return land to its original condition, and to give information on mine ownership and operations. The information must include the area to be mined, methods to be used, starting and finishing dates for compliance with environmental standards, and a complete reclamation plan. The two agencies had a combined budget of $165 million and employed about 4500 in 1979.[15]

The Consumer Product Safety Act of 1972 established the Consumer Product Safety Commission (CPSC) to protect the public against unreasonable risks of injury from consumer products. CPSC does this by issuing enforcement safety standards governing the design, construction, contents, performance, and labeling of more than 10,000 consumer products and by banning hazardous consumer products. The commission had a budget of $39 million and about 900 employees in 1979.[16]

These six agencies spent almost $1.5 billion on their regulatory activities and had a total of 19,000 employees in 1979. They represent only the tip of the iceberg of federal regulatory spending, which grew from $866 million dollars in 1970 to approximately $6 billion in 1980.[17] That explosive burst of regulatory funding expanded the amount and the effects of social-concern regulation and had important consequences for our economy.

THE COSTS OF REGULATION In 1975, most of the social-concern regulatory apparatus was in place and in pursuit of the goals of improved quality of life in America. President Ford released a study by his Office of Management and Budget (OMB) of the economic impact costs of both economic and social regulation. This study estimated the cost of federal regulation alone at $130 billion dollars, or $2000 per family.[18] Assuming that all costs were passed on to the consumer, that was a burden which would make the income tax of 1916 an insignificant issue by comparison.

In a paper prepared for the Subcommittee on Oversight and Investigation of the Committee on Interstate and Foreign Commerce of the House, the General Accounting Office (GAO) assailed the OMB study for a variety of reasons, most of which boiled down to inaccuracies of cost measurement. The GAO review led to the general abandonment of the OMB estimate. But thoughtful public-policy analysts were beginning to wonder about the economic impact of both economic and social regulation.

In 1978, Murray Weidenbaum and his associates at the Center for the Study of American Business did a study of the costs of regulation of business for the Joint Economic Committee of Congress. Their analysts estimated that business had borne total costs of $66 billion in 1976. Extrapolated forward to 1978, this amounted to $96.7 billion. This study resulted in some more sparring regarding the methodology of calculating costs, the definition of costs, and the offset of benefits.[19]

The result of the Weidenbaum study, however, was that policymakers began to recognize that the costs of regulation were probably very large and their impact on the economy should be considered. A beginning of economic balance was on the horizon. A number of thoughtful policymakers realized that, in addition to the inefficiencies of economic regulation, which were now widely under attack, social-concern regulation might be affecting both inflation and productivity in ways not completely understood.

To the extent that $96 billion was a fair approximation of total regulatory costs in 1978 and to the extent that it was passed on to consumers in increased prices, it could be a potent inflationary factor. Federal budget outlays in 1978 were $450 billion, with a $49 billion deficit. Budget deficits are inflationary, and the addition of anything approaching $96 billion in regulatory costs to the $49 billion deficit undoubtedly had a significant inflationary effect. Government regulatory policy was adding hidden and unbudgeted demand to the economy.

In addition, insightful policymakers had obviously concluded that the process of economic regulation had, in several instances, discouraged effective management and innovation. It was logical, therefore, to question whether the design standards of social-concern regulatory legislation might also be impeding innovation in industry and thus dragging down productivity and hampering increases in the supply of cost-competitive goods.

A significant amount of attention, therefore, was given to the Business Roundtable (a group of chief executive officers of some of our major corporations), when it released its "Cost of Government Regulation Study" in March 1979. That study—done in meticulous detail by the highly respected accounting firm of Arthur Andersen & Co.— focused on the direct costs of complying with the regulatory requirements of six agencies and programs by 48 companies in 1977. It was not intended to include the costs arising from the effects of all regulatory agencies on those companies, nor were the conclusions of the study to be extrapolated to all businesses or the economy in general. The study specifically did not attempt to quantify indirect costs such as loss of productivity, construction delays, resource misallocation, lost opportunity, or investment disincentives.[20]

The findings, however, were instructive. For the 48 companies reporting, the direct costs of complying with the regulations of the six agencies and programs were more than $2.6 billion. That was a significant amount for these companies; it represented 15 percent of their net income. It also represented 10 percent of their total capital expenditures and fully 43 percent of their $6 billion research and development expenses.[21]

The Business Roundtable study led policymakers to seek more data on the possible impact of regulatory costs on the economy through inflation and productivity loss. In fact, Christopher E. DeMuth, director of Harvard University's faculty project on regulation, characterized the study as too limited. If the Roundtable Study were used as the basis for calculating regulatory costs, DeMuth argued: "Agencies would be inclined to prohibit certain [new] activities outright rather than require that all activities [new and old] be undertaken in a certain manner—thereby reinforcing the already pervasive tendency of regulation to freeze production technology at the level assumed as the basis of regulation."[22]

That meant that the regulators would use the Roundtable type of cost and data for design standards which would specify the equipment currently being used. Cost analysis might tell us where we were; and it might also help to keep us there.

By the 1980 Presidential campaign, there was fairly general agreement in Washington and among students of regulation that we would spend between $100 billion and $150 billion on regulation of both types in 1980. There was also substantial agreement that we should begin to quantify and measure regulatory costs, particularly those direct costs arising from required compliance with regulations. In order to obviate the problem of freezing current technology where it was, policymakers were beginning to think about setting regulatory standards in terms of overall performance, rather than specific equipment design.[23]

THE BENEFITS OF REGULATION   As the policymakers struggled with the problem of costs, they also struggled with the problem of benefits. There are two methods currently being developed to evaluate whether or not the costs of regulation are worthwhile. They are cost-benefit analysis and cost-effectiveness analysis.

Cost-Benefit Analysis Cost-benefit analysis presents both some practical and some philosophical problems with respect to benefits. Many benefits are difficult to quantify. The benefits to be derived from a highway project, for example, might require an analysis of the value to be placed on time saved by users through the increased capacity and efficiency of the highway, the value to be placed on a decrease in the number of fatalities and injuries, the costs of changes in noise and air pollution, and of course, the scenic attractiveness of the route. If President Eisenhower had been required to quantify such benefits as these for 41,000 miles of our Interstate Highway System, it obviously never would have been built. America would today possess an inadequate national road system.

It also poses severe philosophical problems. Actuaries may be able to estimate the age at death of a group of people killed by a certain kind of injury or disease and compute what their expected future income would have been if they had lived their actuarially calculated life span. That part of future income can then be discounted to the present. That present value of total future income can then be taken as the value of life for the average number of the group; and by dividing the present value by the number of persons in the group, the value of a human life can be calculated. The catch is that, depending upon the rate of discount employed, the value of that human life can vary several hundred percent.[24]

Even if we could find a public figure qualified and willing to select the appropriate discount rate and actual value of our life, the whole process would cut across the grain of humanism in America. When Lyndon Johnson talked about the quality of life in Ann Arbor, he talked in terms of human aspirations. He was right to do so. It would be a double irony if, having neglected the cost of the legislation, we were to bend the human ideals of the legislation back against themselves by requiring their quantification into calculated benefits.

Cost-Effectiveness Analysis Cost-effectiveness analysis is another matter altogether. While there are some similarities between cost-benefit and cost-effectiveness analysis, there is a major difference. With cost-effective studies, the goals are not so explicitly quantified. The analysis is designed to determine which of an alternative group of methods of effectively reaching the goals is the least costly. This moves away from simple design standards and leaves room for the consideration and actual development of new technologies. It is a procedure that should be encouraged because it will include, to some extent, an evaluation of indirect costs.[25]

While 1980 brought increasing awareness of the need to come to grips with the cost of regulation, there were—as might be expected —varied views of the benefits of social-concern legislation.

President Carter said: "Automobile safety standards are saving 9000 lives per year. Deaths in coal mine accidents dropped 47 percent between 1970 and 1977, mainly because of the work of the Mine Safety and Health Administration. The child-proof containers mandated for such products as household cleaners and drugs have prevented as many as 200,000 accidential poisonings of young children."[26]

Douglas Costle said: "The benefits far exceed the costs."[27]

Paul W. MacAvoy, a professor at the School of Organization and Management at Yale University and former member of the Council of Economic Advisers, wrote:

In health and safety regulation the invoking of costly equipment standards has not achieved the specific industry results in improved working and living conditions for which they were designed.[28]

. . . in general health and safety controls operated in the 1970s in ways that increased costs, increased prices, and reduced production, without improving the quality of work conditions or of the environment.[29]

Robert W. Crandall, a regulatory expert at the Washington-based Brookings Institution, criticized the EPA air-quality standard for photochemical smog specifically:

This standard impinges directly upon the agency's need to control automobile emissions since a large share of the constituents of photochemical smog comes from automobile exhaust. EPA's problem is that it cannot demonstrate that low levels are harmful to human health. But, if it relaxes the standard, EPA cannot proceed down the road of further constraining the automobile—programs for requiring three-way catalysts, inspection and maintenance, and even transportation control plans. Therefore, the environmentalists are actively pressing EPA not to relax the air-quality standard, pushing unreplicated studies which are 25 years old as the basis for "concern" over the health effects of smog.[30]

Citing a Carter administration estimate that the standard would cost $14 billion to $19 billion in inspection and maintenance requirements when implemented, Crandall was decidedly skeptical of the EPA's effectiveness.[31]

On the other hand, the Senate Governmental Affairs Committee, in releasing a report by the Center for Policy Alternatives at MIT in March 1980, said that billions of dollars a year are saved as a direct result of regulation in the areas of health, safety, and environment. It endorsed the findings, which included the following:

Air pollution benefits ranging from $5 billion to $58 billion annually, with automobile pollution controls alone worth $2.5 billion to $10 billion each year.

Up to 60,000 lost workday accidents and 350 deaths avoided in 1974 and 1975 due to OSHA rules on workplace safety. . . .

Crib safety standards reducing injuries to infants by 44 percent since 1974, and flammable standards causing a 20 percent reduction in the frequency of burn deaths and serious burns to children in 1975.

Automobile safety controls saving over 28,000 lives in an eight-year period, 1966–1974. Seatbelts alone are said to have reduced injuries by 34 percent and deaths by 20 percent.

Water pollution abatement resulting in a $9 billion gain to the economy through increased recreational use such as boating, camping, fishing and vacationing.[32]

As we came into the eighties, there was decided disagreement on the benefits to our nation from the cumulative effects of social-concern legislation. The important consideration was that the issue was beginning to be debated openly, as any important issue should be in a healthy democracy. That was a good sign.

The original aspirations of social-concern legislation were very general. That was inherent in its pragmatic idealism. An attempt to translate that idealism into a precisely defined and mechanically quantified set of benefits is as impossible as attempting to quantify the effectiveness of basic research at a given point in time. We now know that we need to direct more of our nation's resources into basic research, but no scientific specialist can exactly quantify the right amount. Similarly, we know that the people of America deserve a continued striving of national policy for improved health, safety, and environmental quality of life; and no regulatory specialist can exactly quantify what that means.

Those problems should be addressed by the President and Congress, who are elected to resolve the difficult trade-offs required in setting public policy. We know the resources that we are committing to basic research. We do not have more than a general idea of what we are spending on the regulatory process. Nor are we entirely certain that that process is the best way in which to achieve the desired ends. Our first priority, obviously, should be to determine the cost of the process and its impact on our economy. Only then can policymakers begin to put trade-offs between economic effects on jobs and the effects on the quality of life in their proper perspective.

REGULATORY ANALYSIS UNDER CARTER President Carter defined the issue very clearly: "Our society's resources are vast, but they are not infinite. Americans are willing to spend a fair share of those resources to achieve social goals through regulation. Their support falls away, however, when they see needless rules, excessive costs, and duplicative paperwork. If we are to continue our progress, we must ensure that regulation gives Americans their money's worth."[33]

In March 1978, Carter issued Executive Order 12044, which was binding on the executive agencies and requested cooperation from the independent commissions. It was basically the beginning of an attempt to acquire cost information, minimize compliance costs, and resolve the problem of benefit analysis. It was also an exercise in moral suasion. It took the Ford administration's recognition of the problem one step further.

Under the regulatory analysis program, each agency publishes a semiannual agenda of all the significant rules it expects to propose or complete in the succeeding year. These agendas have helped to provide a government-wide picture of upcoming rules; they are published in a Calendar of Federal Regulations twice a year. That calendar has provided details and a timetable for the 100 to 200 most important upcoming rules. It has been compiled by the Regulatory Council, an assembly of the regulators themselves, which Carter created in November 1978. The regulators who drafted each major rule have written a preliminary regulatory analysis which included the rule's anticipated costs, its benefits (to the extent that they can be realistically identified), and alternative ways to accomplish the goal.

At the same time, President Carter set up a regulatory analysis review group (RARG) within the Executive Branch. It has been chaired by the Council of Economic Advisers, has been staffed by the Council on Wage and Price Stability, and has worked closely with the Office of Management and Budget. The RARG has selected 15 to 20 major proposed rules a year, reviewed their regulatory analysis, discussed them with the agencies that wrote them, and then filed a public report with recommendations for more cost-effective approaches.[34]

While the Calendar of Federal Regulations and the RARG report provide information, the statutorily responsible official still makes the final decision. And because the reviewers have had neither the legal authority nor the political responsibility for issuing final regulations, the regulators have tended to ignore their counsel. Therefore, the review process has not had a significant influence on the substance of regulations.[35]

With this experiment under their belt, the regulators themselves agreed that in 1980 there were 129 major new regulations that would entail direct compliance costs of over $100 million dollars. The total costs of those regulations, as they spread their effects in the economy, was a minimum of $13 billion.[36] The identifiable tip of the iceberg itself was also growing.

That prompted the Carter administration to propose the Regulatory Cost Accounting Act in 1980 to provide for a searching and general review of federal regulation. The proposed act would have created a systematic body of data on the costs of complying with federal regulations which would identify key problems of regulation and, if properly used by policymakers, bring the regulatory process into balance with other national objectives.

OMB would provide the guidance on definitions and accounting standards in order to ensure uniformity of cost measurement throughout the government. The head of each agency would be responsible for designating, with the agreement of the director of OMB, the rules for which compliance costs would be measured. Then the agency would send a report detailing each rule's direct compliance costs and its effects. The OMB, in turn, would prepare a consolidated Federal Regulatory Costs Report which the President would send to Congress together with any suggestions for changes in either the regulatory statutes or the reorganization or consolidation of regulatory programs.[37]

Official Washington was beginning to reach out as far as possible to determine whether or not it could cope with the problem of regulatory cost measurement. George Eads, a member of the Council of Economic Advisers under Carter and a specialist in regulation, believed that, with time and experience, it would be entirely feasible.

FUTURE REGULATORY POLICY DEVELOPMENTS Regulatory specialists both in and out of government caution that we must give serious thought to the implications of systematizing regulatory-cost accounting.

Legislation similar to the Regulatory Cost Accounting Act of 1980 proposed by Jimmy Carter, if enacted, would lead ultimately to a regulatory budget. The proponents of caution suggest that we consider the psychology of government control of private expenditure. As we have indicated, the growth of regulatory involvement in our economy has increased from 10 percent to 25 percent of gross national product. The concern is that a regulatory budget will legitimize this involvement, further erode the traditional distinction between the public and private sectors, and creep across the entire economic spectrum. In effect, a regulatory budget could be the Trojan Horse of national planning which could take over the private sector with complete governmental decision making.

While this is a legitimate concern, it has been raised twenty years too late. If the mid-sixties had been a more thoughtful time, the Landis report might have had a cautionary impact on the cascade of social-concern legislation that erupted from the Johnson White House.

We, therefore, are where we were in 1921 when, after about a decade of study and debate, Congress and the President agreed to the creation of the federal expenditure budget. Three Presidents representing both political parties had participated in the development of events leading to the passage of the Sixteenth Amendment and the reality of the income tax. The only sensible course of action was to develop a system of measuring revenues against expenditures. Just as the income tax became an irrevocable fact of life, the ideals of the social-concern legislation are embedded in public policy. We can neither revoke them nor ignore their costs. To attempt the former would be to rebuke the heritage of humanism in America. To attempt the latter would amount to irresponsibility in economic policy making.

An effective accounting of compliance costs is the missing link in the regulatory process. A regulatory budget would provide the vehicle for limiting total compliance costs and assist the President and Congress to better assess competing social and economic policy goals. It would give the regulators a clear directive to seek cost-effective solutions.

The regulatory budget should be phased in over three to five years to bring all regulatory agencies—both economic and social—under the balanced control of the President and Congress. Direct-cost systems would be developed for the major regulatory agencies in the initial stage in order to perfect the system prior to wider and then complete implementation.[38]

If the regulatory budget were coupled with a balanced economic policy which would require the President to report annually on the major sectors of both aggregate supply and demand in his analysis of the state of the economy, it could be an important analytical tool of economic policy. That combination would do much to ensure that policy is balanced between the need to encourage new technological developments (which will result in increased and productive long-term economic growth) and the national goals of health, safety, and environmental protection.

Of equal importance, the discipline of a regulatory budget would lift the tough trade-off decisions between jobs and social policy into the bright light of policy debate. Rather than watch in dismay as the entities of government interact in technical discord through the court system, the average citizen might be enlightened by a commonsense discussion of decisions that affect all of us. Slowly, the average citizen might be enticed back into the political process. And, with the majority of Americans once again interested in the future of our country, a vision of cooperation, compromise, and consensus might appear on the horizon. Distant perhaps, but on the horizon nonetheless.

8 THE STEEL INDUSTRY: OPPORTUNITY FOR REVITALIZATION

On April 11, 1962, John F. Kennedy opened a Presidential press conference to ignite a dispute and confirm a mutual distrust between government and the steel industry that would continue into the early eighties. He said:

Simultaneous and identical actions of United States Steel and other leading steel corporations increasing steel prices by some $6 a ton constitute a wholly unjustifiable and irresponsible defiance of the public interest. In this serious hour in our Nation's history . . . at a time when restraint and sacrifice are being asked of every citizen, the American people will find it hard, as I do, to accept a situation in which a tiny handful of steel executives whose pursuit of private power and profit exceeds their sense of public responsibility can show such utter contempt for the interest of 185 million Americans.[1]

Those were strong words, uttered in a national confrontation between the President of the United States and Roger Blough, the chairman of the board of U.S. Steel. They convey an image of the President locked in verbal combat with the representative of a tough, lean, competitive, and powerful steel company.

Eighteen years later, Robert J. Petris, director of the United Steelworkers District 38, returned from a visit to Japan. He had toured Nippon Kokan's Ohgishima steelworks, which we described in Chapter 4. Eighteen years after the Kennedy-Blough confrontation, the union leader Petris compared the American steel industry with Ohgishima. He said:

It's unbelievable! They way they are making steel at the new works we visited appears to me to be at least five to ten years ahead of anything we can build here in America even if we start right now.[2]

... the biggest single difference is the kind of engineering, plant technology, the size of the blast furnaces and the computerized processes that they employ compared with what I was used to working with and what I see here in America today. They must pour far more money into the steel business than our American companies do. I don't see how we can compete with such a modern steel complex with our worn-out facilities.

I'm not an economist, but when I see a straightline system of production from the self-contained harbor, where the basic ingredients arrive from literally thousands of miles away, to the final product shipments by Japanese-owned freighters, it tells me that they haven't missed a single trick in increasing their productivity.[3]

Eighteen years after the President of the United States and the chairman of U.S. Steel had locked horns in confrontation, a steel union man candidly stated that our worn-out facilities could not compete with the modern steel complex of Ohgishima.

This observer was not an economist. He was not a spokesman for the American Iron and Steel Institute. He was not the chairman of Nippon Kokan. He was not the head of the Council on Wage and Price Stability. He was not the chairman of U.S. Steel. He was not a Wall Street security analyst. He was not the head of the congressional steel caucus. He was a steel union man who, with years of experience on the plant floor, brushed aside the curtain of sophisticated debate then raging among those other individuals and told us the stark truth: that we are no longer competitive in the world steel market. The United States cannot compete with the Japanese in steel.

Something had happened to our steel industry in the previous twenty years. A deep sickness and internal decay had developed in the basic underpinning of our industrial society. Make no mistake about it: steel is the basic material of the manufacturing process. If we are to revitalize America, the American steel industry must once again be vital and be able to stem the tide of trade imbalance and deteriorating productivity. The first step in regaining health is for chronically ill persons to look in the mirror, see themselves as they really are, and admit that they are sick. Our steel industry is uncompetitive because of management, labor, and government. They all need to look in the mirror and recognize reality.

Whether it is Nippon Kokan or Texas Instruments, the benchmark of a healthy company and a healthy industry is the same. Texas Instruments' successful business performance has been based on an increased amount of fixed assets per worker, economies of scale with the emphasis on global market expansion, use of human ingenuity and involvement of labor, effective use of research and development in all phases of its business, aggressive involvement in the continuous evolution of the technological process, a responsible reaction to properly conceived, long-term government policy, and a total focus by management on a planned and integrated use of resources.

Ohgishima is not the last generation in steel-making facilities. Some other Japanese, Korean, Taiwan, or new third-world company will improve upon it in the relentless competitive fight for cost reduction and market share. That process is anything but static. If we are to revitalize America, we are going to have to take advantage of the lowest-cost steel to cut inflation and increase productivity. And our own steel industry should participate. The first step is for all of us to recognize the problem.

Early in 1980, the American Iron and Steel Institute issued a major white paper titled *Steel at the Crossroads.* It failed to honestly recognize the problem. It said: "The American steel industry is efficient today, by global standards, and is competitive with most of its worldwide rivals. Indeed, under recent actual operating conditions, the industry has been and is a lower cost steel supplier to domestic markets than most of its foreign competitors."[4]

The white paper on steel went on to state the primary reasons why we are losing our competitive edge:

· Persistently low rates of return coupled with outdated tax measures that fail to provide adequate capital recovery;

· Capture of a significant portion of the domestic market by steel imports at "dumping prices";

· Excessive government control and regulation, which significantly increase steelmaking costs and mandate the spending of funds that would otherwise be available for replacement and modernization of productive equipment;

· Reduced earnings as a result of unwarranted government interference in the marketplace determination of steel prices, which has restricted the recovery of cost increases;

· Escalation of steelmaking costs at a rate in excess of increases in steel prices.[5]

Eighteen years after the Kennedy-Blough dispute, the American steel industry was still blaming the government for its problems. The statement was characteristic of over twenty years of circular reasoning by government, management, and labor, which has resulted in the continuous decline of the American steel industry.

Instead of using a Marshall-Plan approach by creating a positive environment for productive investment and cooperation between business and labor, government has gradually become intertwined in the process of decay. Steel management has not had an outward-looking strategy on increased market share, lowered production costs, and increased world market share. Labor has contributed to the problem by pricing itself out of the world market. By continuously solving the labor problem "this year only," government has encouraged a cycle of wage and price increases which has repeatedly led business and labor back to government for another short-term quick fix. There is plenty of blame to be shared. The shared blame should be accepted and something constructive should be done about the problem.

An analysis of the present weakness of our steel industry requires an assessment of both our decline in world market share and of the ever-increasing involvement of business, labor, and the government in a cycle of weakness.

THE DECLINE OF AMERICAN STEEL In 1947, when General Marshall went to Harvard to offer United States aid to Europe in a framework of cooperation for reconstruction and recovery, the United States steel industry exported 6 million tons of steel.[6] We were the world leader in steel. In fact, the U.S. steel industry assisted with technology, advice, and business planning in both the recovery of Western Europe and the reconstruction of Japan.

In 1947, the U.S. steel industry produced 57 percent of world output. By 1958, the last year in which we had a positive trade balance in steel, we produced 28 percent of world output. Twenty years later, our share of world output was 17 percent and we were a chronic importer of steel from all parts of the world. In 1978, we imported 21 million tons of the steel we used in America.

Table 8-1 graphically illustrates our shift from world strength to weakness in steel. In 1956, eleven years after the end of World War II, the American steel industry was still very strong. That year marked the beginning of the Eisenhower highway program, when automobile sales were soaring. The future was very bright. Japan, still recovering from the war, was a factor of relatively small significance in world steel. We outproduced Japan ten to one during President Eisenhower's second term and our period of strength.

Then came 1959 with the bitter 116-day steel strike. The consensus achieved during the war was beginning to be strained. Business and labor in the steel industry were at each other's throats. That was our first trade-deficit year in steel. The first signal of weakness on the trade

Table 8-1   U.S. AND JAPANESE STEEL PRODUCTION,
EXPORTS, AND IMPORTS *(In Million Net Tons)*

	United States			Japan	
Year	Crude Steel Production	Exports	Imports	Crude Steel Production	Exports
1956	115.2	4.2	1.3	12.2	1.3
1957	112.7	5.2	1.2	13.9	1.0
1958	85.3	2.7	1.7	13.3	1.7
1959	93.4	1.7	4.4	18.3	1.7
1960	99.3	3.0	3.4	24.4	2.5
1961	98.0	2.0	3.2	31.2	2.5
1962	98.3	2.0	4.1	30.4	4.2
1963	109.3	2.2	5.5	34.7	5.8
1964	127.1	3.4	6.4	43.9	7.2
1965	131.5	2.5	10.4	45.4	10.5
1966	134.1	1.7	10.8	52.7	10.4
1967	127.2	1.7	11.5	68.5	9.6
1968	131.5	2.2	18.0	73.7	14.1
1969	141.3	5.2	14.0	90.5	17.2
1970	131.5	7.1	13.4	102.9	19.4
1971	120.4	2.8	18.3	97.6	25.6
1972	133.2	2.9	17.7	106.8	23.0
1973	150.8	4.1	15.1	131.5	27.3
1974	145.7	5.8	16.0	129.1	35.5
1975	116.6	3.0	12.0	112.8	31.9
1976	128.0	2.7	14.3	118.4	39.7
1977	125.3	2.0	19.3	112.9	37.8
1978	137.0	2.4	21.1	112.6	34.5

SOURCE: Robert W. Crandall, *The United States Steel Industry in Recurrent Crisis: Policy Options in a Competitive World,* The Brookings Institution, Washington, D.C., 1981.

side of our economic triangle came with the deficit. At the same time, Japanese steel production increased 38 percent.

Even in 1962, it was not too late for recovery. The United States imported about 4 million tons of steel and exported 2 million tons. That was not a chronic deficit. If the steel industry had been oriented to the management philosophy of world market share, it could have turned outward and recognized the Japanese competitive challenge for what it was. If it had been oriented to a dramatic effort to increase production and lower unit costs, it would have been prepared to meet that challenge. If there had not been created a mounting adversarial relationship between the steel industry and the government, the two might have worked together in areas such as the investment tax credit to prepare to meet that challenge. Instead, the industry fought with its government while Japanese exports began to gain enormous strength.

Between 1962 and 1965, Japanese steel production increased 50 percent and more than doubled in exports. Our chronic trade deficits in steel began in 1965. That year, of course, was also when the build-up for the Vietnam war and the Great Society was underway. That these events came together in 1965 was not entirely coincidence. Cooperation, compromise, and consensus were rapidly vanishing from the land.

In 1968, after three years of divisiveness in government, Lyndon Johnson got his war tax. But it was too late for steel. Imports increased from 11.5 to 18 million tons. It was then time for hat-in-hand supplication to Washington. The effort was well received. But while the Japanese began building the second generation of steelworks like Ohgishima, with automated energy and pollution-control systems merged into a computerized steel-making process, we sought refuge in protection from imports and began a bitter wrangle over the introduction of the social-concern legislation for higher standards of air and water quality and human safety. Led again by a chairman of U.S. Steel, Edwin H. Gott, the American steel industry began a decade of descent into decay, with plenty of help from government and labor. Our imports stayed high and the technology of our plants and equipment became relatively deteriorated, while the Japanese not only modernized, but also more than doubled their exports from 1968 to 1978.

The deterioration of our world competitive position in steel depicted in Table 8-1 is explained by the analysis of costs and prices presented in Table 8-2. The two tables combined explain the shift in the American steel industry from world strength in 1956 to weakness in 1978 and the growth and expansion of the Japanese steel industry. In any business, cost affects prices and prices determine sales. Therefore, if market share—sales—is to be increased, costs must be lowered.

Table 8-2 compares the basic cost of American and Japanese steel from 1956 to 1976. This figure includes both raw-material (iron ore, scrap, oil, coal, natural gas, and electricity) and labor costs. Table 8-2 compares U.S. steel prices with average import prices (including importation charges) for five major finished steel products. Although the data does not provide a precise cost-price comparison on a product-by-product basis, the correlation of the data in Table 8-2 does explain the dynamics behind the deterioration of the American competitive position.

In 1956, when the United States was still a net exporter of steel, our basic cost was below that of Japan; obviously, as a competitive exporter, our domestic prices and finished products were substantially below import prices from Japan (and other countries). We had an $8 dollar basic-cost advantage.

However, by 1959, the second Japanese modernization program was nearing completion, and Japanese production costs were now about $22 less than our's. Those lower costs were responsible for the 50 percent burst in Japanese exports in 1960. While we were em-

Table 8-2   UNITED STATES AND JAPANESE COST AND
PRICE DATA IN U.S. MARKETS *(In Dollars Per Net Ton)*

| | Basic Cost of Finished Steel | | | Import Price Including |
Year	U.S.	Japan	U.S. Price	Importation Charge
1956	$100.55	$108.72	$111.94	$172.20
1957	99.79	120.85	122.38	166.86
1958	100.84	89.49	128.18	133.21
1959	103.40	81.68	130.18	131.13
1960	109.03	77.18	130.97	149.93
1961	111.13	83.09	130.53	130.73
1962	107.72	73.99	130.44	129.94
1963	105.24	71.70	130.54	124.85
1964	104.30	68.22	133.16	119.81
1965	102.50	69.29	133.26	122.24
1966	102.70	65.19	133.52	115.74
1967	106.78	63.08	133.88	115.72
1968	108.32	61.49	137.27	115.49
1969	113.63	63.44	141.69	122.60
1970	124.49	70.81	151.56	145.79
1971	132.43	73.74	161.61	147.24
1972	140.71	75.81	173.00	161.17
1973	146.25	91.60	183.10	192.48
1974	195.55	133.63	241.11	302.43
1975	245.19	144.48	267.48	296.94
1976	267.30	146.90	281.34	248.88

SOURCE: Robert W. Crandall, *The United States Steel Industry in Recurrent Crisis: Policy Options in a Competitive World,* The Brookings Institution, Washington, D.C., 1981.

broiled in our 116-day steel strike, the Japanese were lowering their costs. While government, business, and labor were looking inward in the United States, the Japanese steel industry was spanning the globe.

During the sixties, our cost structure was fairly stable, and that was reflected in a relatively stable price structure. But during the period from 1959 to 1968, the Japanese continued their modernization and cost reduction programs in steel. While our nation was moving from economic strength to weakness, the Japanese reduced their basic cost of production 25 percent through productivity improvements and increased their exports sevenfold. Two sides of their economic triangle were strengthening. Steel was leading in the weakening of two sides of our economic triangle. By 1968, import prices of steel products were decidedly lower than domestic prices.

Then government, business, and labor interaction began to work to increase costs in this country. Coherent long-term economic policy continued to deteriorate with a change in administrations, the years of management neglect began to take their toll, and labor costs initiated dramatic increases. Between 1968 and 1976, the basic cost differential widened dramatically from $46 a ton to $120 a ton in favor of the Japanese. The United States was forced to resort to subtle measures to prevent steel imports from ballooning even further and completely destroying the American steel industry.

In 1973, both Japan and the United States were hit with the price impact of the oil embargo. As energy prices shot up, so did the basic cost of steel in both the United States and Japan. Because Japan is resource-poor and imports most of its energy sources, its industry had been conscious of energy costs during modernization. As might be expected, Japanese plant and equipment was far more energy-efficient than its United States counterpart. Basic costs—including oil, coal, natural gas, and electricity—were brought under control in 1975 and 1976 in the Japanese steel industry. They were not in the United States. Thus, a weakened position in energy completed the weakening of our economic triangle and contributed to the American steel industry's relative decline. The United States steel industry was not world competitive and was on the verge of partial liquidation by the end of 1976. Driven by higher energy costs and lower productivity in the United States, steel imports reached a new high of 19.3 million tons in 1977.

THE REASONS FOR THE DECLINE OF AMERICAN STEEL Management, labor, and government have all played roles in the decline of the United States steel industry. An understanding of these roles is important to understanding why the industry is in trouble and to deciding how best to make it world competitive again.

The Role of Management   When an industry declines the way the American steel industry has, an assessment should be made of the people in charge: management. In the case of steel, an analysis is very simple: successive managements of leading companies have not had competitive management strategies. They did not employ the basic Texas Instruments or Nippon Kokan strategy of success: use profits to introduce new products and processes to lower costs and increase market share and profits; then roll those profits right back into the cycle.

In the aftermath of the Kennedy press conference in 1962, Roger M. Blough, board chairman of U.S. Steel, was asked: "Could you explain just how you meet competition by raising your price?"

He replied: "Your problem, as I tried to explain before, is to have enough to buy the machinery and equipment to make the kind of products—to make the quantities of them—that will enable you cost-wise to get the business which, in turn, provides the employment."[7]

Chairman Blough left his successors a legacy from which they would not deviate. In 1971, when its competitive fate was all but sealed, U.S. Steel's chairman Edwin H. Gott, addressed the question of competing by lowering prices in order to increase business: "We're different. It's not part of our way of life in this country."[8]

That philosophy did seal the fate of the American steel industry. We watched and reacted as the Japanese took the leadership in world steel away from the American industry. The Japanese integrated developments in raw materials, plant location, and technology into modern, efficient plants like Ohgishima.

In raw materials, the United States once had a decided competitive advantage. In 1956, coking coal cost $9.85 per ton in the United States and $22.14 a ton in Japan. Iron ore was $9.63 a ton in America and $16.69 per ton in Japan. We produced 24.2 percent of the world's iron ore and agglomerates in 1956. America was rich in two major raw materials which are required in the modern integrated steel-making process and had easy and relatively inexpensive access to them.

However, that advantage was destined to change; by 1965 the U.S. percentage of world iron ore production dropped to 14. Meanwhile, the Japanese steel companies worked closely with the trading companies, such as Mitsui, as we described in Chapter 4. Forward-thinking management sought out new sources of raw materials around the globe. Larger and lower-cost bulk freighters were developed for shipping iron and coal. Long-distance water transportation costs were lowered dramatically, and raw material costs were gradually reduced.

In 1965, American coking coal costs were $9.65 per ton versus $14.27 for the Japanese. American cost of iron ore was $11.80 per ton versus $12.17 for Japanese steel makers. But this American advantage in critical raw material costs gradually evaporated.

By 1976, with their relentless global approach of seeking out resources in all parts of the world and importing, processing, and exporting, the Japanese steel companies now had a cost advantage in both coking coal and iron ore. With the crunch of the oil embargo, the price of coking coal increased substantially; but in Japan it was $53.60 a ton versus $56.04 in the United States. The Japanese advantage in iron ore was far more dramatic. From 1965 to 1976, iron ore had increased $3.64 a ton in Japan to $15.81, while in the United States the cost increase was $15.82 to $27.62. In 1976, the Soviet Union, Brazil, and Australia all outproduced the United States in iron ore and agglomorates, and India produced half as much as we did. With twenty years of market- and price-oriented competitive management, the Japanese had lower-cost resources than their insular and complacent counterparts in the United States.

This twenty-year raw material cost advantage reversal clearly proves that the Japanese, with their market share and lower price strategy, have had superior management to ours in the steel industry. While our steel management has been blaming others for their problems—as they did in the 1980 white paper—the Japanese steel management has outperformed them. There is no other explanation for the loss of our decided raw-material cost advantage since 1956.

Plant location is another developmental area in which Japanese management has strengthened their steel industry. As part of their superior management strategy based on a worldwide business outlook, the Japanese steel managers built a substantial portion of their modern facilities close to deep-water harbors. By 1976, 82 percent of their plant capacity had access to deep-water harbors, compared with only 10 percent in the United States. In addition to a savings on transportation and handling costs, access to deep-water harbors creates economies of scale in receiving raw materials and shipping production, as steel union leader Petris recognized during his visit to Ohgishima. However, our steel industry capacity has virtually shrunk inwards into middle America, in reflection of the management philosophy of our industry.

While domestic rail transportation costs doubled from 1967 to 1977, ocean transportation costs became relatively more attractive. By 1976, relative raw-material transportation costs showed only a modest differential between the two countries. Transportation costs for coal averaged $6.89 a ton in the United States against $8.62 in Japan. The average transportation costs of a ton of iron ore were $5.00 in both countries. When those raw materials were processed into finished steel products in Japan, they cost slightly in excess of $57—including import duty—to export to the United States. With a basic cost advantage of $120 a ton, there was still ample margin for profits, overhead or indirect costs, and price discounts from the domestic price of finished steel products.

Technology is the third area in which decisions by Japanese management have resulted in modern, efficient plants. By integrating the advantages of the deepwater harbor, the automated handling of raw materials, and technology developed around the world, the Japanese have built modern, integrated steelworks with a minimum efficient size of 6 million tons. By capitalizing on technology that has been diffused throughout the world, they have put together large-scale coke batteries, blast furnaces, basic oxygen furnaces, continuous casting machines, and a computerized integration of process control, energy recycling equipment, and pollution controls into streamlined new steelworks. While during the sixties and seventies their American counterparts were cautiously adding new technology to old plants and equipment in a process called rounding-out, the Japanese were boldly building completely new facilities.

Table 8-3 illustrates the fallacy of the defensive U.S. steel industry's strategy as opposed to the aggressive modernizing strategy of the Japanese. As our steel industry rounded out and added gradually to its older facilities in the sixties, the basic cost of finished steel remained about constant and capacity increased only slightly. As the Japanese built integrated steelworks, their cost came down and capacity expanded dramatically.

As we moved into the seventies, the relative inefficiency of the approach of rounding out old plants began to be apparent. Basic costs in the United States began to creep steadily upwards while capacity remained relatively flat. In Japan, raw-steel capacity was increased three and one-half times from 1962 to 1972, and basic costs were kept flat.

In May 1971, in "The Steel Industry Today," the American Iron and Steel Institute said: "There is some evidence that Japan's headlong expansion may have started to slow down because of shortages of labor, rising costs of raw materials and increasing concern about the environment and other demands for capital in its economy."[9]

Table 8-3 UNITED STATES AND JAPAN CRUDE STEEL
CAPACITY AND FINISHED STEEL PRODUCTION COSTS

	United States		Japan	
Year	Capacity (in million net tons)	Basic Cost (in dollars per net ton)	Capacity (in million net tons)	Basic Cost (in dollars per net ton)
1956	129.9	$100.55	13.7	$108.72
1957	132.9	99.79	16.3	120.85
1958	136.3	100.84	19.4	89.49
1959	139.8	103.40	23.3	81.68
1960	142.8	109.03	27.7	77.18
1961	143.5	111.13	33.1	83.09
1962	144.7	107.72	37.8	73.99
1963	145.9	105.24	42.0	71.70
1964	147.5	104.30	47.6	68.22
1965	148.2	102.50	54.3	69.29
1966	149.4	102.70	62.4	65.19
1967	150.6	106.78	74.1	63.08
1968	152.2	108.32	85.4	61.49
1969	152.8	113.63	98.8	63.44
1970	153.8	124.49	114.3	70.81
1971	154.8	132.43	121.4	73.74
1972	156.2	140.71	131.0	75.81
1973	156.7	146.25	142.3	91.60
1974	157.0	195.55	154.5	133.63
1975	157.4	245.19	165.3	144.48
1976	157.7	267.30	166.4	146.90

SOURCE: Robert W. Crandall, *The United States Steel Industry in Recurrent Crisis: Policy Options in a Competitive World*, The Brookings Institution, Washington, D.C., 1981.

That statement was made two years after the plans for Ohgishima got underway. In order to increase the productivity of the workers, cut raw material costs, and anticipate environmental concerns, Nippon Kokan was moving into the next generation of integrated steel making. Capacity increases might slow in Japan, but modernization and cost reduction would continue. In 1971 the management of the American steel industry simply did not seem to understand the dynamics of world steel competition.

In 1971, the basic cost differential was about $60 dollars a ton. By 1976, that differential had increased to $120 dollars a ton.

From 1965 to 1969, the American steel industry spent $10.2 billion on capital improvements. From 1966 to 1970, the Japanese steel industry spent $6.2 billion dollars on new plants and equipment. The Japanese spent less money for more capacity and lower-cost production. The American strategy of rounding out was very costly from a competitive perspective. From 1960 to 1980, there was only one new integrated mill constructed in the United States. That was the 3-million-ton Burns Harbor steelworks of Bethlehem Steel Corporation, which was completed in 1970.

By 1976, the average annual production capability of the ten largest U.S. plants was 5.4 metric tons. The average for the ten largest Japanese plants was 10.4 tons. This was the result of the difference between rounding out old facilities and building new, integrated mills. At the end of 1976, Japan's larger capacity included a substantially greater number of very large blast furnaces, more efficient use of basic oxygen furnaces, three times as much continuous casting, and a 32 percent lower energy consumption per ton of crude steel. The Japanese management strategy had resulted in a much more efficient steel industry.

One of the standard measurements of steel production efficiency is the amount of raw steel made in the basic oxygen furnace (or other type of furnace) that is processed into finished products. The percentage of finished products processed from raw steel is known in steelmaking as "yield." In 1976, the U.S. industry yield was 71 percent. In Japan it was 86.2 percent. By 1979, the yield at the ultramodern Ohgishima works was 95 percent. Over twenty years of different management strategies in a competitive world had resulted in the relative decline of our steel industry against that of the Japanese. We were no longer competitive with the Japanese in steel because their more efficiently produced steel cost substantially less than ours. They had put together raw materials with modernized large-scale facilities in strategic locations. They had gone forward; we had not. Their steel industry had been well managed; our steel industry had been badly managed.

The Role of Labor   Beginning in 1968, the United Steelworkers of America began to get contract settlements that were remarkable in America. The significance of these settlements is revealed by the figures in Table 8-4.

With the exception of 1970, steel wages increased every year more than the rate of inflation; from 1968 to 1973 wages increased substantially more than the rate of productivity growth in this country. In each contract year, the union negotiated successfully in its own best interest.

From 1966 to 1978, productivity in the U.S. steel industry increased at an annual rate of 1.4 percent. In 1967, the average steel worker was paid about 38 percent more than manufacturing workers in general. By 1974, this differential had increased to 60 percent, and after the 1977 steel settlement, steel workers received 71 percent more than their counterparts in American manufacturing, on the average.

The message of Table 8-4 is very simple: from 1968 to 1978 steel workers in America had compensation increases far in excess of their increases in productivity. For this reason they led the inflation rate in this country by a substantial margin. In doing that, they contributed to the decline of international competitiveness of our steel industry. They were demanding more than other Americans, and when they got it, they helped to price their industry and themselves out of the world market. Steel labor has played a very important role in the decline of the U.S. steel industry.

The Role of Government Government involvement in our steel industry has contributed to the industry's decline in several ways. On

Table 8-4 STEEL WAGES, INFLATION, AND PRODUCTIVITY IN THE UNITED STATES *(In Percentage Increase from Previous Year)*

Year	Steel Wages	Consumer Price Index	Output Per Person
1966	2.1	2.9	3.2
1967	1.3	2.9	2.0
1968	5.7	4.2	3.3
1969	6.1	5.4	.2
1970	4.4	5.9	.7
1971	9.4	4.3	3.3
1972	12.7	3.3	3.5
1973	7.4	6.2	1.9
1974	17.6	11.0	−3.0
1975	11.9	9.1	2.1
1976	9.9	5.8	3.5
1977	12.2	6.5	1.9
1978	9.9	7.7	.5
1979	11.4	11.3	−.9

SOURCE: "Annual Statistical Report: American Iron and Steel Institute 1979," "Economic Report of the President, January 1980."

July 15, 1959, what was to be a long and increasingly bitter steel strike began. The walkout ended with the injunction of the Taft-Hartley national emergency strike clause on November 7. Negotiations, however, boiled on throughout the remainder of the year.[10]

What started as only a modestly popular strike on the part of the rank-and-file workers hardened into bitterness in October, after industry negotiations injected the issue of local work rules and management prerogatives. In an era of postwar prosperity, that issue was seen as a threat to jobs and union security. It unified the membership behind its leader, David McDonald.

In a time of adversarial relationships between business and labor in the steel industry, there was a rigidity in the workplace that could erupt into open hostility. Productivity was frequently interpreted by both sides to mean: work harder. The industry wanted to eliminate contract clauses that prohibited them from making unilateral changes in local work practices. Understandably, labor balked; and they won, with the help of Vice President Nixon and Secretary of Labor James Mitchell.

Nixon and Mitchell worked through Blough and McDonald personally, beginning in early December. They suggested that the government would recommend a formula, but only if the parties agreed to accept it as a basis for a "voluntarily" negotiated settlement. When it was all over on January 4, 1960, Mitchell was very careful to say that Nixon had not threatened the executives, although he had painted a very realistic picture of potential legislation, if the strike continued.[11]

After fifteen years of the wage-price increase cycle, the American steel-industry position of world superiority had eroded, and now it came to an end. World costs had changed; and as Table 8-2 indicates, U.S. import prices and domestic producer prices had come close to equilibrium. The dramatic shift in 1959 to a negative trade position in steel was not recognized for what it was: the beginning of the competitive decline of the American steel industry. Having achieved a "voluntary" settlement, the politicians went on to a Presidential election and left labor and management to their own devices.[12]

After the Kennedy victory, two years went by in a status quo. Steel prices were stationary, and there was a developing hostility toward the new President in the executive suites of Pittsburgh. Four days after a contract was signed that raised the cost of steel labor 2.5 percent, U.S. Steel announced a 3.5 percent price increase on April 10, 1962. The White House orchestrated a counterattack. On April 13, Inland Steel announced that it would hold its original price, Bethlehem Steel rescinded its increase, and Roger Blough was beaten.[13]

At that time *U. S. News and World Report* summarized the reasons for the Blough-led price increase:

· Business was aware that government would step into problems that arose in basic industries. The full power of government would be called upon when officials interpreted the public interest as being at stake.

· In raising prices, the companies asserted their freedom to act under the rules of a private-enterprise system. It was a challenge to a system of economic planning by government through the use of guidelines and productivity formulas.

· Industry prefered to generate its own capital for investment in modernization and expansion rather than accept "investment credits" within the tax system. Profits were regarded as a vital source of investment funds. With a price increase, the industry sought to add to its profits and at the same time retain its own freedom of action in the use of these profits.[14]

By the time the 1965 negotiations came, the importance of letting business and labor reach a voluntary settlement was disregarded by Lyndon Johnson. The President inserted himself forcefully into the negotiations. The contracts were extended from May 1 to September 1 with an interim wage increase, and President Johnson sent special mediators to Pittsburgh on August 28. The following week he called the parties to the White House, participated in the mediations, and on September 3, forced an agreement.[15]

Then came 1968. The Vietnam war was tearing at the country and bringing Lyndon Johnson's Presidency to a close. There was pure and unenlightened selfishness throughout America. And there was militancy on the steel-mill floors: all the business managers wanted the biggest quarter of their careers, and all the labor leaders wanted a bigger settlement than they had ever gotten. Leadership and consensus completely disintegrated. People were simply looking out for themselves.[16] That was the year that steel wage increases exceeded both the Consumer Price Index and the national increase in productivity. The basic cost of steel broke out of a ten-year pattern of stability, and steel imports exploded from 11.5 to 18 million tons.

With demand-oriented economic policy in disarray and the steel industry—both labor and management—rushing head-on into competitive disaster, the industry turned to Washington for relief. The State Department negotiated voluntary restraint agreements (VRAs) with the Japanese and European Economic Community (EEC) steel producers. These were thinly disguised protectionist devices which limited Japan and the EEC to 5.75 million tons each in 1969, with 5 percent increases in 1970 and 1971. Imports from both Japan and the EEC were reduced in 1969 and 1970, increased again in 1971, and then lowered again.[17]

In 1971, U. S. Steel chairman, Edwin Gott, said: "Nobody likes quotas. But at the moment, it's the only way we can live."[18]

This implied that the American steel industry was taking measures to rectify its competitive position. It was not. Through the VRAs, our government helped industry and labor continue their self-deception.

The voluntary arrangements with the Japanese and EEC were renewed in 1972 and extended through 1974. Steel imports from Japan had been cut from 7.3 million tons in 1968 to 6.2 million tons in 1974. EEC imports were reduced from 8.4 million tons to 6.4 million tons. Imports from other countries which did not participate in the voluntary restraint agreements, however, increased from 2.3 million tons to 3.4 million tons during the life of the VRAs.[19] Steel was coming into the United States from around the world.

With the 1971 and 1973 dollar devaluations and the VRAs, the industry had some breathing room, and domestic production increased from 120.4 million tons to 150.8 million tons in that period. In view of the strength of domestic business, the industry and the union agreed to an Experimental Negotiating Agreement (ENA) in 1973. In exchange for limitations on the right to strike during future contract negotiations, the industry agreed to a 3 percent per year wage increase for the following three years, in addition to a liberalized cost-of-living escalator and a modest bonus. The ENA foreclosed any hope of keeping steel labor costs in any sensible relationship to productivity increases.

In 1974, the Antidumping Act of 1921 was amended with the assistance of an active lobbying effort by the industry. The new definition of dumping included sales in the United States below the cost of production.[20] The Treasury Department—and the Commerce Department since 1979—was given the responsibility of determining whether dumping occurred. The U.S. International Trade Commission then had to determine whether the industry had suffered and the workers had been hurt. This was a very time-consuming process and set the stage for the trade crisis of 1977.

As the economy faltered in 1974 and dropped in 1975 into the most severe recession since the Great Depression, domestic steel production fell from 145.7 million tons to 116.6 million tons. When the recovery came, so did increased steel imports. Domestic production increased 3.3 million tons from 1976 to 1977, but imports rose by 5 million tons. Encouraged by the Carter administration, dumping suits were filed with the Treasury Department, a steel caucus of over 200 senators and representatives was formed to aid the industry, and the Carter administration shifted its Undersecretary for Monetary Affairs in Treasury, Anthony Solomon, from the dollar problem to the steel problem.

While labor was walking with the steel industry in the halls of Congress, another inflationary settlement was made under the experimental negotiating agreement. In the midst of Lloyd McBride's successful campaign to succeed I. W. Abel in the union leadership, a three-year settlement in excess of 9 percent per year was reached.

As the union told its membership: "The 1977 Settlement marks our second impressive success in bargaining conducted under the Experimental Negotiating Agreement (ENA) and exceeds the gains achieved in the outstanding ENA settlement in 1974. . . . No other industrial union in the United States has matched this record."[21]

By early January 1978, Solomon suggested establishing a "trigger" pricing mechanism (TPM), based upon production costs of the Japanese industry. These were benchmarks upon which to base antidumping investigations in which penalties, if justified, could be imposed within sixty to ninety days. In addition, smaller companies in declining areas became candidates for loan guarantees under the Economic Development Administration and a tripartite committee of labor, industry, and government was formed to work out further policy options. The effort was to prove to be just another political Band-Aid.

Against the background of reality the Solomon report said: "We expect that the industry and labor will cooperate by taking advantage of this opportunity to improve their efficiency, reduce their costs, and expand utilization of their productive capacity, thus restoring the steel industry to a sound health."[22]

Government, business, and labor all turned their backs on the mirror of reality and sat down at the tripartite table to while away the time, while Ohgishima came on-stream in Japan. This definitely was not cooperative vision in the spirit of the Marshall Plan.

By 1979, U.S. Steel junked its plans for constructing its first new integrated steel mill in 26 years at Conneaut, Ohio, and prepared to start writing off old facilities. Chairman David M. Roderick said: "Assuming no changes in steel's cost-price relationship, there is no question that the domestic industry is going to continue to shrink."[23]

In November 1979, U.S. Steel shut fifteen plants employing 12,500 workers and recorded the largest write-off in American corporate history. In February 1980, it signed a three-year contract for technical aid from Japan's Nippon Steel Corporation to increase the productivity of its blast furnaces. And in March 1980, it temporarily shut down three major plants, laid off 25,000 of its 95,000-person work force and filed antidumping complaints against producers in seven European countries.[24] The Commerce Department suspended the "trigger" pricing mechanism.

Then in the midst of the tough 1980 Presidential campaign, during the politically strategic month of October, U.S. Steel withdrew its antidumping suits with the encouragement of the Carter administration. The trigger pricing mechanism was reintroduced at an average of 12 percent higher than when it was suspended in March. While the candidates sparred about who would do more to "revitalize" the steel industry, a Commerce Department news release noted that: "The TPM is being reintroduced for a transition period (three to five years) during which the U.S. industry is expected to modernize. . . ."[25]

This statement had a poignant echo of the past. The politicians were at it again. Lacking the toughness of Truman, Hoffman, Harriman, and Eisenhower, or the insight of John Kennedy, they walked away from one of America's most deeply troubling problems, leaving political rhetoric in their wake.

HOPE FOR THE FUTURE   The American Iron and Steel Institute white paper of 1980 played on most of the familiar industry themes; but there was one important difference. The industry was now fully behind tax incentives for businesses; they would now take all the tax help they could get. Understanding had taken a long time. There was also hope for increased understanding, if for no other reason but necessity.

In 1980, contracts came up for renegotiation. The settlement was again high, at about 9 percent a year for the next three years. However, it was within the Carter administration's 7.5 to 9.5 percent guidelines. In addition, in order to finance improved pension benefits for retired steelworkers, the union gave up its last cost-of-living agreement under the old contract and agreed to forego any improvement in the cost-of-living adjustment.[26]

Most important, the union and the nine major steel companies agreed to attempt to improve worker-management relationships outside of the normal contractual mechanisms (such as the grievance procedure). They agreed to set up Labor-Management Participation Teams (LMPTs) right down to the department level.[27] By giving the workers a voice in improving the job environment, work schedules, and production processes, it was hoped that labor could help management cut costs. This, of course, was a variation of the United Auto

Workers and General Motors Quality of Work Life program that saved the Tarrytown plant, the Team Improvement Program at Texas Instruments, and the JK activities that have been pervasive throughout Japanese manufacturing companies for many years.

Both sides were cautious, but as USW negotiator Sam Camens said: "Our union recognizes the fact that many problems the steel industry has are our problems. The union and the company are attempting to develop an in-plant relationship whereby workplace, environmental, working conditions, quality control, and production problems will be discussed and attempted to be solved through department committees in a cooperative effort."[28]

At the same time, seventh-ranked Inland Steel—the company that backed President Kennedy in 1962—was putting the final months of work into the installation of the first 4000-cubic-meter inner-volume blast furnace in the United States at its Indiana Harbor steelworks. That would increase the capacity of that facility, the largest in the United States, to 10 million tons. Other industry experts had maintained that the U.S. steel technology was second to none, but several years ago Inland decided to work with Nippon Kokan and adopt its blast-furnace technology. They brought the Japanese company in right at the start of the construction of the blast furnace in 1976.

Inland Steel is one company in our steel industry that believes in lowering costs and integrating its mill. However, it does not have the capital to do it all at once. Inland has the will to compete, but it needs new tax incentives to provide the financial resources to speed up the rounding-out process into a modern integrated steelworks. Other major steel companies need the same incentives.

Many students of the steel industry believe that with high U.S. construction costs it would be too expensive to build an American version of the next generation of ultramodern facility beyond Ohgishima. This assessment may overlook several important factors. Operating costs will probably continue to rise, and they certainly will in the rounding-out process. Add-on environmental controls destroy the opportunity for using energy-saving recycling technology. Rounding out does not take advantage of maximal computerization and layout efficiency. A joint venture with a company like Nippon Kokan with their superior construction know-how would certainly reduce construction costs.

The Reagan administration should step back from the failure of the Carter tripartite involvement and let management and labor work out some alternatives to shrinkage of the work force by gradual liquidation, sudden bankruptcies, and unexpected plant closings. There should be a gradual and planned lowering of the work force through attrition and government-funded retraining and relocation programs. This should be coupled with new tax incentives to encourage construction of new steel-making capacity to replace relatively unproductive steelworks. Government should underwrite the redeployment of our human resources, once a sensible plan is worked out. Government should assist the American steel industry to return to normal health.

Improved depreciation rates and higher cash-refundable investment tax credits will help. But what is necessary is for a leading steel company and its union to work out a planned work-force reduction in conjunction with those incentives for the building of an ultramodern facility within the U.S. marketplace. Such a facility would fairly soon become the low-cost producer in the United States, and its employees would be guaranteed security by their own productivity. In the spirit of the Marshall Plan, the initiative to reconstruct our steel industry must be provided by labor and management themselves.

It is important that the American steel industry be revitalized. No ally or adversary can take us seriously in our commitment to re-strengthen our triangle of trade, energy, and productivity if the most basic industry in our nation is not turned around. If steel continues as an overwhelmingly negative factor in our merchandise trade—while tying government up with periodic threats of costly and time-consuming dumping suits—all other positive trade efforts will be penalized. If steel continues to use energy-inefficient plants, our OPEC adversaries will continue to question our national will. If industry and labor continue to work unproductively in union-leader Petris' old worn-out plant and continue an unchecked spiral of wage and price increases, the nation as a whole will suffer.

If we establish a rational and balanced long-term economic policy with equal attention given to supply and demand, there will be growth of steel production in a revitalized America. If that long-term revitalization policy is coupled with a well-planned, long-term commitment by a program to help one or two major companies and their employees to become efficient world-class producers, it will logically follow that some financial institutions in the United States will see the opportunity forming. Some will be willing to take a risk if government sets the right long-term balanced policy and labor and management grasp the initiative to develop a long-term plan within that policy framework.

Labor and management in the steel industry in America have the opportunity to turn the tide of adversarial antagonism and help provide the leadership necessary to return cooperation, compromise, and consensus to our nation in order that it may function once again.

9 AGRICULTURE: MODEL FOR REGAINING OUR COMPETITIVE EDGE

An idea can be a powerful force. A vision of the possible can mold that force into concrete action. An idea and a vision were embodied in the Agricultural Trade Development and Assistance Act of 1954, commonly known as Public Law 480. The idea was a variation and an outgrowth of the theme General Marshall had stated at Harvard seven years earlier. It was very simple: the United States should use its large agricultural surplus to promote international trade and develop an export consciousness among the producing farmers. Instead of regarding the surpluses as an expensive threat to the domestic market, the American farmer could export these surpluses. The federal government would help the farmers create a long-term program for expanded production based upon the development of a total global market.

What helped to turn this idea into a reality was a program of letting other countries pay for surplus agricultural commodities with their own currencies. Some of the proceeds paid in these currencies was then used for two purposes: first, for marketing and sales campaigns abroad to increase the demand for American agricultural products overseas and develop local markets; second, for local economic development in programs designed to increase the standard of living and therefore increase demand for food products. Use of local currencies for market and economic development thus raised the demand for agricultural imports from the United States.

Although not stated as an objective at the time, this concept redirected our agriculture policy toward a framework of world market share.

The success of Public Law 480 resulted from the confluence of three events. The most important was the passage of Public Law 480 itself, with its significant shift of agricultural policy to a global perspective. The second was a law (passed prior to Public Law 480 in 1954) which moved our agricultural attachés from the Department of State to the Department of Agriculture. While they still worked with ambassadors abroad, after 1954 they reported and were responsible to the Secretary of Agriculture. The third event (which took place in 1953) was the restructuring of the Office of Foreign Agricultural Relations (OFAR) into the Foreign Agricultural Service (FAS). OFAR had been primarily a statistical and information-gathering entity within the Department of Agriculture, with limited trade-policy authority. As the FAS, it would become an action agency with the new mission of developing markets and expanding agricultural trade.

The net result of these three events was a partnership between the federal government and commodity producers that altered the course of American agricultural history. With this cooperative relationship, with government funding of a market development program, with overseas market and economic development financed by proceeds from the sale of surpluses, and with an important public and private policy shift to a global, outward-looking perspective, our agricultural balance of trade moved from a deficit in the early fifties to a strong surplus as we entered the eighties.

The history of American agriculture is exactly the opposite of that of American steel in the last thirty years. In agriculture, we have combined human resources, technology, and a cooperative interaction between the government and private sectors into an increasingly productive growth industry based upon a strong trading emphasis. American agriculture has been a powerful, positive force in promoting trade and productivity.

A direct philosophical child of the Marshall Plan, agricultural export policy was funded in its early stage through Public Law 480, it gathered strength and adherents as the FAS and the producing farmers learned that they could in fact cooperate, and it evolved into a strong underpinning of our economy. Born in our period of strength, that export policy survived our decline, and gathered renewed vigor following the Vietnam war-Watergate period. It is an important illustration of how we can resharpen our competitive edge.

THE BACKGROUND OF PUBLIC LAW 480   We have not always enjoyed the enlightened export-oriented agricultural policy that we have today. On May 26, 1933—in the depths of the Depression, when unemployment and poverty were very severe—the Secretary of Agriculture and officials of the Agricultural Adjustment Administration met with spokesmen for wheat producers, processors, and distributors to discuss a proposal to pay farmers to plow under part of the wheat crop. With the prospects of a sharp decline in the winter wheat crop because of adverse weather conditions, however, the threat of an increased surplus was lessened, and on June 16, 1933, an outline of the wheat program was announced. Under a domestic allotment plan, contracting producers who agreed to limit wheat acreage for the 1934 and 1935 crops would receive payments on the basis of their proportionate share of wheat production consumed in the United States.

Cotton farmers, on the other hand, experienced weather conditions that would produce an increased surplus. Cotton, which had fallen from 29 cents a pound in 1923 to 6½ cents a pound in 1932, had a carry-over supply which was three times normal size. If acreage were allowed to increase, the supply and price relationship would only get worse. Thus, on June 19, 1933, a plow-under campaign was announced for cotton. Its first-year objective was to eliminate 10 million acres, or one-fourth of the growing crop, in return for cash payments.

Corn producers, like wheat producers, experienced weather conditions that would reduce their crop in 1933. While the pressure to plow under corn was thus defused, the smaller corn crop would not result in reduced hog production until the 1934–1935 season. A major expansion in hog breeding had resulted from the cheap corn of the preceding year. Therefore, an overabundant supply of hogs was expected to come to market in the winter of 1933–1934. To keep supply down and prices up, the government purchased 6.2 million pigs weighing less than 100 pounds and 222,000 sows about to farrow and had them slaughtered.

The media termed this emergency slaughter program "the killing of little pigs." The public was shocked. Farmers were distressed. Agriculture Secretary Henry A. Wallace commented: "To have to destroy a growing crop is a shocking commentary on civilization. I could tolerate it only as a cleaning up of the wreckage of unbalanced production."[1]

The surplus problem, however, was not fully cleaned up. It did not go away. On August 24, 1935, the Agriculture Administration Act was amended to give the President authority (among other things) to impose import quotas on farm products when these imports interfered with the agriculture adjustment program.

Prior to World War II and the Marshall Plan, our agricultural policy consisted of plowing surplus under, cutting supply back, and further reducing world trade with the implied threat of import quotas. As in steel today, we thought defensively in agriculture.

The Second World War, of course, changed the economic situation dramatically. In its aftermath came the Marshall Plan, a cooperative effort with the Europeans to revive Europe, the world economy, and world trade with an investment in self-help and self-initiative.

Watching the Marshall Plan unfold in Europe was an individual who would later play an important role in translating its ideas into Public Law 480. Gwynn Garnett, who had grown up on a farm in Iowa, was director of the food and agricultural section of the U.S. High Commission in Germany in the late forties. He saw the Marshall Plan counterpart funds constructively used to revitalize agricultural research and rebuild flour mills.

At the same time, there was again a farm surplus problem in the United States. In 1949, Garnett briefed a group of farm leaders—including Allan B. Kline, head of the American Farm Bureau Federation—on the program in Germany. His message was that the American farm surplus should not be plowed under or given away. It should be used as capital for economic development around the world. By helping Europe and Japan to rebuild their economies and assisting other nations to develop theirs, we were encouraging those countries to build up exports of their own; the proceeds from the sale of those exports would permit those countries to buy more United States farm products. A continuously regenerating cycle of economic development and agricultural trade would benefit all and result in worldwide economic growth.

Kline was responsive to Garnett's idea, and despite the laissez-faire orientation of the Farm Bureau, he hired Garnett to serve as a member of his legislative staff in Washington, with a special emphasis on foreign affairs. This was an unusual linkage. The Farm Bureau's laissez-faire orientation meant that government should stay out of the private sector—completely and unequivocally out. Furthermore, the farming community, the government, and the universities, all tended to view America as the residual exporter: we would supply what others were not able to supply. When Gwynn Garnett joined the Washington office of the Farm Bureau on January 1, 1950, agriculture was riding a crest of economic strength along with steel. From a trade perspective, both industries were order takers, not marketers. But Garnett had Kline's backing, and as the surpluses grew, so did the power of his idea.

When the Korean war broke out on June 25, 1950, the Department of Agriculture shifted its supply constraint programs to encourage the production of sufficient food and fiber to meet any possible need associated with the war. Acreage allotments and marketing quotas were suspended for the 1951 and 1952 crops of wheat, rice, corn, and cotton. That, of course, exacerbated the already festering surplus problem.

While the surpluses continued to build, Garnett went to work with

Senator Andrew F. Schoeppel of Kansas and other senators and congressmen from farming states. On July 24, 1953, Schoeppel and ten other senators introduced the bill which ultimately became Public Law 480.

Of the three events which affected the reshaping of agricultural policy and the passage of Public Law 480, the first to occur was the organization of the Foreign Agriculture Service within the United States Department of Agriculture (USDA). On the initiative of Assistant Secretary John H. Davis, the Foreign Agricultural Service was set up on March 10, 1953, to handle all USDA activities related to the development, expansion, and maintenance of foreign markets. Raymond A. Ioanes, who had joined the government directly out of college in 1940 and who would later play an important role in the development of an aggressive agricultural export policy, was one of the young public servants who scented action in the FAS and got himself transferred into the newly energized agency.

"In effect," said Assistant Secretary Davis a year later, "the Foreign Agricultural Service functions as American Agriculture's eyes and ears abroad, constantly searching for market opportunities and always working to overcome obstacles to the flow of United States farm products in world trade."[2]

Davis endorsed three principles that would guide the FAS effort in developing export markets.

- Government should assist, not displace, the private trade. Export trade should be carried on through established private trade channels wherever possible.

- U.S. export prices must be competitive. We cannot expect to maintain or expand exports of farm products if our prices are higher than those charged by other exporters. However, at the same time we must not be aggressive in pushing down world prices.

- Bold, imaginative, and new steps must be taken both by private trade and government to pave the way for such trade efforts.[3]

Davis's principles were given additional force by a companion piece of legislation to Public Law 480. That legislation, spearheaded by Senator George Aiken of Vermont with the support of the White House and spokesmen for the farm states in Congress, called for the transfer of the agricultural attachés from the State Department to the Department of Agriculture. On August 28, 1954, the attachés became part of the FAS, where they had the mission of developing, penetrating, and expanding markets for farm products around the world.[4]

This gave the Department of Agriculture action-oriented, market-oriented, and results-oriented individuals working in U.S. embassies around the globe.

Meanwhile, Public Law 480 was being enacted. Outsiders like Garnett worked with insiders like Davis. With the help of Schoeppel and others on the Hill, the legislation slowly developed a supporting coalition as it worked its way through Congress. At the same time, of course, the surplus was building. By February 1954, the federal government, through the Commodity Credit Corporation of the USDA, owned $6.25 billion of price-supported commodities, three-fourths of which were wheat, cotton, and corn. That was a record high.[5]

With an accelerating economic recovery in the world, world agricultural supplies were at record levels. The sellers' market which both the American agriculture and steel industries had known was vanishing. Competition was developing from other countries. World price levels were declining. Foreign exchange controls, differential exchange rates, bilateral trade agreements, and other trade complexities impeded our export of agricultural products.[6]

On the other hand, vestiges of the Marshall Plan's financial mechanisms were still alive. In March 1954, the Commodity Credit Corporation (CCC) announced the sale of $20 million worth of wheat to the Spanish government for Spanish currency. That currency would be used by the Defense Department and other agencies to defray local construction and operating costs in Spain. Here was a concrete example of how the farm surplus could be exported to benefit the United States.

The Second World War, the Marshall Plan, and Garnett's original idea of using our agricultural surpluses as capital for market and economic development had unquestionably moved our policy away from the plow-it-under approach of the Depression. As the coalition around the idea of foreign agricultural development broadened, it attracted supporters like Douglas Dillon of the State Department and other members of the foreign-policy establishment.

The legislation moved through both the agriculture and foreign policy committees of both houses of Congress. Its proponents argued that the President should be empowered "to make agricultural surpluses available to any nation . . . friendly to the United States for such purposes as to maintain economic progress, to increase consumption, to encourage economic development, to promote new or expanded markets and trade, to promote defense strength, to purchase strategic materials, and pay United States obligations."[7] With purposes such as those, the legislation could not miss. It was a self-help program like the

Marshall Plan, except this time we were helping ourselves as we helped others.

What had started with the conservative Farm Bureau had been expanded to attract the liberals. Senator Hubert Humphrey of Minnesota sensed a good idea and joined the coalition. The Agricultural Trade Development and Assistance Act of 1954 was a prime example of the use of cooperation, compromise, and consensus in the development of legislation that could be translated into viable public policy. Like the Marshall Plan, the act was the result of a broad coalition of interests that came together over an extended period of time. Signed into law by President Eisenhower on July 10, 1954, it stated:

The Congress hereby declares it to be the policy of the United States to expand international trade; to develop and expand export markets for United States agricultural commodities; to use the abundant agricultural productivity of the United States to combat hunger and malnutrition and to encourage economic development in the developing countries . . . that are determined to improve their own agriculture production; and to promote in other ways the foreign policy of the United States.[8]

The crucial part of Public Law 480 was Title I, which provided for the sale of United States agricultural commodities to foreign governments for local currencies. As previously mentioned, those currencies would be used for such purposes as promoting local economic development and developing new foreign markets for American farm products; but they could also be used for meeting expenses of U.S. government agencies in foreign nations.[9]

The export expansion part of the act was implemented in three phases, as the Act was amended in 1959 and 1966. The first phase was the surplus phase. The second was the development phase. The third was the drive for market share.

THE SURPLUS PHASE, 1954–1959 To the surprise of few, the Farm Bureau's Garnett was appointed administrator of the FAS in January 1955. His mandate was to constructively export our farm surplus and develop cooperation between the industry and the government. Garnett was a logical choice. He had a farm background and government experience, and of course, he had participated in shaping the enabling legislation. The implementation of Public Law 480 would require imagination, the support of Congress, and the staunch backing of the senior people in the USDA. Garnett was an innovator and had both the necessary support around town and out in the farm groups.

His executive assistant was Ray Ioanes. Ioanes would move up to Deputy Administrator in 1957, and then run the Foreign Agricultural Service as its administrator from March 1962 until his retirement on September 1, 1973.

In 1955, the farm community was clearly not concerned about exports. Assistant Secretary of Agriculture Davis had made this point when he testified before the House Committee on Agriculture in the Spring of 1954:

We hear reports that some of our exports in the past have not lived up to grading standards. While Federal Appeal Inspection has been available to foreign buyers, some were not aware of this. United States soybeans faced real resistance in some countries until importers requested Federal Inspection which has resulted in an improvement in quality of shipments. Similar problems are currently being faced by United States wheat exporters in Europe because certain foreign millers have claimed that some shipments have contained more than permitted amounts of substandard grain.[10]

When the customer has to seek a quality product, the seller is obviously not market oriented. Gwynn Garnett therefore had to begin working with the farmers on basic fundamentals like the quality of the export product itself. He had two primary tasks: to export the surplus and to convince the farmers that exporting was in their interest.

Table 9-1 illustrates the results of these efforts begun in 1955. From a negative balance before Public Law 480 was passed in 1954, agricultural trade gradually increased through the surplus, development, and drive-for-market-share phases into the early seventies, when years of emphasis on farm exports paid large national returns in a much more competitive world. Table 9-1 illustrates the long and gradual shift from an agricultural trade deficit to a significant surplus.

In the period 1951 to 1955, total U.S. exports were 17.9 percent of total world exports. By 1978, our percentage of total world exports had dropped to 10.8 percent. The United States's share of agricultural exports, on the other hand, increased from an average of 12.3 percent of world agricultural exports in 1951 to 1955 to 15.5 percent in 1978. For agriculture, it was a tough, lengthy, but rewarding marketing effort.[11]

The surpluses did not go away very fast. As Table 9-1 suggests, there was a quick burst of agricultural exporting in 1956 and 1957, as the Foreign Agricultural Service began to function effectively and the funding provisions of Public Law 480 were implemented. There were no miracles. But the pioneers of the early program were as important to the building of agricultural marketing momentum as the scientists

Table 9-1 U.S. AGRICULTURAL AND MERCHANDISE
TRADE BALANCES *(In Billions of Dollars)*

| Year | Agricultural Trade | | | Merchandise Trade |
	Exports	Imports	Balance	Balance
1953	2.8	4.2	−1.4	1.4
1954	3.1	4.0	−.9	2.6
1955	3.2	4.0	−.8	2.9
1956	4.2	4.0	.2	4.8
1957	4.5	4.0	.5	6.3
1958	3.9	3.9	.0	3.5
1959	4.0	4.1	−.1	1.1
1960	4.8	3.8	1.0	4.9
1961	5.0	3.7	1.3	5.6
1962	5.0	3.9	1.1	4.5
1963	5.6	4.0	1.6	5.2
1964	6.3	4.1	2.2	6.8
1965	6.2	4.1	2.1	5.0
1966	6.9	4.5	2.4	3.8
1967	6.4	4.5	1.9	3.8
1968	6.3	5.0	1.3	.6
1969	6.0	5.0	1.0	.6
1970	7.3	5.8	1.5	2.6
1971	7.7	5.8	1.9	−2.3
1972	9.4	6.5	2.9	−6.4
1973	17.7	8.4	9.3	.9
1974	22.0	10.2	11.8	−5.3
1975	21.9	9.3	12.6	9.0
1976	23.0	11.0	12.0	−9.3
1977	23.6	13.4	10.2	−30.9
1978	29.4	14.8	14.6	−33.8
1979	32.0	16.2	15.8	−29.5

SOURCE: "Economic Report of the President, January 1980"; Department of Agriculture; Department of Commerce, Bureau of Economic Analysis.

at Bell Labs were to the present state of our expanding semiconductor business.

In the first year, shipments under Public Law 480 were valued at $384 million. Two years later, the value of Public Law 480 shipments was up dramatically to $1.5 billion.[12] While there was an emphasis on surplus shipments, the really significant developments took place in the structural initiatives and changes in farmers' attitudes. In addition to bringing many action-oriented professionals like Ray Ioanes into FAS, Garnett began to structure relationships with farm groups, primarily commodity-producing groups. He recognized that he had to arouse their interest in exports if Public Law 480 were to succeed.

He therefore set to work with the American Soybean Association (ASA), a not-for-profit association of soybean producers run by George Strayer in Hudson, Iowa. This organization was basically a one-man operation run by a farmer who had never been to Japan, a country that would develop into the major market for soybean exports as the FAS gathered strength. Using the local currencies from surplus sales to Japan, Garnett sent Strayer off to Tokyo with FAS sponsorship to begin one of the early cooperative marketing missions to Japan. In 1956, the American Soybean Association signed a cooperator's agreement with FAS and became one of the early producer groups to enter an exporting partnership with the federal government. In a short time, this association had come a long way from laissez-faire Farm Bureau attitudes—at least in the export part of agricultural policy.

The Japanese had long been users of soybeans, primarily for human consumption. They mixed ground soybeans with water to obtain tofu, a high-protein food. By fermenting whole cooked soybeans, they made miso, a nutritious product that was added to other foods. In one of the early market development studies done by the cooperating FAS and ASA, it was learned that the Japanese did not like tofu and miso when they were made from the green soybeans produced in America. Since these foods accounted for about one-half of all soybeans used in Japan, this information was of considerable importance to American soybean farmers. Responding to the demands of the Japanese market, the American soybean producers shifted to growing the preferable varieties. By the end of the surplus phase of the market development program in 1959, very few green soybeans were produced in the United States.[13]

The American Soybean Association also broadened the food market in Japan by employing a Japanese home economist, Yoshiko Kojima. Starting in 1956, she toured Japanese schools to show educational officials how an artificial hamburger could be made out of soybeans and used in the school lunch programs. Because she was persistent and well informed on her product, she sold them on the idea, and a substantial new market was opened in Japan, with the school system as the third cooperating party.

The ASA also hired Karl Sera, a Japanese animal nutritionist who had received his masters degree from Iowa State University. Knowing that the Japanese swineherders and poultry farmers typically used a feed ration of 31 different ingredients, Sera set up demonstration trials. In doing so, he used soybean meal and corn as a carbohydrate source and proved that this combination would produce a much greater weight gain in swine and poultry at lower cost than the 31-ingredient ration. This led to the development of another new market in Japan for soybeans—soybean meal.

By going directly to the user, the ASA had bypassed the Japanese cooperative farmer's organization that had a vested stake in selling the 31 different ingredients to the swineherders and poultry farmers. Not surprisingly, an explosion ensued, and powerful political pressure was applied to have the ASA thrown out of Japan. However, with the help of the U.S. agricultural attaché, the ASA worked with the farmers at the grass-roots level until a counterpolitical pressure developed. The issue eventually got resolved in favor of the swineherders and poultry farmers and, of course, the American soybean farmers.

These were two early examples of market plans developed by the ASA in conjunction with the FAS. In both cases, local currencies were used for market development. Furthermore, by working with third parties in Japan, the ASA-FAS partnership showed the Japanese how they could gain nutritional advantages on the one hand and economic advantages on the other hand through using soybeans and soybean meal.

The American soybean farmer—tough, intelligent, and practical in the use of self-initiative—was beginning to respond to the new export initiatives. The trading standards of quality, price, reliability, and service were beginning to be understood. The bold, imaginative steps called for by Assistant Secretary John Davis were beginning to unfold.

Between 1955 and 1959, exports of soybeans, soybean oil, and soybean meal doubled. The carryover of soybeans was down to 62 million bushels; in 1960 it was down to 23 million bushels; and by 1961 the soybean surplus was only a memory. A beginning had been made, and the soybean producers moved along with the rest of the farming industry into the development phase of the trade expansion program.

THE DEVELOPMENT PHASE, 1959–1966 By 1959, a number of studies of Public Law 480 had been made, and the job of food-for-peace administrator had been created at the White House level. Senator Humphrey summarized the studies for the Senate Committee on Foreign Relations:

- [The Law] was administered as surplus disposal with little attention to humanitarian and foreign-policy goals.

- Friends abroad felt that they were doing the United States a favor by taking surplus commodities.

- The program was not seen as a continuing one because authorizations were limited to one year.

- The machinery for administering the program was inadequate.[14]

In his 1959 farm message to Congress, President Eisenhower called for the use of American farm commodities to promote the well-being of friendly countries throughout the world. He announced that he was combining all farm-surplus export programs into one Food for Peace program. In extending Public Law 480 in 1959, Congress changed the title to the Food for Peace Act of 1959.

The 1959 legislation provided that at least 5 percent of the Title I sales proceeds in local currencies be made available for agricultural market development activities. In 1961, Congress further provided that 2 percent of the foreign currency in each sales agreement should be convertible into currencies of other countries for market development.

Of equal importance was the amendment to authorize long-term credit sales of agricultural commodities for dollars to friendly nations. Commodities could be delivered annually for periods of up to ten years, with payments to be made over a period of up to twenty years. [15]

The thrust of the 1959 amendments was to permit a transition into multiyear development programs and long-term supply contracts, with or without the use of the long-term dollar financing.

The outstanding example of a multiyear program was the four-year 1960 agreement with India, which provided for the shipment of 600 million bushels of wheat and 22 million bags of rice. This was a commitment to a better way of life for its people on the part of the Indian government; once the decision was made to increase the level of food on a sustained basis, there was no turning back. The use of the multiyear program ultimately led, by 1980, to India's being the only developing country in the world to have a grain reserve.

Under the leadership of Secretary of Agriculture, Orville Freeman, from 1961 the twin thrust of market and economic development prospered. Freeman gave both aspects of the program more personal attention than had any other Secretary. He believed that Public Law 480 "made a direct contribution to the achievement of the rising expectations of people in developing countries."[16] There was, he told the House Subcommittee on Foreign Agricultural Operations in 1964, an increasing direction of programs "along channels that promote economic growth and enhance the ability of those receiving assistance to provide for themselves. Commodities that otherwise would have been surplus in American stockpiles (were) being transformed into capital investments that (would) return rich dividends in the future."[17]

As we moved into the early sixties, Europe and Japan joined a group of other economically strong countries in the hard-currency block. With their strong currencies, this group became known as the developed countries. The direction of our agricultural export policy shifted toward increasing commercial sales for dollars to the developed countries, while at the same time using Public Law 480 for funding sales of agricultural commodities to the less developed countries. There was a subtle but gradual shift of emphasis away from surplus reduction toward market development in both hard- and soft-currency countries and economic development in the less developed countries.

In the developed countries of Western Europe, in Latin America, and in Japan, FAS worked with the cooperators and third-party entities in setting up and running trade fairs and in developing new marketing programs. These included a wide range of activities, such as product demonstrations, conferences, seminars, and exchange of technical and management personnel.[18] While the FAS and the cooperators continued to work with foreign governments on educational programs for health and improved nutrition, they also developed specific relationships with foreign industry cooperators such as retail food chains.

Discrete product-marketing programs were developed in jointly financed ventures with foreign processors and distributors. In this middle phase, relationships were opened up with foreign agricultural businesses and joint efforts were undertaken to help them prosper and penetrate their own consumer markets. If they did, the FAS reasoned, the markets for American agricultural commodities would be expanded.

One of the new methods of assisting foreign manufacturers in their product promotion was the introduction of utilization research. The Northern Utilization Research and Development Division of the Agricultural Research Service in Peoria, Illinois, for example, cooperated with the FAS, the ASA, and Japanese food processors. When the Japanese manufacturers reported that our soybeans did not have the right characteristics for the manufacture of tofu and miso, two Japanese scientists were brought over to work at the Peoria laboratory. An improved process using full fat grits was developed that resulted in uniform soaking and cooking and a 50 percent reduction in fermentation time. Thus, the cooperative program helped the Japanese manufacturers serve their own consumers better.[19]

Because the program was working, the FAS gained both increased stature and experience. An integral part of its market-development program was a continuous emphasis on liberalization of trade. As the program expanded, the FAS management, the attachés, and the cooperators became very knowledgeable about tariff and nontariff barriers to agricultural trade. They gave continual attention to detail in this complicated area, and little victories here and there kept the momentum going. The important consideration was that the FAS was working for the farmers. The partnership was growing stronger.[20]

At the same time, the concessional sales—those subsidized below the cost to the Commodity Credit Corporation—continued in the lesser-developed countries under Public Law 480.[21] The emphasis on economic development was expanded under the strong support of Secretary Freeman. As a result, Ioanes and the FAS moved the programs along much more effectively and rapidly. This strong support was continued by Earl Butz when he was Secretary in the early seventies.

Korea was an example of a very successful economic development program. When Freeman became Secretary, our agricultural trade with Korea was inconsequential. Today, it is over $1 billion. In support of the FAS, he fought a classic battle for economic development. Jamie Whitten, chairman of the House Agricultural Sub-Committee for Appropriations, questioned him closely about spending funds in Korea to develop agriculture that would ultimately compete with American exports. The congressman wanted to know why the Secretary wanted the United States to create its own competition.

The Secretary explained that we were not doing that. Instead, by helping Korea to expand its own economic development, the standard of living would be raised in that country. An increased standard of living meant consumption of a broader variety of agricultural products and processed foods. By helping Korea with its economic development, our development program would in the long run create a very good customer for our exports. With increased nutrition, there would be a corresponding increased demand for more proteins. That would mean more demand for meat and poultry, which would result in increased exports of American soybeans and corn. Economic development in Korea would expand exports of U.S. farm products. And that is exactly what happened.

From 1959 through 1966, as Table 9-1 indicates, our agricultural exports increased steadily from $4 billion to $6.9 billion. That was a 72 percent increase during the developmental phase of our program to increase agricultural exports. During that period, our balance of agricultural trade moved from a deficit of $1 billion to a surplus of $2.4 billion. That development phase put our agricultural trade balance decidedly into the black. In 1966, the $2.4 billion agricultural trade surplus represented fully 63 percent of our $3.8 billion merchandise trade surplus.

By the time the third phase of the export market development program approached, we had progressed a long way from the time when Japanese importers of our soybeans had to request a Federal Appeal Inspection in order to ensure a quality shipment of soybeans. As we moved into the phase of driving for market share, the FAS and the cooperators fully understood trade. In the classroom, in the extension services, in the experiment stations, and on the farm, they focused on the suitability of the export product. They were focusing on what the consumer wanted. They were focusing on price. And, of equal importance, they were emphasizing a three-way promotional effort between the FAS, the cooperators like the ASA, and the foreign third parties, like the soybean processors in Japan.

THE DRIVE FOR MARKET SHARE Increased productivity, of course, was one of the primary reasons for the success of the agricultural export program. From the passage of Public Law 480 in 1954 to the beginning of the drive for market share in 1966, farm output per hour of farm work increased 119 percent.[22]

It was a classic case of trade and productivity working to reinforce each other. As markets were penetrated, the defensive policies of the thirties were completely discarded, the program of rigidly high price supports was adjusted to world prices, and the farmers became export oriented. The good farm managers expanded their operations and plowed their earnings right back into the acquisition of more land, more efficient farm equipment, and more sophisticated use of fertilizers, pesticides, and higher-yielding strains of seeds.

From 1954 to 1966, crop production per acre increased 37 percent. Fueled by the expansion of trade, an increasing number of productive acres were taken out of the soil bank and returned to active farming. That, of course, increased the productivity, or output per hour, of the farmer and made the United States the low-cost producer; with an increased export effort leading to increased sales abroad, the cycle of increased trade and increased productivity continued to expand.

Farm output per hour of farm work doubled again from 1966 to 1979; exports of farm products increased from $6.9 billion to $32 billion during the same time.

The Public Law 480 financing program reached its peak in 1966 and 1967. With the nation embroiled in Vietnam, some of the urgency went out of the idea of food for peace and the idealism of helping other nations in their economic development. The deterioration of cooperation, compromise, and consensus in America damaged the economic development part of Public Law 480. At the same time, some of the largest nations who received aid from us had poor crop years; their needs placed strains on world supplies of farm commodities. This naturally nudged the program of export expansion toward the creation of additional commercial demand.[23]

Concurrent with this modest tightening of world supply were the 1966 amendments to the Food for Peace Act, which recognized the underlying market trends and shifted the emphasis of the program from surplus disposal to planned production for exports to meet world food needs. The act called for an orderly transition to sales exclusively for dollars by the end of 1971.[24]

It was therefore natural that the cooperator associations would begin to take an increasingly major role in the ongoing export program. In order to focus on the increasing role of the domestic producing cooperators in the third phase of our agricultural export development program, we will consider the growth of the American Soybean Association. As Table 9-2 indicates, the ASA had been very much the junior financial partner in the cooperator relationship. But that was about to change.

American Soybean Association In 1966, the ASA developed a pilot program—the check-off system—for raising operating funds from its members. The check-off system permitted the soybean farmer, at the first point of sale, to automatically transfer part of his profit to the ASA. As Table 9-2 indicates, the dollar contribution of the ASA to the cooperative export promotion effort between the FAS, the ASA, and foreign third parties did not begin to increase dramatically until 1970. The assumption of leadership by the producers during the third phase of the program was gradual.

At the same time, the major processing companies were having philosophical problems with the arrangement between the ASA and the Soybean Council. As the FAS and the ASA began to develop relationships with third-party processors in foreign nations, competing processing plants were built, particularly in Europe. The processors,

Table 9-2 SOYBEAN COOPERATOR EXPENDITURES
(In Thousands of Dollars)

Year	FAS Expenditures	ASA Expenditures	Soybean Council*	Third Party	Total
1956	5	–	–	–	5
1957	85	37	47	20	189
1958	167	20	164	45	396
1959	214	20	301	298	833
1960	377	23	363	348	1,111
1961	579	28	328	494	1,429
1962	973	32	355	665	2,025
1963	1,423	18	402	895	2,738
1964	1,471	23	291	800	2,585
1965	1,119	35	273	481	1,908
1966	825	53	263	488	1,629
1967	863	43	363	790	2,059
1968	857	49	223	624	1,753
1969	664	50	228	772	1,714
1970	600	120	0	497	1,217
1971	690	174	0	1,412	2,276
1972	846	379	0	2,040	3,265
1973	1,190	624	0	1,761	3,575
1974	1,178	1,055	0	2,353	4,586
1975	1,221	1,246	0	2,152	4,619
1976	1,266	1,124	0	2,588	4,978
1977	1,582	1,361	0	2,385	5,328
1978	1,980	1,645	0	3,266	6,891
1979	2,583	4,001	0	4,932	11,516

SOURCE: Foreign Agricultural Service, U.S. Department of Agriculture.

*The Soybean Council was a joint effort between the ASA and a group of processing companies.

who wanted to export by-products—soybean meal and oil—not the soybeans, finally terminated their participation in the program in 1969. Therefore, the ASA had to expand its small initial group of check-off states to include all of the soybean producing states.

The transition from the development phase to the drive for market share was not without its difficulties. The Vietnam war, of course, complicated the situation by shifting foreign policy away from assistance programs for economic development in less-developed countries. Between 1966 and 1970, as Table 9-2 illustrates, total cooperator expenditures in the soybean export program sputtered. Since the surplus problem which initially triggered the program was clearly solved, the FAS began to diminish its financial support. The basic message was: If you want continued government participation, you are going to have to mobilize your own resources. As Table 9-2 indicates, that was done. ASA cooperator expenditures increased dramatically from $120,000 dollars in 1970 to over $4 million at the end of the decade.

The basic idea of the Marshall Plan—cooperation mixed with self-initiative—was translated by Gwynn Garnett into a government-led shift in agricultural policy to expanding exports to solve our surplus problem, while at the same time harnessing our natural, human, and technological resources to continue that export expansion to enhance our own economic well-being. Government had provided the vision and had nurtured the program. Now that it was in the process of shifting from the development stage to the really expansive stage, it was time for the self-initiative of the private sector to play a fuller role. Jimmy Minyard, the knowledgeable and highly professional current head of the market development program, succinctly characterized the third phase: "Government should do what it does best; and the private sector should do what it does best. We facilitate; and they produce and sell."[25]

The real genius of the agricultural market development program throughout its three phases has been the carefully nurtured triangular relationship between the FAS, the American cooperators such as the ASA, and the foreign cooperators. As Table 9-2 indicates, this triangular relationship has been strengthened with increased financial participation by all three parties during the third phase of soybean export expansion. In practically every country, the ASA has been able to find a third party with a similar interest in expanding soybean trade directly or indirectly. As this relationship has matured over time, the marketing leadership now comes from the ASA, with full and careful planning participation on the part of the FAS.

In fact, the FAS leads the budgetary planning process, which is based on a long-term contract that is periodically updated; covers the worldwide activities of the ASA; and is funded for eighteen months to two years, depending upon the availability of funds. In July of each year, the ASA submits its annual market plan to the FAS. That plan is both structured and budgeted on a country-by-country basis, including estimates of third-party funding. This gives the FAS a good idea of the proposed activities and the goals the ASA is trying to accomplish. When the program is mutually agreed upon, it is up to the ASA to implement it.

The day-to-day supervisory aspects of program spending, particularly the use of government funds, are the responsibility of the agricultural attachés. But it is very clear that the attaché is less of a police officer and more of a partner and marketer. As a result, when the ASA is developing its marketing plan, its field representatives work very closely with the attachés. The attachés, in turn, review the plans for the country and send their comments to the FAS in Washington. The accomplishments of the attachés are still very clearly understood to be measured by our agricultural export success in the country in which the attaché is stationed. The attachés are an unusual combination of skilled diplomats and bottom-line-oriented marketers.

Table 9-3 shows the importance of soybeans in our agricultural trade expansion program. When the first phase of the program began in 1955, soybeans accounted for only 6 percent of our agricultural exports. They increased to 10 percent when the development phase began in 1959. As the overall program moved into the drive for market share in 1966, the soybean percentage of total agricultural exports increased to 16 percent. Despite the sputtering of cooperator expenditures as the marketing leadership changed to the ASA in the early years of the drive, soybean exports were 22 percent of total agricultural exports in 1972. This was the same year that the Soviet wheat crop and the Peruvian fishing failures completely tightened world supplies and sent a price shock wave throughout the international economic system.[26] By the end of the seventies, soybean exports accounted for fully 24 percent of our overall farm exports.

During the period of the three-phase implementation of Public Law 480, Japan had become our major soybean export market. We were doing in agriculture in general, and soybeans in particular, what the Japanese were doing in steel: expand trade with export subsidies in the early stages; increase productivity; then take the strength of that productivity and drive it right back into market expansion. Again and again. From a small $50 million soybean market in 1955, Japan became a $1 billion soybean market by the end of 1979. The United States's share of Japanese soybean imports was 93 percent, and the ASA was fighting to keep it there.

This great trade expansion accomplishment has been the result of the dedication and hard work of many individuals and entities within the agricultural community. Most important, of course, have been the American farmers themselves. The Foreign Agricultural Service and the American Soybean Association have acted as pathfinders in this expansion. The FAS has only 750 employees out of more than 81,000 in the Department of Agriculture. Of those, 127 employees serve on the front line of agricultural trade in 63 countries.[27] The ASA has only

Table 9-3 U.S. SOYBEAN AND AGRICULTURAL EXPORT DATA

Year	Total Agricultural Exports (in billions of dollars)	Total Soybean Exports (in billions of dollars)	Soybean Exports to Japan (in billions of dollars)	Total Soybean Cooperator Expenditures (in millions of dollars)
1955	3.2	.2	NA	NA
1956	4.2	.3	.05	.005
1957	4.5	.3	.06	.19
1958	3.9	.3	NA	.40
1959	4.0	.4	NA	.83
1960	4.8	.5	NA	1.11
1961	5.0	.5	NA	1.43
1962	5.0	.6	NA	2.03
1963	5.6	.7	NA	2.74
1964	6.3	.8	NA	2.59
1965	6.2	1.0	.16	1.91
1966	6.9	1.1	.21	1.63
1967	6.4	1.2	.18	2.06
1968	6.3	1.2	.22	1.75
1969	6.0	1.2	.20	1.71
1970	7.3	1.8	.31	1.22
1971	7.7	2.0	.31	2.28
1972	9.4	2.1	.38	3.27
1973	17.7	3.9	.78	3.58
1974	22.0	5.0	.76	4.59
1975	21.9	3.8	.66	4.62
1976	23.0	4.5	.70	4.98
1977	23.6	5.8	.99	5.33
1978	29.4	7.0	1.04	6.89
1979	32.0	7.9	1.08	11.52

SOURCE: U.S. Department of Agriculture, American Soybean Association, "Economic Report of the President, January 1980."

160 employees, but the combined cooperator expenditures of $11 million in 1979 covered 175 different projects in 76 countries of the world. Currently run by Dr. Kenneth Bader (who grew up on a farm in Ohio, was educated as an agronomist, and was a vice president of the University of Nebraska prior to taking over the management of ASA in 1976), the ASA has been a powerful force in the positive contribution to our trade balance.

In the Japanese section of its 1980 marketing plan, the ASA wrote, in part:

We are most pleased with the success of our market development effort over the past ten years. Because of our work, we enter the decade of the Eighties having established a solid base on which to continue the growth of this major market. It presently represents America's largest market for soybean exports and, of significant importance, what may be our largest potential market.[28]

As we define our objectives and outline our strategies to achieve them, we must be aware of the competition with which we will have to deal. Ranging from the significant marketing efforts of the Canola producers and the reemergence of China into the export food bean market to the growing emphasis of the Government of Japan to diversify its food supply, we are facing the potential for significant inroads into our major soybean export market. How successful we are in maintaining these markets will, to a great degree, depend on the willingness of those who provide our funds to insure the necessary support throughout the 1980s. Many of the strategies which we will propose will be of a multi-year nature, several establishing a base on which future strategies will be established. We must be prepared to either see them through or forget about beginning. The latter really does not represent an alternative because, to do so, will be to abandon the field to our competition.[29]

Having come in twenty-five years to a 93 percent market share in Japan, Bader of the American Soybean Association, Minyard of the Foreign Agricultural Service, and the soybean farmers of America have no intention of letting that happen.

LESSONS FOR AMERICAN BUSINESS AND LABOR As Orville Freeman, former Secretary of Agriculture and now President of Business International Corporation, would attest, the American farmer is as tough, as independent, and as much against government interference in his affairs as any business person in the United States. However, that same American farmer is now as much a seasoned believer in the concept of trade expansion for market share as is the management of Texas Instruments. That same American farmer is also a believer in the possibility of cooperating with government. Properly structured, with government facilitating and the farmers producing and selling with the assistance of their producer associations, that cooperative relationship has proven mutually rewarding to the American farmer and the American people.

There now seems to be a growing understanding among the representatives of labor, government, and business of the significance of trade and global market share to our economic well-being. Cooperation between these central participants in our country's economy may be on the horizon again.

If it is, then cooperation should be understood in its proper context. The role of government should be one of fostering self-initiative and promoting the public interest. The role of business and labor should be the application of self-initiative. In order to ensure that cooperative ventures succeed in an environment of mutual trust, the government participants—like the key people who have made the history of the FAS so successful—should be both very knowledgeable about the industry with which they work and prepared to use that knowledge to enhance the public good. Professionalism is an absolute requisite. In addition, any cooperative effort between government and industry should be oriented toward achieving specific objectives. All of these were the ingredients of both the Marshall Plan and the cooperative relationship between the FAS and the ASA. That is why the Marshall Plan was successful, and that is why the FAS market development program is a real-life prototype of how we should structure a national program for trade expansion.

America is not Japan. We are not a homogeneous, hierarchical society. While we have much to learn from the Japanese, we have also had our own experience in successful trade expansion and productivity increases. We should adapt the agricultural success story to American industry. Directly under the Secretary of Commerce and with the strong backing of the President, we should establish a tough and hard-hitting foreign-market development service. Our commercial attachés should report to the head of that new service and that foreign-market development service should be given all of the governmental responsibility for commercial trade.

We do not need a Ministry of International Trade and Industry. It is good for Japan, but it is not our form of cooperation, compromise, and consensus. What we do need is an action-oriented trade entity run by professionals who know both trade and specific industries. That new foreign-market development service should be charged with selecting a few pilot programs with cooperating industries that have both a desire to compete and the ability to become a world, low-cost producer. Working with invigorated trading companies enhanced by the legislation outlined in Chapter 4, this new service-oriented trading entity should set targets for export success. This would not involve subsidies for trade. Rather, its most important characteristic would be a tough, hardnosed facilitation of trade for the management and employees of a few industries that have the ability and the desire to compete internationally.

If there is the necessary national will to do so, the coal industry infrastructure—from the mine to the sea lanes—would be a good place to start. That would begin a very real and long-term program to work simultaneously on a recovery of strength on all sides of our triangle of trade, energy, and productivity.

10 THE CALL TO ACTION

America had both domestic and international economic strength at the end of World War II. By the mid-sixties, however, we were headed into the decline that has brought us to our present weakened economic condition.

THE PRESENT SITUATION Central to the development of our economic weakness was the decline of our post-World War II strength in the economic triangle of trade, energy, and productivity. Our first merchandise trade deficit came in 1971. Our domestic production of oil peaked in 1970, world supplies tightened irrevocably, and we lost control of our energy destiny to OPEC in the 1973–1974 embargo. The impact of that loss was underscored again with the price shocks in 1979. In 1967, productivity began to deteriorate seriously. The favorable trend of productivity increases, compared with inflation, was shattered by the policies of the mid-sixties. With 1967 as a base of 100, the productivity index of 1950 had been at 61 and the consumer price index at 72.1. From 1967 to 1979, the index of productivity increased from 100 to only 118.1, while the consumer price index rose from 100 to 217.4. That was it. We were a nation weakened in trade, energy, and productivity.

Policy Consequences of the Johnson-Nixon Years Two important consequences of the policies of the Johnson-Nixon decade have compounded our economic deterioration and weakened our position in trade, energy, and productivity. The first is the confusion and blurring of the functions of the different levels of the federal government. Government has become ineffective, and the American people know it. The second consequence is the increasingly short-term orientation of our economic policymakers, as they attempt demand-side .trade-offs between the twin evils of inflation and unemployment. In short, the stability of government and the stability of economic policy during the Truman-Eisenhower period of strength have deteriorated into instability and confusion.

The Functions of Government. The Great Society's purpose was to deal with social concerns and social problems. In the past fifteen years, the ideals of social concern—environmental protection, highway safety, occupational safety, and consumer protection—have been submitted to the litigious and adversarial regulatory process. We are now at the point at which the political leaders of states announce support for legislation which would give governors the power to overrule federal regulatory agencies. We are now at the point at which estimates of the annual cost of regulation—both social and economic—run over $100 billion, but no one really knows the true costs because there is no budgetary process by which to measure them. Within our federal system, regulation—the outgrowth of the social-concern legislation of the sixties—is working at functional cross-purposes, and its real economic effect is unmeasured.

At the same time, we have government programs resulting from social-problem legislation of the thirties, fifties, sixties, and the Great Society, which frequently have multiple goals and have become increasingly difficult to administer and evaluate. Compounding these problems of making government work effectively is the variety of funding procedures. Categorical grants for specific programs are intended to give coherent national direction with tight controls on the state and local recipients to ensure uniformity of result. Revenue sharing, on the other hand, delegates the spending decisions away from the federal government, which raises the funds from the taxpayer. In between are block grants with functional and philosophical elements of both categorical grants and revenue sharing. As a consequence, there is serious confusion about who spends the taxpayers' money and how it is spent. The social-problem legislation of the Great Society—after partial reorganization of the structure and funding process in the Nixon administration—has now lost the coherent positive effect it was intended to have on our society. The American people are confused as to just who at what level of government should be held accountable for effective delivery of government services and programs.

Short-Term Demand-Management Policy. Since 1966, our economic policy has become increasingly oriented towards the short term. The shift came to be symbolized by the elimination in 1966 of the investment tax credit, which had been part of President Kennedy's long-term economic program to get America moving again. Both the investment tax credit and accelerated depreciation allowances of 1954 were suspended in October 1966. They were restored in March 1967. The investment tax credit was again repealed in April 1969. Then it was reinstated in April 1971. In August 1971, wage and price controls were applied, to be phased out in four segments by 1974. We turned up the burner of investment in April and then put on the lid of controls in August.

In 1973 and 1974, credit was tightened, with the resulting credit crunch in the summer of 1974; that, in conjunction with the first oil-supply shock, led to the 1974–1975 recession, which was then the deepest since the Depression. That, in turn, led to the tax cut of 1975 and the enormous budget deficits of 1975 and 1976.

The second oil shock came in 1979. From a postrecession low of 5.8 percent in 1976, inflation went over 11 percent in 1979, and in October of that year the Federal Reserve Board tightened credit hard again. By the first quarter of 1980, the consumer price index advanced at an 18 percent annual rate. In mid-March, President Carter asked for discipline and sacrifice, and the Federal Reserve applied selective credit controls. In April, the Composite Index of Leading Indicators dropped by the greatest percentage ever. By late May, the Federal Reserve Board relaxed many of the controls it had placed on credit only a couple of months earlier, and the Secretary of the Treasury said it was "time now to go back to a more balanced approach . . . in which we seek to correct inflation by moderation and not by draconian measures."[1]

Whether it was fiscal or monetary policy, our economic policy was short term and demand oriented as we entered the eighties. It created an environment of such instability that making serious long-term plans was increasingly difficult for anyone in America.

Positive Trends for the Eighties Despite more than a decade of alternating short-term actions and reactions on the part of economic and political policy managers, there were some positive underlying trends as we moved into the eighties. The most important was in energy. The problem of world price differentials had been broken by President Carter with the legislated phased-in decontrol of natural gas in 1978 and phased-in decontrol of crude oil in April 1979. (The latter was, in turn, partially offset by the Crude Oil Windfall Profit Tax Act of 1980.) With energy conservation having become a watchword, there was a dramatic shift to Japanese fuel-efficient cars in particular and to numerous other consumer methods of saving energy. On the positive side of supply, the Energy Security Act was passed in the summer of 1980. It established the Synthetic Fuels Corporation with initial funding of $20 billion and a goal of synthetic fuels production of 500,000 barrels per day by 1987 and of at least 2 million barrels per day by 1992.

On the trade side of our economic triangle, there was the shift of the commercial attachés from the Department of State to the Department of Commerce. That, of course, was reminiscent of the beginning of our agricultural trade policy. There was also some bipartisan support for legislation that would completely exempt activities of export trading associations from antitrust liability and permit financial institutions to acquire equity participation in export trading companies for the financing of exports.

With the publication of *Accounting for Slower Economic Growth* by Edward F. Dension in 1979, our serious deterioration in productivity began to get widespread attention. There was a Presidential focus on the need to increase our national spending on research and development. There was bipartisan agreement that we should legislate further tax incentives to modernize our plant and equipment. There was discussion of how to increase savings on the part of the American people. Labor and management—even in the steel industry—were talking about more effective use of our human resources through cooperative self-initiated efforts on the plant floor. And, finally, in a Presidential election year when the two-and four-year political cycles coincided, there was a focus on the stability of the budget process and the absence of a tax cut. Decisions in these areas would wait until after the election, when a new four-year Presidential cycle would permit more informed discussion of their productivity impact and relieve the pressure for political expediency.

As Ronald Reagan came to the Presidency, America was poised at the juncture of a turn to revitalize the American economy, to resharpen our competitive edge. Muammar al-Qaddafi's June 11, 1973, nationalization of the Bunker Hunt assets in Libya had gone largely unnoticed in an America consumed by internal discord at that time. By contrast, the November 4, 1979, seizure of the American Embassy in Iran and the taking of the American hostages, the use of the American flag for carting away trash from the occupied American Embassy compound, and the imprecations of the Ayatollah Ruhollah Khomeini were both noticed and heard. The American people felt helpless and frustrated, and they began to recognize that our international frustrations were partly based upon our own economic decline. People began to recognize that our economy was seriously off track and that it would take a long time to get it back on track; but they also wanted revitalization to begin.

The Harvard and Washington Conferences At Harvard University on April 25 and 26, 1980, there was a conference on United States competitiveness. The theme was a question: "Can the United States remain competitive?" The conference was sponsored by the Subcommittee on International Trade of the Senate Finance Committee, the New York Stock Exchange, and Harvard University.

Chaired by Dean Henry Rosovsky of Harvard, New York Stock Exchange Chairman William M. Batten, and Connecticut Senator Abraham Ribicoff, the conference brought together senators and congressmen from both parties, business executives, academicians, and a few representatives of labor. Its purpose was to determine whether these different groups of Americans shared a common concern about the deterioration of America's economic position in the world.

There was a symbolic irony in both the location and the theme of the conference. At the same university thirty-three years before, General George Marshall had initiated the development of a major economic plan by offering cooperative assistance to all of Europe on behalf of the United States, then the strongest nation in the world. Now, in a nation seeking leadership, a group of leaders from the key segments of our society gathered to assess whether we could cooperate to help ourselves.

One important conclusion was that the participants did indeed share a concern about our weakened economic position, and an overwhelming majority of them issued a strong consensus statement of their concern. An extensive poll that was conducted for the benefit of the conference participants showed that a very large majority of the American people understood the severity of our economic weakness and were prepared to accept short-term financial sacrifices if these would restore economic stability and growth.[2]

The Harvard conference was followed by a bipartisan congressional economic conference on December 10, 1980, in the historic Senate Caucus Room in Washington. It was sponsored by the Joint Economic Committee, the Lyndon Baines Johnson School of Public Affairs, and the leaders of the Harvard conference. It, too, brought together a diverse group of Americans, including this time leaders of environmental and consumer groups and a much stronger representation of labor leaders. Lane Kirkland, president of the AFL-CIO was one of the keynote speakers. The purpose of the Washington conference, as articulated by another keynote speaker, Professor Barbara Jordan, was to bring leaders with different positions together to begin to get to know and understand each other so as to begin to form the coalition needed to get the economy and the country moving again.

A companion poll to the one done for the Harvard conference was undertaken for the Washington conference and produced similar conclusions about what the American people were thinking.

- 77 percent believed that our economy is seriously off on the wrong track.

- 61 percent believed that our economy is in a real crisis and not just going through minor problems.

- 60 percent of those who believed we are in a real crisis thought that it would last three to five years or more.

- 52 percent believed that we could suffer a depression like the one of the thirties over the next two or three years.

- 67 percent believed that it would take three to five years or more to solve our inflation and unemployment problems.

- 54 percent expected major changes in our economic policies in the next several years.

- 93 percent believed that nothing seemed to work and that Ronald Reagan should be given a chance to try his economic policies, even if they don't totally agree with them. Significantly, 94 percent of the union members polled took this position.

- 77 percent were willing to endure a higher rate of inflation for a year if it would mean a stronger economy in the long run.

- 83 percent were ready to accept almost any economic program that had a chance of reducing inflation, even if it made things difficult for a short period of time.

- 80 percent believed that there has been too little cooperation between government, business, and labor in trying to solve our economic problems.

- 83 percent believed that greater cooperation between government, business, and labor should be a top priority in the next five years. Significantly, 85 percent of union members polled held this view.[3]

As the Reagan administration was being formed, leaders of different parts of our society and certainly the American people in general understood that our economy is seriously weak (with a real chance to return to the horrible conditions of the thirties); that new policy directions are required; that policy changes will take a long time to work; and that the cooperation of government, business, and labor will be required to form policies that can be legislated and implemented. Conditions were ripe for new directions of change. There was a parallel in these conditions to those that made possible the Marshall Plan, the Employment Act, and the Hoover Commission.

POLICIES FOR A RETURN TO WORLD LEADERSHIP It took a long time for our economic strength to decline. And it will take a long time —certainly more than a single Presidental term or even two—to fully resharpen our competitive edge and regain world economic leadership. Therefore, it is imperative that we reassess our position and begin to revitalize America as soon as possible. In order to do so, we must undertake two fundamental tasks. One is to establish a Commission on More Effective Government. The other is to update the Employment Act to focus on the creation of productive jobs and not just jobs themselves. There are also some specific actions we can take simultaneously to strengthen—slowly but irrevocably—our triangle of trade, energy, and productivity.

The Commission on More Effective Government Just as the Hoover Commission needed bipartisan support and the prestige, backing, and cooperation of both Presidents Truman and Hoover, so also will the Commission on More Effective Government need similar support. President Reagan will be unable, by himself, to generate the kind of power that is necessary to achieve restructuring of government to the extent necessary for viability in the eighties. In order to lay the groundwork for a return to coherent government, we have to take a hard look at the relationships between the federal government and its programs, as well as all of the other state, county, and municipal programs that are related to it or depend upon it. For this reason, the effort must involve both political parties and the independents in the country if it is to lead to the re-creation of a governmental system that works.

This commission should be a high-level entity that includes members who are truly independent of party ties. Nine members of the commission should come from the executive branch, the House, and the Senate; an equal number of public members (not public servants) should be appointed to the commission, three each to be named by the

President, the Speaker of the House, and the Senate Majority Leader. This eighteen-person commission would thus involve people who have some expertise in one or another level of government as well as people who have a broad understanding of the United States and its history.

The mandate of the commission—ideally chaired by a former President—should be to design a more efficient and economical executive branch and straighten out the functions, the relationships, and the effectiveness of government at all levels. The objective should be to give the American people reassurance that the government is theirs and that it is responsive and accountable to them at all levels.

An Amended Employment Act The Employment Act should be updated to bring it into the current framework of supply limitations. There should be a new emphasis on job creation through maximum interrelated use of human resources, technological resources, natural resources, and capital resources. The President should be required to report annually on determinants of both aggregate supply and aggregate demand. The intent should be full employment through production of an increased supply of goods and services, achieved by pursuing long-term policies that will ensure demand for those goods and services. Of equal importance, economic policy should be refocused on long-term policies to ensure a return to policy stability that will enable business and labor to base their planning on more rational expectations in the future.

A balanced economic policy would naturally lead to new attitudes on the part of investors, management, and labor. Investors would again seek to make long-term investments in growth. Management would be encouraged—in fact, the market place would demand it—to plan, not just for the next quarter, but for long-range results. And that would mean a concentration on the quality of work life and productivity. It would mean a partnership with labor to improve the work place and the intelligent use of human resources.

Policies for a Strong Economic Triangle On the basis of these two high-level commitments—to make government more responsive to the people and to seek stable and real long-term economic growth with a balance between supply and demand—we should move simultaneously to strengthen trade, energy, and productivity. An excellent first step would be to mount a major effort in coal. This would include a productive modernization of the infrastructure from the mine to the sea lanes, and it would require the cooperative interaction of business, labor, and government all along the line. It would also include a major effort to export coal, using the example of our agriculture market development program as a blueprint. Government's role would be important in such an undertaking to ensure the balance of public interest.

The effort in coal should be the centerpiece of our program to regain economic strength, and it would involve more than coal exports alone. Just as the FAS and the ASA have developed trade marketing programs for soybean by-products, the coal-technology innovations sponsored by the Synthetic Fuels Corporation should be exportable. The same should be true of innovations in pollution-control equipment. Our coal program should be a coal-technology program. It could strike a blow at the heart of OPEC's greedy cartel-controlled price spiral. With a balanced supply of energy in the world, we could once again regain economic leadership. Having now recognized the importance of energy to noninflationary world economic growth, we could return once again to the very practical idealism of the Marshall Plan and Public Law 480. We could once again become a positive force for noninflationary economic development in energy-starved nations around the world.

We have accomplished this type of large-scale national program before with the Marshall Plan, the Eisenhower highway program, and the Kennedy space initiative. Government, representing the public interest, can be the facilitator that makes possible the private mobilization of our human, technological, natural, and capital resources. Our goal now should be to become a net exporter of energy within a decade.

The government's role should be to guarantee the success of the program with energy price supports that will underwrite the costs of safeguards for the environment and human safety. A further role would be to bring business and labor together and coordinate the transportation improvements in both rail and pipeline necessary to move the coal and the synthetic by-products from the mines to the ports rapidly and productively. Government should take the lead in helping to modernize our ports on the East, Gulf, and West Coasts in order to substantially increase an efficient export capacity. And government should cooperate with the exporters in helping them to secure profitable long-term contracts around the world.

If we increase our own energy productivity to the point where we can become a net exporter of energy, we will once again be in a position to steady the world price of energy and eliminate future inflationary shocks like those of 1973–1974 and 1979. And, if we succeed, we will begin again to become strong in the vital economic triangle of trade, energy, and productivity.

This program should be a contemporary Marshall Plan for America itself, but it will have ultimate implications for the entire world. It should be coordinated by the Office of the President. This program should be given President Reagan's personal attention and be a centerpiece of our domestic and international economic activity.

Trade   As part of a new national trade program, all aspects of commercial trade should be concentrated into a tough, hard-hitting, and results-oriented foreign-market development service reporting directly to the Secretary of Commerce. Export trade associations should be given antitrust exemption in foreign-market development efforts and the opportunity to enter joint ventures with financial institutions for financing purposes. The new foreign-market development service should seek out a few industries, like the machine-tool industry, in addition to coal, and help them establish viably financed trading associations and work toward a long-term export program, just as the Foreign Agricultural Service did with the American Soybean Association.

Energy.   In addition to a major national commitment to the coal program for a net energy export position within a decade, the activities of the Synthetic Fuels Corporation should be directed at the widest possible diversification of our sources of energy. We have learned a bitter lesson by our dependence on OPEC oil. In order to proceed as efficiently as possible, the legislation establishing the Energy Mobilization Board should be passed. There should be careful attention given to environmental safeguards and, where necessary, the cost of these should be built into the price of the fuel.

We are going to have to pay for progress. Our gasoline is half as expensive as in most European countries and Japan. We are still subsidizing consumption. Through a gasoline tax, we can encourage additional conservation and pay for the supply increases that are the key to regaining our economic strength without incurring budget deficits.

We must also continue to encourage the unexpected breakthrough with a continual serious commitment to research and development. While an immediate solution should not be anticipated, long-term basic research in solar energy and other presently untapped available sources should continue to be vigorously pursued. We cannot overemphasize the importance of research and development and the long-term need to diversify energy supply.

And, of course, we must continue to reduce demand for energy through programs for more fuel-efficient transportation, housing, and manufacturing plants and equipment.

Productivity. One of our primary objectives in productivity should be to work smarter. There should be a national emphasis on making better use of our human resources. This is not something that requires an actual government program. But government can heighten the awareness of the importance of this objective and create an environment that encourages business and labor to develop Quality of Work Life programs and improve upon them. Government can help to disseminate information on successful voluntary programs from one company and one industry to the next. Government can use its moral leadership to stress human-resource development. This emphasis on quality of work life and effective use of human resources—by asking the person who knows, how to do the job better—can be the cornerstone of a cooperative relationship between business and labor which government can facilitate.

In steel, we should experiment with a program for retraining and relocating workers, coupled with special tax incentives so that one or more major companies can build ultramodern steelworks in the heart of our domestic market. If the industry and labor are willing to cooperate in creating a much higher rate of efficiently automated fixed capital per worker, government should facilitate that cooperation by underwriting the cost of retraining and relocating workers and by providing the investment incentives for new construction. Government can make a fast transition to a highly automated steelworks possible. The American steel industry does not have the Ohgishima luxury of job attrition and relocation to jobs in other steel facilities. In the long run, such a program will be much cheaper than higher trigger prices, more inflation, and more decay in our steel industry.

Generally, we must introduce more well-thought-through tax incentives to modernize our plants and equipment. The more efficient the equipment, the more productive the worker.

While we are assisting business to modernize, we should give the American people a strong incentive to save and invest. Instead of tax cuts for consumption, we should have tax cuts for savings and investment. Thus, savings and investment would flow into a broad range of activities from new housing construction to investments in new small companies, which present the best job-creating possibilities.

We should legislate a new concept: an investment tax credit for individuals. This incentive to save would be a credit against the amount of income tax owed by the taxpayer. It would come right off the taxpayer's bill, provided it is put into a long-term savings-and-investment account with a financial institution. The investments in that account could be changed or rolled over, without any tax payment, as long as they remained in the account. Taxes would be paid only when funds above the original capital investment were taken out and spent on consumption. In order to achieve a degree of equity, the amount (including yearly individual investment tax credits and other capital contributions) allowed to be put into the savings-and-investment account by one taxpayer should be capped at $50,000.

There should also be a new emphasis on research and development by business, with a special investment tax credit and an immediate write-off for investment in R&D facilities. We must regain our lead in research and development.

In order to determine the real impact of both economic and social-concern regulation, we should introduce the regulatory budget discussed in Chapter 7. This regulatory budget should be a companion piece of legislation to the modernizing of our economic policy, with its new, balanced emphasis on analyzing the determinants of both supply and demand within a predictable long-term framework. There should be a careful annual reevaluation by both the Council of Economic Advisers and the Joint Economic Committee of the effectiveness of these programs on productivity.

The Council of Economic Advisers and the Joint Economic Committee are neither legislative nor policy-implementation entities. Together, however, they can and should be the overseers of coherent long-term economic policy. Until the Special Study on Economic Change of 1980, economic policy in this nation had not been seriously reviewed since the Employment Act was written in 1946. We have certainly learned, in the hardest way possible, that we must regularly look objectively at where we have been and where we are going economically. Twice—in 1979 and 1980—Senator Lloyd Bentsen of Texas, chairman of the JEC, produced unanimous bipartisan annual reports.

And, finally, we must foster an outward-looking market expansion approach on the part of business and labor. Expanded output is an important part of productivity and one that forces us to consider the trade side of the economic triangle. Indeed, all three sides of the triangle must be given equal and simultaneous attention.

THE COALITION AND THE LEGISLATIVE PROCESS As the Reagan administration unfolds, we fully recognize the political reality of a Republican President, a Republican-controlled Senate, and a Democratic-controlled House. The polls from the Harvard and Washington conferences clearly reflect the fact that Ronald Reagan was given a mandate by the American people to develop new initiatives—not quick fixes—to restore our domestic economy to health and our international position to one of strength. That will undoubtedly mean different (Republican) agendas and ideas from the ones we propose.

However, the current political reality ensures that the Reagan agenda will take the customary circuitous path through Congress. No legislation ever materializes exactly as it enters the legislative process, as our discussion of the legislative history of the Employment Act, the Sixteenth Amendment, and the Carter energy program illustrates.

Nevertheless, we believe three of our recommendations are essential to the economic revival of America. These three are a Commission on More Effective Government, an amended Employment Act, and a program for a net energy export position within a decade. These proposals are so essential that they should be treated in a bipartisan framework with a major effort by President Reagan to develop broad national coalitions for their support, legislative enactment, and implementation.

These three tasks represent the key goals for America in the next decade. They are not utopian. They are essential. If they are not achieved—and achieved relatively promptly—our society will not survive in anything like its present form. Unless they are accomplished, we face a real risk that we will lose our ability to peacefully and drastically change our governments on election days. We will lose our ability to maintain the orderly and peaceful processes whereby such dramatic changes in policy can be made. The American people clearly recognize our problems and yearn for solutions and the leadership to implement those solutions. If the right combination of programs and leadership is not put together to accomplish these goals, the American people may turn inward again, and that will ensure our ultimate failure.

We have seen the overriding importance of coalitions in the passage and implementation of several key pieces of policy-making legislation —the Marshall Plan, the Employment Act, the Eisenhower highway program, and agriculture's Public Law 480. Each of these was passed by a coalition much broader than an aggregation of like-minded special-interest groups within a political party at the executive and congressional levels. Not one of these important pieces of legislation was passed by a President alone, a Congress alone, or interest groups alone.

There was a significant difference in the breadth, depth, and conscious timing of the different coalitions which were formed to work for the adoption of these policies. The Marshall Plan coalition was the best designed of the four; it included the broadest cross section of our society.

As we have discussed, the failure of some of President Johnson's most cherished social programs resulted from a lack of coalition building. Those programs were not the result of the efforts of broad bipartisan coalitions that represented a majority of our society. They were therefore not acceptable to whichever political administration came to power in Washington. It is clear, then, that we must return to the bipartisan coalition process of the pre-Johnson era. While some may yearn for government by party, the major policy changes that are now required can only be achieved through the building of broad-based coalitions. This is the only way to restore confidence in government and to develop an economic policy satisfactory to a majority of the American people.

The development of new policies that command broad and general support will require real compromises among the various interest groups that make up the coalition. Only through compromise will the policies be acceptable to (though not necessarily preferred by) a substantial majority of Americans.

An economic policy is not going to work if it suits only business and labor, or labor and agriculture, or any other narrow combination of groups. It is doomed to failure if it ignores the perceived needs of one or more of the largest interest groups or the felt interest of a number of small but very active groups in this country. In order to develop effective long-term domestic economic policies, the basic interests of all of the people in our society must be taken into account. Those policies must be perceived by the overwhelming majority of Americans as being *reasonably fair to strong and weak groups alike.*

The principal policy leader should be the President, as was the case in the Marshall Plan. But inaction by the President should not impede the coalition-building process. The Marshall Plan is the most effective example of the coalition-building process with the President of the United States as the leader. But on occasions in the past (such as with Public Law 480) it was not the President who initiated the coalition building for a specific piece of important legislation, although he later supported and took some credit for it. A coalition in support of a major issue may start outside the formal political process, led by one or a few public-spirited citizens or interest-group leaders.

Today there is a new President and a new political alignment in Congress. The situation has many similarities to the political relationships that existed during both the Truman and Eisenhower administrations. President Reagan has his mandate and his programs. It may be a little while before the President and his supporters can move forward given the monumental size and difficulty of the task before them. But even that delay should not prevent the leaders of business, finance, labor, agriculture, and hundreds of other groups from moving ahead to create the beginnings of effective national coalitions.

The Coalition-Building Process There are nine steps in the co-alition-building process, including the legislative process (which we will treat separately). While we will analyze the steps in chronology, it is important to remember that in actual practice some of them may take place simultaneously.

The first is for the President to gather the leaders of Congress together to discuss an issue he thinks holds major importance to the national interest. Just as Harry Truman did on June 22, 1947, Ronald Reagan should arrange a small bipartisan meeting at the White House to discuss the three major tasks we have enumerated as being important to the future of this country.

As with the Marshall Plan, the second step is for the bipartisan meeting to recommend that a special high-level study committee be established to analyze the issue and establish a factual basis for subsequent discussion. The actual analysis, the third step, is important to achieving that "acceptable" end result and leads to the President's decision to propose a major policy. In the fourth step, he makes his initial determination of what his ideal goal is, what he really thinks should be done in the national interest. This step includes formation of solutions and a tentative but carefully developed proposal.

If the President decides to have a high-level, bipartisan citizen's study committee—which later can provide the nucleus of a national committee to lobby for support of the legislation—its members must be picked with infinite care. The chairperson must be a well-known and respected individual who is deeply if not publicly committed to the ideas and purposes which will be contained in the eventual legislation.

A cleverly fixed or rigged committee will not do. The analysis of the issue and the ultimate recommendations of the study committee must be genuine and must be perceived to be genuine. The people of the country and the media are often misled by phony study committees, but the people of the country very rarely are fooled on matters that fundamentally affect their own interests. And these bills will.

It can be weeks or even months before the study committee has completed what should be a thorough and well-publicized examination of the issue, and the President's tentative solutions may be changed, perhaps in a major way. This important step of analysis is more complex than it may seem. The complicated set of facts that underlie the issue have to be established and then perceived as valid by the many different interest groups who will eventually have to agree on what policy solutions will work and are desirable.

The President must be satisfied that the facts are there, that the recommendations can be sustained, and that the proposals will be accepted by a substantial majority of the people. He must be satisfied that he and his advisers have developed a policy good enough in an ideal sense to be politically viable to most of his supporters and to a wide range of regional, state, and local leaders. And it must be important enough to be worth a long and difficult fight for enactment, one that will require enormous effort on his part, on the part of his staff, and on the part of the leaders of the all-important coalition that he hopes to build.

The fifth step is for the President to decide what portion of his ideal goal *must* be attained if the program is to be truly effective and worth passing into law. On economic policy, for example, the President must decide how much of a shortfall on his inflation and unemployment goals can be tolerated and still leave a policy which works well enough over a ten-year life span to promote the various national interests. At the same time, the President must continue to engage the support of a majority of the people who ultimately will become part of the coalition, which is responsible for the enactment and implementation of the policy.

He knows his goal: passage through the United States House of Representatives and the United States Senate of a bill, which, in its final form, will almost surely not be the first policy choice of any major interest group, including possibly a majority in his own political party. If possible, however, his initial proposal should be fashioned to ensure the support of this group.

If he is satisfied that he is in a position to proceed, the sixth step is the President's decision on how to begin building the actual coalition. He must decide what groups he can bring in to support him and how he will do so.

The announcement of the now fully developed proposal is the seventh step. When announced, the proposal must have enough appeal to the general public to gain attention and sympathy. The atmosphere surrounding the announcement of the proposal needs to be friendly. This is where prior contacts with leaders and subleaders by the President and his representatives are important. The response to the proposal by the experts and the specialists in the policy area must be positive. The media decision makers must conclude that the issue is important and newsworthy. The leaders of Congress from the President's party must react with enthusiasm; and if not all-out enthusiasm, at least some tentative and modified support should be obtained from the other party. The leadership of the two parties in Congress, the committee and subcommittee chairmen, and ranking minority members of the committees to which the bill eventually will be referred must now join in a chorus of support: "all out," "modified," or "skeptical, but we'll give it a chance," as their strategy and tactics may dictate.

Outside of Washington, the governors, the mayors, the county executives, the public opinion leaders, the media personalities, the heads of chambers of commerce, the labor unions, the League of Women Voters, religious organizations, academic groups, and the leaders of as many interest groups as possible must be as positive as good organization and a "hard sell" through communication can make them.

This process evolves into the eighth step—public education to begin building the coalition itself. The tremendous effort just to begin the process properly cannot be overstated. Before it is over, there will have to be hundreds of thousands of contacts designed to influence the 100 senators and 435 representatives who with the President make our laws. Some of those contacts will be made by the President on a one-to-one basis with individual leaders of large interest groups. Many more will be made by the President with a collection of leaders of various groups and with the membership of specific groups. The President may bring the leaders of these groups together into a national committee for the support of the legislation.

The Cabinet and subcabinet will have to be mobilized and sent out on the campaign trail to generate support for this specific proposal. The congressional liaison team of the White House will have to contact and organize its opposite members in all the departments and agencies. The role of the public information people of the bureaus and the subdivisions of government will supplement this broad educational campaign. And this leads to the final step, which is the legislative process itself.

The Legislative Process   The legislative process consists of building a great coalition of people in support of a proposal which is in their general interest. When the proposal is drafted into an actual bill and introduced as legislation, the coalition-building process must be intensified. This requires more than mobilizing a party, more than Presidential power, more than governmentwide action, more than a combination of President, party, and Congress. It requires that the President lead the people of the United States to help him pass the legislation through Congress and implement a complicated policy that is acceptable to them and is in their collective interest.

In the process of moving through the incredible maze of the U.S. Congress, this particular piece of legislation will be affected by every other piece of legislation which is moving toward action in Congress. No matter how minor all these other bills may seem, the treatment of them by the administration will affect the attitude of their individual legislative sponsors, whose support and votes will be needed to move the President's bill through Congress. Even the most knowledgeable outside observers frequently fail to understand that the legislative process is a "seamless web" with progress of a bill intricately interwoven into the progress of other legislation.

It is conceivable that overwhelming public support, reinforced by overwhelming media support, will rush the bill like a hurricane through some or all of the legislative process, overcoming those persons and things which stand in its way. Public opinion can be incredibly powerful in its effect on Congress; but that rarely happens. When it does, it is usually only at one of the many key points in the legislation's progress. The Budget and Impoundment Control Act of 1974, for example, finally passed the House and Senate by near-unanimous votes. However, a key component of the bill, which made its passage possible in the House, survived on several occasions only by a narrow margin of two or three votes.

The legislative process is by no means an exact science. It is more of an art. It can be affected by external factors—assassinations, a volcanic eruption, an invasion, a domestic riot—that change the atmosphere in the country and in Congress in a few days.

In attempting to push his legislation through this maze, the President must remember that the legislative process must be fair to the bill's proponents and opponents alike. If the opponents cannot be convinced of the bill's virtues, they may have to be placated to some degree, particularly if they are key committee members or represent blocks of members. Compromise becomes an important element of the legislative process.

In the writing of the bill, the President, his advisors and staff, and the leaders of Congress and their colleagues must always be looking for the right goal. That goal is the *final enactment* of a bill which (despite all the changes, compromises, improvements, or damaging amendments that will surely take place) will still serve the purposes of the President's original proposal. It will have to satisfy the bottom-line position which he has previously decided upon.

Once the President's bill has been drafted and introduced to Congress, it begins to move through six steps to its final signature by the President.

1. Hearings before the appropriate committees of the House and Senate on the bill as introduced by the chairmen of the respective committees.

2. Mark-up (or rewriting) of the bill in the committees.

3. Scheduling of the bill by the majority party in the House and Senate for debate.

4. Passage of the bill in each house.

5. Reconciliation of the differences in the two bills by a committee of conference.

6. Passage of that identical reconciled bill in each house.

From the beginning to the end, constant effort by many people is absolutely necessary. There really are few hours and no days off for the leaders of the effort on behalf of the President.

The Participants in the Legislative Process   In the legislative process, the first participants are the President's people. The leader may be a Cabinet officer or an Assistant Secretary. From the White House or perhaps the Executive Office of the President come one or more additional policymaking individuals and the senior congressional liaison person who is an "operator" or a "mechanic." There will be a few more top-level people representing the Administration who come from outside the White House—perhaps six or eight in all. The top person may be in direct charge of passage of the bill, directly responsible to the President. On the other hand, this responsibility may be delegated to the head of congressional liaison or some other person especially chosen for the task.

Joining the President's people will be a similar small group from the Senate and the House. This may consist of the chairmen of the committees involved and perhaps a top strategist from the Steering and Policy Committee of the President's party. The President must know who is in charge of that group (which is sometimes hard to know) because he will have to deal with that group of congressional leaders when his bottom line on compromise becomes subject to the bottom line of the congressional leaders.

The President must also determine which are the other interest groups in Congress on whose support the final legislative decision may rest. He must know their leaders too because his bottom line of compromise may be subject to the bottom line of these diverse interest groups.

And now, the shape of the legislation passes into the blur of the legislative process, and the policy is much more questionable than it seemed when it was initially announced by the President.

Compromise and Building a Coalition Around the Legislation The hearings in the full committees or the subcommittees begin—perhaps in the House, the Senate, or both at the same time. The hearings may also involve more than one committee in one or both houses. Because of the bill's overriding importance, it might be possible to have joint hearings.

During this step, in the mark-up on the floor of both houses and in the conference, compromise takes place. It is necessary for a consensus bill to develop. The sophisticated and experienced observer will know that many types of interchanges take place, like those listed below. They are articulated perhaps in much more elegant and subtle language, or sometimes they are only signaled and understood. But in colloquial shorthand, some of the interchanges necessary for compromise to take place are these:

· I can't pass this bill without your help, so what does it take to get your support?

· I have the key votes you need. What are you going to give me?

· If you can't beat 'em, join 'em.

· If we don't hang together, we'll hang separately.

· If it ain't this, it ain't nothin'.

· (And most often) This is not fair to the poor (or to the taxpayer or to my ego). What are you going to do to correct this terrible mistake?

During this legislative process, the President and his allies in and out of Congress are patiently—sometimes quietly and sometimes with wide publicity—pursuing the never-ending task of building a coalition in the country, in the House, and in the Senate. They develop dozens of contacts, from top labor leaders to hundreds of local union presidents and on to thousands of union members. They have the help of dozens of corporate leaders through their channels to thousands of stockholders. They mobilize support through agriculture, small business, the educational system, the health-care system, insurance, public-interest groups, and others, until ideally the 220 million Americans in their homes, at their work, and on vacation have been contacted, persuaded, and convinced.

It takes this kind of effort to develop the compromise which leads to the coalition necessary to pass major policy initiatives or changes. There are exceptions, but those are almost always "bad" pieces of legislation, such as that which passes with "a whoop and a holler" when many members of Congress are at their worst—just before election time.

But most of the "good" bills which are of major importance to the general interest of the country do require this enormous effort. Certainly the three we propose as essential to the survival of our system of government and the viability of our society—reform of our government, a balanced economic policy, and a massive program to become a net energy exporter within a decade—will require such an effort.

The whole process may take six months, a year, two years, or the bill may be divided up and passed in pieces. At each step, the President and his people must pay constant and almost fanatic attention to detail of language, to attitudes of individual members of Congress, to outside groups, and to public opinion. There must be a constant, balanced effort to build support throughout the country and in Congress. There must be an infinitely patient willingness on the part of the President to listen, to compromise (but never too far), to adjust language, to modify substance, to flatter, to cajole, to co-opt, to educate, to lead. If these things are done, the bills will succeed.

The President must make hundreds of thousands of contacts with people to achieve support of his policy, even though that policy will not be finally and precisely detailed until the very last step in the legislative process, the final vote of both houses. These hundreds of thousands of contacts must be complemented by hundreds and perhaps thousands of judgments on large and small issues which may affect the final outcome of the effort.

The process of legislating a major policy in our democracy is perhaps the most intricate, least definable, and least predictable of any human activity. It is like attempting a master chess game in which the board is far larger and the squares and pieces are far more numerous. And in this master game the squares are erratically and unpredictably changing their colors and the pieces are changing their values. It is an act of faith to say that our system works.

It has worked in the past with the Marshall Plan. And once again the President has the opportunity to work for compromise on the part of the vast and different interests in our society. Around that compromise he can develop the great national coalition necessary to turn the future of this country in a positive direction.

In order to reform our government, develop a balanced economic policy, and undertake a challenging national program to become a net energy exporter within a decade, we must develop a new spirit of cooperation, compromise, and consensus in America. We must also develop a new bipartisan national coalition through which this new spirit can be translated into action. To do so will require the effort of President Reagan, dozens of national leaders, hundreds of regional leaders, thousands of local leaders, and millions of our citizens.

THE CALL TO ACTION Our problems are not insurmountable, but they are severe. There should be no mistake about the urgency of our need to rectify them. If our decline is not reversed, Qaddafi and Khomeini will be followed by other adversaries who will prey upon our economic weakness and our dependency on Mideast oil. The war between Iraq and Iran underscores the general and continued instability of the Persian Gulf and the Mediterranean.

As the aborted guerilla attack on the Grand Mosque in 1979 should grimly remind us, Saudi Arabia itself is not invulnerable to political change. And political change in Saudi Arabia would almost certainly be unfriendly to the interests of the United States. In the absence of forceful national action to regain our economic strength, we will continue to hang—dangling—on the end of a tenuous thread to Saudi Arabian oil. It is essential, therefore, to mobilize our national will and seek the necessary compromise that will make a national coalition for change possible.

There are positive signs of movement in the three areas important to our survival and revitalization. Senator William Roth of Delaware, the new Republican Chairman of the Senate Governmental Affairs Committee, has publicly stated that he will make the Commission on More Effective Government a legislative priority of his committee in this session of Congress. That is an important development which could be the beginning of strong bipartisan support in both houses of Congress.

In December 1980, the Joint Economic Committee published its "Special Study on Economic Change," which was initiated in 1977 by the late Senator Hubert Humphrey, Representative Richard Bolling of Missouri, and former Senator Jacob Javits of New York. The publication of this study was completed as a major bipartisan undertaking under the leadership of Senator Lloyd Bentsen and Representative Clarence Brown of Ohio. The conclusion of this bipartisan study was that future economic policy developments should be directed to the need for renewed economic growth.

This bipartisan report emphasized that these policies should bring about:

- A gradual reduction in the percentage of federal spending in relation to GNP to free more resources to the private sector, and a gradual reduction in the rate of growth of the money supply.

- More incentive to save, invest, conduct research, innovate, produce, develop human skills, participate in export business, and provide more secure sources of energy and materials.

- Better coordination of policies which remove unwarranted growth barriers and which reduce the chances of programs working at cross-purposes.[4]

This, too, is an important beginning. If the Reagan administration follows up on this initiative, America would begin the turn to a long-term balanced economic policy.

After the Venice Summit in June 1980, the free-world leaders declared: "Together we intend to double coal production and use by early 1990. We will encourage long-term commitments by coal producers and consumers."[5] That declaration spurred a great amount of interest and the study of the possibility of the development of coal export programs. Among the many important studies was the work of W. W. Rostow and the study *Energy and the Economy* by the Council of Energy Resources at the University of Texas, which was released at the December 1980 Washington conference.

That and other similar studies have fostered considerable interest among business, labor, and other groups in the idea of a net energy export program. It is an idea which lies waiting to be seized by a President with the vision of a Harry Truman and a George Marshall.

But our country, after all, belongs to its citizens. As the Washington conference poll clearly indicates, we all have a desire for action on these important issues. President Reagan and his advisors may have the vision to pick up these ideas and mold them into their own programs for action. We hope they do. But the desire for action and the desire to provide action may never merge into a legislative program that is enacted and then implemented. That requires the participation of the American people.

There are several initiatives of action that can be taken by interested citizens. The first is to write to President Reagan, to your senator, to your representative in Congress, to congressional leaders of both parties, to the editors of your newspaper, to television and radio stations. Tell them of your concern about these problems and your desire for action to find solutions.

Most Americans today belong to at least one public-interest or special-interest group. Yours may be a professional group, a labor group, a student group, a religious group, the League of Women Voters, the World Affairs Council, an agricultural organization, or an academic group. Organize a debate or a conference for your organization to hear speakers and to discuss how our nation can regain its competitive edge. There are plenty of knowledgeable speakers on the subject to help you think about the problems and debate the solutions.

And then you, and other Americans—all of us—can begin to consciously think about our differences. We will not be able to bring a new coherency to government, to develop a new balanced economic policy, and to mount a major national coal and coal-technology export program without the backing and participation of the American people. There are still some bitter differences between regions and interest groups in our country. If we do not begin to look for trade-offs and compromises, we may well render the Reagan Presidency impotent and turn in upon ourselves once again. It is important, therefore, that every American begin to recognize that others have honestly held differences. It is important that each of us begin to try to understand those differences, openly discuss them with each other, and begin to seek out compromises.

In the end, only a majority of Americans can forge the new coalition needed for our nation to regain its economic strength. If we do not, a decline into a severe depression is an ugly alternative. It is time that each of us hear the call to action. It is time that all of us begin to develop a new national coalition for America's future.

REFERENCES

CHAPTER 1

1. Frank L. Kluckhohn, "Marshall Pleads for European Unity," *The New York Times,* June 6, 1947, p. 1, col. 5; p. 2, col. 3. Richard Bissell, W. Averell Harriman, interviews, 1980.
2. Charles P. Kindleberger, Ford Professor of Economics Emeritus, M.I.T., interview, 1980.
3. *The New York Times,* p. 2, col. 4.
4. Ibid., cols. 5–6.
5. Ibid., col. 6.
6. William Manchester, *American Caesar,* Little, Brown, Boston, 1978, pp. 497 f.
7. Ibid., pp. 499 f.
8. Ibid., p. 507.
9. Dean Acheson, *Present at the Creation,* W. W. Norton, New York, 1969, pp. 548 f.

CHAPTER 2

The background information in this chapter is derived primarily from the following sources:

America's Highways: 1776–1976, U.S. Department of Transportation, U.S. Government Printing Office, Washington, D.C., 1976.

Stephen Kemp Bailey, *Congress Makes a Law,* Columbia University Press, New York, 1950.

W. Averell Harriman; Richard Bissell; Stephen Kemp Bailey, Francis Keppel Professor of Educational Policy and Administration, Harvard University; Robert Lenhart, former Vice President Administration and Secretary of Research and Policy Committee, CED; James H. Rowe, Jr., Esq., Corcoran, Youngman and Rowe; Don K. Price, Weatherhead Professor of Public Management, Harvard University; interviews, 1980.

Harry Bayard Price, *The Marshall Plan and Its Meaning,* Cornell University Press, Ithaca, N.Y., 1955.

1. John Gimbel, *The Origins of the Marshall Plan,* Stanford University Press, Stanford, Calif., 1976, p. 8.
2. Ibid.
3. W. Averell Harriman, interview, 1980.

4. Gimbel, *Origins of the Marshall Plan,* p. 250.
5. Ibid., pp. 5, 265.
6. "European Recovery and American Aid," President's Committee on Foreign Aid, U.S. Government Printing Office, Washington, D.C., November 7, 1947, pp. 3–11.
7. Dean Acheson, *Present at the Creation,* W. W. Norton, New York, 1969, p. 235.
8. "European Recovery and American Aid," pp. iv f.
9. Richard Bissell, interview, 1980.
10. "European Recovery and American Aid," p. 11.
11. Price, *The Marshall Plan,* p. 47.
12. Ibid., p. 63.
13. Harriman interview.
14. Price, *The Marshall Plan,* p. 94.
15. Joint Economic Committee research.
16. Bailey, *Congress Makes a Law,* p. 54.
17. Ibid., p. 224.
18. Ibid., pp. 165 f.
19. "Employment Act of 1946."
20. Ibid.
21. "United States Statutes at Large," vol. 61, part 1, report 344, U.S. Government Printing Office, Washington, D.C., June 24, 1947, p. 5.
22. Ronald C. Moe, *Executive Branch Reorganization: An Overview,* Congressional Research Service, Washington, D.C., November 18, 1977, p. 16.
23. Herbert Emmerich, *Federal Organization and Administrative Management,* The University of Alabama Press, University, 1971, p. 86.
24. James H. Rowe, Jr., interview, 1980.
25. Charles Aikin and Louis W. Koenig, "The Hoover Commission: A Symposium," *The American Political Science Review,* vol. 43, October 1949, p. 939.
26. U.S. Bureau of the Census, *The Statistical History of the United States,* Basic Books, New York, 1975, p. 716.
27. Ibid., p. 718.
28. *America's Highways,* p. 172.

CHAPTER 3

The background information in this chapter is derived primarily from the following sources:

Leslie H. Gelb with Richard K. Betts, *The Irony of Vietnam: The System Worked,* The Brookings Institution, Washington, D.C., 1979.

Doris Kearns, *Lyndon Johnson and the American Dream,* Harper & Row, New York, 1976.

W. W. Rostow, *The Diffusion of Power,* Macmillan, New York, 1972. Copyright © 1972 by W. W. Rostow.

1. Harry Bayard Price, *The Marshall Plan and Its Meaning,* Cornell University Press, Ithaca, N.Y., 1955, p. 175.
2. Joint Economic Committee Staff Report.
3. Associated Press, May 30, 1980.
4. Kearns, *Lyndon Johnson,* pp. 65 f.

5. *Congress and the Nation,* vol. II, "1965–1968," Congressional Quarterly Service, Washington, D.C., 1969, p. 664.
6. *Time,* June 2, 1980, p. 19.
7. Walter D. Heller, *New Dimensions of Political Economy,* Harvard University Press, Cambridge, Mass., 1966, p. 118.
8. Helen W. Dalrymple, *Significant Domestic Programs of the Johnson Administration, 1964–1967,* Congressional Research Service, Washington, D.C., 1968, p. 1.
9. Rostow, *The Diffusion of Power,* pp. 330 f.
10. Ibid.
11. Kearns, *Lyndon Johnson,* p. 290.
12. Bert H. Cooper, *Statistics on U.S. Participation in the Vietnam Conflict, with Addendum,* Congressional Research Service, Washington, D.C., August 15, 1972, p. 4.
13. "Federal Government Finances, January 1980," U.S. Government Printing Office, Washington, D.C., p. 12.
14. George F. Break, "Intergovernmental Fiscal Relations," in Joseph A. Pechman (ed.), *Setting National Priorities: Agenda for the 1980s,* The Brookings Institution, Washington, D.C., 1980, pp. 256 f.
15. Charles L. Schultze, "Sorting Out the Social Grants Programs: An Economist's Criteria," *Papers and Proceedings of the American Economic Association,* vol. 64, no. 2, May 1974, p. 181.
16. Break, "Fiscal Relations," pp. 261 f.
17. Alice M. Rivlin, "Social Programs in the United States: Some Lessons of the Last Decade," *The Canadian Business Review,* vol. 2, no. 1, Winter 1975, p. 13.
18. Break, "Fiscal Relations," p. 250.
19. Ibid., p. 255.
20. Chester L. Cooper, *The Lost Crusade: America in Vietnam,* Dodd, Mead, New York, 1970, pp. ix–xi, 28–39.
21. Gelb, *Irony of Vietnam,* p. 41.
22. *Time,* June 2, 1980, p. 19.
23. Kearns, *Lyndon Johnson,* pp. 267, 283.
24. Cooper, *U.S. Participation in Vietnam,* p. 3.
25. Gelb, *Irony of Vietnam,* p. 171.
26. Kearns, *Lyndon Johnson,* p. 349.
27. Cooper, *U.S. Participation in Vietnam,* p. 15.
28. Henry Kissinger, *White House Years,* Little, Brown, Boston, 1979, p. 194.
29. Cooper, *U.S. Participation in Vietnam,* p. 3.
30. Kissinger, *White House Years,* pp. 434, 505, 511.
31. Charles Lally, "Kent State Remembers Four Slain by Guardsmen," *The Hartford Courant,* May 4, 1980, p. 1, col. 1.
32. Kissinger, *White House Years,* pp. 512 f.
33. Ibid., p. 514.
34. Ibid., pp. 1406, 1446, 1472.
35. William Watts and Lloyd A. Free, *A Policy Perspective: America's Hopes and Fears —1976,* Potomac Associates, Washington, D.C., 1976, p. 2.
36. Theodore H. White, *Breach of Faith: The Fall of Richard Nixon,* Atheneum, New York, 1975, p. 7.
37. "Submission of Recorded Presidential Conversations to the Committee of the Judiciary of the House of Representatives by President Richard M. Nixon, April 30, 1974," U.S. Government Printing Office, Washington, D.C., 1974, pp. 172 f.
38. White, *Breach of Faith,* p. 7.
39. Ibid., p. 350.

CHAPTER 4

The background information in this chapter is derived primarily from the following sources:

Craufurd D. Goodwin (ed.), *Energy Policy in Perspective: Today's Problems, Yesterday's Solutions,* The Brookings Institution, Washington, D.C., 1981.

Mike Mansfield, U. S. Ambassador to Japan; William Sherman, Chargé d'Affaires, U. S. Embassy, Tokyo; William Piez, Director, Office of Economic Policy, Bureau of East Asian and Pacific Affairs, U. S. Department of State; Yoichi Miyagawa, Japanese Ministry of Finance; Tadakatsu Sano, Deputy Director, Iron and Steel Administration Division, Bureau of Basic Industries, MITI; Shigeru Ishihara, General Manager, Mitsui & Co., Ltd.; Shanae Yamado, Sr. Vice President, Mitsui & Co., U.S.A., Inc.; Yoshito Tokumitsu, Assistant General Manager, Ken Matsumoto, and Mr. Ninomiya, Nippon Kokan K.K.; Yasumasa Saito, General Secretary, Japanese Federation of Iron and Steelworkers Union; Joe T. Franklin, Statistical Director, and James A. Gray, President, National Machine Tool Builders Association; James A. D. Gier, President and CEO, and Clifford R. Meyer, Director, Cincinnati Milicron; Dario Scuka, Analyst in International Trade and Finance, Library of Congress; Craufurd D. Goodwin, Dean, Graduate School, Department of Economics, Duke University; Stuart Jackson, Correspondent, *Business Week*; Philip Jones, Director, Ohio Trade Office, Far East; Frank W. Luerssen, President, and Robert J. Darnall, General Manager, Inland Steel Co.; Kiyoshi Kawahito, Business and Economic Research Center, Middle Tennessee State University; interviews, 1980.

Burton I. Kaufman, "Mideast Multinational Oil, U.S. Foreign Policy, and Antitrust: the 1950s," *The Journal of American History,* vol. LXIII, no. 4, March 1977.

"Mitsui & Co., Ltd., Annual Report 1979."

Mitsui & Co., Ltd., descriptive pamphlet 7806.

Mitsui & Co., Ltd., 1978–1979 statistics on general trading firms, prepared by Information and Research Division.

"Multinational Oil Corporations and U.S. Foreign Policy," Subcommittee on Multinational Corporations, Senate Committee on Foreign Relations, U.S. Government Printing Office, Washington, D.C., January 2, 1975.

"Ohgishima: The Ultramodern Steelworks on the Sea," Nippon Kokan, Tokyo, 2–3 AAA, November 1979.

On-site visit to Ohgishima steelworks, Japan, 1980.

"The Steel Industry of Japan, 1979," The Japan Iron and Steel Foundation, Tokyo, 1980.

"United States–Japan Trade: Issues and Problems," Report by the Controller General of the United States, General Accounting Office, Washington, D.C., ID-79-53, September 21, 1979.

Yutaka Takeda, "J-K Activity (Autonomous Self-Management Activity): A Key to High Productivity at Nippon Steel Corporation," speech before Japan Society, Inc., May 9, 1980.

1. Robert Stobough and Daniel Yergin (eds.), *Energy Future,* Random House, New York, 1979, p. 22.
2. Dean Acheson, *Present at the Creation,* W. W. Norton, New York, 1969, p. 501.
3. Stobough, *Energy Future,* p. 22 f.
4. Kaufman, *Mideast Multinational Oil,* p. 953.
5. Dario Scuka, *OPEC: Organization of the Petroleum Exporting Countries, Background, Review, and Analysis,* Congressional Research Service, Washington, D.C., HD 9560, 74-189E, October 24, 1974, p. 5.

6. Stobough, *Energy Future,* p. 24.
7. Scuka, *OPEC,* p. 7.
8. Ibid., p. 8.
9. "Middle East Oil: A Chronology 1967–1974," Congressional Research Service, Washington, D.C., June 2, 1980, p. 1.
10. Henry Kissinger, *White House Years,* Little, Brown, Boston, 1979, pp. 434, 503 ff.
11. "Middle East Oil," p. 3.
12. Ibid., p. 4.
13. "Multinational Oil Corporations," p. 134.
14. "Middle East Oil," p. 5.
15. Kissinger, *White House Years,* p. 955–962.
16. "Middle East Oil," p. 7; "Multinational Oil Corporations," pp. 137, 143.
17. "Middle East Oil," p. 7.
18. "Multinational Oil Corporations," pp. 138 f.
19. Stobough, *Energy Future,* p. 27.
20. "U.S. Oil Companies and the Arab Oil Embargo: The International Allocation of Constricted Supplies," Subcommittee on Multinational Corporations, Senate Committee on Foreign Relations, U.S. Government Printing Office, Washington, D.C., January 27, 1975, p. 14.
21. "Middle East Oil," p. 8.
22. *The White House Transcripts,* Bantam Books, New York, 1974, p. 865.
23. "U.S. Oil Companies," pp. 14 f.
24. Ibid., p. 15.
25. *The White House Transcripts,* p. 866.
26. "U.S. Oil Companies," p. 1.
27. "Multinational Oil Corporations," p. 151.
28. "The Oil Crisis: In Perspective," *Daedalus,* vol. 104, no. 4, Fall 1975, p. 85.
29. "Summary of H.R. 3919," Joint Committee on Taxation, U.S. Government Printing Office, Washington, D.C., 58-344 O, JSC-7-80, February 28, 1980.
30. "Achievements of the Economic Summit," White House Press Release, June 30, 1980.
31. Edward F. Dennison, *Accounting for Slower Economic Growth,* The Brookings Institution, Washington, D.C., 1979, p. 4.
32. "Economic Report of the President, January 1980," U.S. Government Printing Office, Washington, D.C., p. 86.
33. Ibid., p. 88.
34. "Declaration on the 25th Anniversary of the Productivity Movement," Japan Productivity Center, March 18, 1980, p. 1.
35. "The United States Steel Industry and Its International Rivals: Trends and Factors Determining International Competitiveness," Staff Report of the Bureau of Economics to the Federal Trade Commission, November 1977, p. 377.
36. Ibid., p. 378.
37. Ibid., p. 385.

CHAPTER 5

The background information in this chapter is derived primarily from the following sources:

Ernest Braun and Stuart MacDonald, *Revolution in Miniature,* Cambridge University Press, Cambridge, England, 1978.

"Science Indicators 1978," Report of the National Science Board, National Science Foundation, U.S. Government Printing Office, Washington, D.C., 1979.

Mark Shepard, Jr., "The U.S. Corporation Within the Competitive Environment," Remarks to Harvard Conference by Chairman and Chief Executive Officer, Texas Instruments, Incorporated, April 25, 1980.

John E. Tilton, *International Diffusion of Technology*, The Brookings Institution, Washington, D.C., 1971.

Justin L. Bloom, Counsellor for Scientific and Technological Affairs, U.S. Embassy, Tokyo; Mark Shephard, Jr., Chairman and CEO, Texas Instuments, Incorporated; Thomas W. Folger, Vice President, Kidder, Peabody and Co.; Thomas J. Perkins, General Partner, Kleiner, Perkins, Caufield and Byers; interviews, 1980.

1. Samuel Eliot Morison, *The Oxford History of the American People*, vol. 3, "1869–1963," New American Library, New York, 1972, p. 292.
2. "Stimulating Technological Progress," Committee for Economic Development, New York, January 1980, pp. 13 f.
3. Justin Bloom, interview, 1980.
4. "Texas Instruments, Incorporated, 1979 Annual Report."

CHAPTER 6

The background information in this chapter is derived primarily from the following sources:

Ray G. Blakey and Gladys C. Blakey, *The Federal Income Tax*, Longmans, Green, London, 1940.

Congress and the Nation, vol. I, "1945–1964," Congressional Quarterly Service, Washington, D.C., 1965.

Congress and the Nation, vol. II, "1965–1968," Congressional Quarterly Service, Washington, D.C., 1969.

Stanley Pratt, Publisher, *The Venture Capital Journal*; Don V. Harris, Covington and Burling; Bernard M. Shapiro, former Chief of Staff, Joint Committee on Taxation; William F. Ballhaus, President, Beckman Instruments, Inc.; Thomas J. Perkins, General Partner, Kleiner, Perkins, Caufield and Byers; Thomas W. Folger, Vice President, Kidder, Peabody and Co.; interviews, 1980.

1. Champ Clark, *My Quarter Century of American Politics*, vol. I, Harper, New York, 1920, p. 440.
2. Blakey, *Federal Income Tax*, p. 64.
3. Ibid., p. 65.
4. Samuel Eliot Morison, *The Oxford History of the American People*, vol. 3, "1869–1963," New American Library, New York, 1972, p. 162.
5. Ibid., p. 165.
6. Blakey, *Federal Income Tax*, p. 366.
7. Ibid., p. 402.
8. "Tax Policy and Capital Formation," Joint Committee on Taxation, U.S. Government Printing Office, Washington, D.C., April 4, 1977, p. 17.
9. Blakey, *Federal Income Tax*, p. 440.
10. *Congress and the Nation*, "1945–1964," pp. 407 f.
11. Ibid., p. 408.

12. Ibid., p. 419.
13. Joseph A. Pechman, *Federal Tax Policy,* The Brookings Institution, Washington, D.C., 1977, p. 302.
14. "Economic Report of the President, January 1980," U.S. Government Printing Office, Washington, D.C., p. 263.
15. *Congress and the Nation,* "1945–1964," p. 427.
16. Ibid., p. 434.
17. Gary Fromm, "Introduction," *Studies of Government Financing: Tax Incentives and Capital Spending,* The Brookings Institution, Washington, D.C., 1971, p. 2.
18. Carl J. Palash, "Tax Policy: Its Impact on Investment Incentives," *FRBNY Quarterly Review,* vol. 3, Summer 1978, p. 30.
19. "Tax Policy and Capital Formation," pp. 43 f.
20. "Siltec Corporation 1979 Annual Report."

CHAPTER 7

The background information in this chapter is derived primarily from the following sources:

Paul W. MacAvoy, *The Regulated Industries and the Economy*, W.W. Norton, New York, 1979.

"Special Study on Economic Change," Joint Economic Committee, U.S. Government Printing Office, Washington, D.C., December, 1980.

Robert W. Crandall, Senior Fellow, The Brookings Institution; Christopher C. DeMuth, Lecturer in Public Policy and Director, Harvard Faculty Project on Regulation; George C. Eads, former member, President Carter's Council of Economic Advisors; Simon Lazarus, III, former Associate Director, President Carter's domestic policy staff; interviews, 1980.

1. Wallace Turner, "Business and Political Leaders in Utah Backing U.S. Steel in Fight with EPA," *The New York Times,* August 19, 1980, p. A12, col. 1.
2. Steve Grant, "State May Be Joined in Expected Anti-Pollution Suit," *The Hartford Courant,* August 21, 1980, p. 19, col. 1; "Excess Smoke Prompts Utility to Suspend Use of High Sulphur Oil," *The Hartford Courant,* August 30, 1980, p. 3, col. 1.
3. Lester C. Thurow, *The Zero-Sum Society,* Basic Books, New York, 1980, p. 13.
4. "Government Regulation: Achieving Social and Economic Balance," Joint Economic Committee Staff Study, U.S. Government Printing Office, Washington, D.C., June 1980, p. iii.
5. "Regulatory Reform: President Carter's Program," White House Paper, August 1980, p. 1.
6. "Special Study on Economic Change," vol. 5—Government Regulation, Joint Economic Committee, U.S. Government Printing Office, Washington, D.C., December 8, 1980, p. 2.
7. Ibid., p. 3.
8. Julius W. Allen, *Costs and Benefits of Federal Regulation: An Overview,* Congressional Research Service, U.S. Government Printing Office, Washington, D.C., Report 78-152 E, July 19, 1978, p. 75.
9. Ibid., p. 76.
10. "Regulatory Reform," pp. 4 f.
11. "Special Study on Economic Change," p. 176.

12. Ronald J. Penoyer, *Directory of Federal Regulatory Agencies,* 2d ed., Center for the Study of American Business, St. Louis, 1980, p. 27.
13. Ibid., p. 74.
14. Ibid., p. 68.
15. Ibid., pp. 62, 67.
16. Ibid., p. 23.
17. "Government Regulation," p. ii; Murray L. Weidenbaum, "The High Cost of Government Regulation," *Challenge,* vol. 22, November–December 1979, p. 35.
18. Julius W. Allen, *Estimating the Costs of Federal Regulation: Review of Problems and Accomplishments to Date,* Congressional Research Service, Washington, D.C., Report 78-205 E, pp. 26 ff.
19. Ibid., pp. 29, 31.
20. "Cost of Government Regulation Study for The Business Roundtable," Executive Summary, Arthur Andersen & Co., March 1979, pp. i f.
21. Ibid., p. iii.
22. Christopher C. DeMuth, "The Regulatory Budget," *AEI Journal on Government and Society: Regulation,* vol. 4, March/April 1980, p. 38.
23. "Government Regulation," pp. ii f.
24. *Costs and Benefits of Federal Regulation,* pp. 43–48.
25. "Government Regulation," p. 11.
26. "Regulatory Reform," p. 3.
27. Douglas M. Costle, Environmental Protection Agency, interview, 1980.
28. MacAvoy, p. 28.
29. Ibid., p. 29.
30. Robert W. Crandall, unpublished paper for government regulation conference, December 7, 1978, p. 14.
31. Ibid., p. 15.
32. "Government Regulation," p. 12.
33. "Regulatory Reform," p. 2.
34. Ibid., pp. 6–10.
35. Christopher C. DeMuth, "The White House Review Programs," *AEI Journal on Government and Society: Regulation,* vol. 4, January/February 1980, p. 20.
36. "The 1980 Joint Economic Report," Joint Economic Committee, U.S. Government Printing Office, Washington, D.C., Report 96–618, March 4, 1980, p. 42.
37. "Regulatory Cost Accounting Act of 1980."
38. "Government Regulation," pp. 13, 21 f.

CHAPTER 8

The background information in this chapter is derived primarily from the following sources:

Robert W. Crandall, *The United States Steel Industry in Recurrent Crisis: Policy Options in a Competitive World,* The Brookings Institution, Washington, 1981.

Kiyoshi Kawahito, "Anatomy of Conflicts in the U.S.-Japan Steel Trade," Middle Tennessee State University, Business and Economic Research Center, Murfreesboro, Conference Paper 60, April 1980.

Reprinted by permission of Westview Press from *The American Steel Industry: Problems, Challenges, Perspectives* by Luc Kiers. Copyright © 1980 by Westview Press, Boulder, Colorado.

Robert W. Crandall, Senior Fellow, The Brookings Institution; Robert A. Hageman, Vice President, Kidder, Peabody and Co.; Frank W. Luerssen, President, and Robert J.

Darnall, General Manager, Inland Steel Co.; Yoshito Tokumitsu, Assistant General Manager, Nippon Kokan K.K.; Sam Camens, Assistant to the President, United Mine Workers; interviews, 1980, 1981.

1. "Public Papers of the President of the United States, John F. Kennedy, 1962," U.S. Government Printing Office, Washington, D.C., 1963, pp. 315 f.
2. Kiers, *American Steel Industry*, p. 157.
3. Ibid., p. 158.
4. "Steel at the Crossroads: The American Steel Industry in the 1980s," American Iron and Steel Institute, Washington, D.C., January 1980, p. 1.
5. Ibid.
6. "The World Battle for Steel," *Business Week*, June 4, 1966, p. 60.
7. "What the Crisis in Steel Means," *U.S. News and World Report*, April 23, 1962, p. 92.
8. "The Steel Industry Negotiates to Survive," *Business Week*, Special Report, May 15, 1971, p. 2.
9. Kiers, *American Steel Industry*, p. 18.
10. "Bargainers Press for Steel Peace," *Business Week*, July 27, 1968, p. 102.
11. "Steel Now—Bill Still to Come," *Business Week*, January 9, 1960, pp. 25–28.
12. Ibid., p. 26.
13. "What the Crisis in Steel Means," p. 37.
14. Ibid., p. 38.
15. "Bargainers Press for Steel Peace," p. 102.
16. Ibid., pp. 103 f.
17. Hans Mueller and Kiyoshi Kawahito, "Steel Industry Economics," International Public Relations Co., Ltd., Japan Steel Information Center, New York, January 1978, p. 2.
18. "The Steel Industry Negotiates to Survive," p. 2.
19. Mueller, and Kawahito, "Steel Industry Economics," p. 2.
20. Kiyoshi Kawahito, "The Recent American-Japanese Discord Over the Steel Dumping Issue," Middle Tennessee State University, Murfreesboro, Conference Paper 39, January 1979, p. 7.
21. Kiers, *American Steel Industry*, p. 107.
22. Ibid., p. 61.
23. "Big Steel's Liquidation," p. 78. Reprinted from the September 17, 1979 issue of *Business Week* by special permission. © 1979 by McGraw-Hill, Inc.
24. Agis Salpukas, "U.S. Steel: Shrinking to Survive," *The New York Times*, July 20, 1980, p. F3, col. 1; Douglas R. Sease, "Nippon Steel Receives U.S. Steel Contract . . . ," *The Wall Street Journal*, February 14, 1980, p. 4, col. 1.
25. "The Steel Trigger Price Mechanism (TPM)," *United States Department of Commerce News*, International Trade Administration, Washington, D.C., p. 2.
26. Philip Shabecoff, "Steel Negotiators Reach Tentative Pact on Wages," *The New York Times*, April 15, 1980, p. 16, col. 3.
27. Ibid.
28. Sam Camens, Assistant to the President, United Mine Workers, interview, 1981.

CHAPTER 9

The background information in this chapter is derived primarily from the following sources:

Kenneth Bader, American Soybean Association; Orville Freeman, Business International; Gywnn Garnett, American Farm Bureau Federation; Raymond A. Ioanes, Foreign Agricultural Service; Jimmy Minyard and Fred W. Traeger, U.S. Department of Agriculture; interviews, 1980.

Wayne D. Rasmussen and Gladys L. Baker, "Price-Support and Adjustment Programs from 1933 Through 1978: A Short History," U.S. Government Printing Office, Washington, D.C., U.S. Department of Agriculture Information Bulletin 424, February 1979.

Representative Thomas S. Foley, State of Washington; Gene Moss, Staff Analyst, Committee on Agriculture, House Agriculture Committee; interviews, 1980.

1. Rasmussen and Baker, "Price-Support and Adjustment Programs," p. 8.
2. John H. Davis, testimony given before the House Committee on Agriculture by the Assistant Secretary of Agriculture, April 27, 1954, p. 9.
3. Ibid., pp. 10 f.
4. "Foreign Market Development," Foreign Agricultural Service, U.S. Department of Agriculture, August 1977, p. 11.
5. Davis, testimony, p. 7.
6. Ibid., pp. 2 f.
7. Ibid., p. 28.
8. "Food for Peace, 1954–1978—Major Changes in Legislation," Congressional Research Service, U.S. Government Printing Office, Washington, D.C., April 26, 1979, p. 31.
9. "American Foreign Food Assistance," Senate Committee on Agriculture and Forestry, U.S. Government Printing Office, Washington, D.C., August 13, 1976, pp. 2, 5.
10. Davis, testimony, p. 6.
11. "Agriculture Food Policy," U.S. Department of Agriculture, U.S. Government Printing Office, Washington, D.C., 1980, p. 2.
12. "Food for Peace," p. 4.
13. Raymond A. Ioanes, "Foreign Markets for Farm Products," remarks before North Iowa Soybean Processing Association, Mason City, December 15, 1980, p. 11.
14. "Food for Peace," p. 4.
15. "American Foreign Food Assistance," pp. 6 f.
16. "Food for Peace," p. 7.
17. Ibid.
18. Ioanes, "Foreign Markets," pp. 3–9.
19. Raymond A. Ioanes, "A Review of Policies to Expand the Demand for Farm Products," paper presented at Second Annual Farm Policy Review Conference, North Carolina State College, Raleigh, November 29, 1961, pp. 11 f.
20. Raymond A. Ioanes, "Distribution of World Commodities," statement before Tenth Kentucky World Trade Conference, Louisville, November 9, 1959, pp. 7 f.
21. Ibid., p. 9.
22. "Economic Report of the President, January 1980," U.S. Government Printing Office, Washington, D.C., p. 310.
23. Raymond A. Ioanes, "Discussion of the Public Law 480 Program," paper for U.S. Department of Agriculture, Washington, D.C., 1970, p. 2.
24. "American Foreign Food Assistance," p. 8; "Food for Peace," p. 9.
25. Jimmy Minyard, interview, 1980.
26. Raymond A. Ioanes, "Outlook for U.S. Trade in Farm Products," talk before National Agricultural Outlook Conference, Washington, D.C., February 20, 1973, pp. 1–4.

27. "Foreign Market Development," p. 10.
28. "ASA Marketing Plan for the 80s," American Soybean Association, Washington, D.C., 1980, p. 2.
29. Ibid., p. 5.

CHAPTER 10

1. Steven Rattner, "Controls on Credit Cut Back Sharply by Federal Reserve," *The New York Times,* May 23, 1980, p. D8, col. 4.
2. "America's Economic Challenge—Public Expectations," Garth-Friedman-Morris-Inc., poll for the New York Stock Exchange, 1980.
3. Ibid.
4. "Special Study on Economic Change," Joint Economic Committee, (a ten-volume series consisting of: Human Resources and Demographics, Energy and Materials, Research and Innovation, Stagflation, Government Regulation, Federal Finance, State and Local Government, Social Security and Pensions, The International Economy, and Productivity), U.S. Government Printing Office, Washington, D.C., December, 1980.
5. "Text of the Declaration of the Venice Economic Summit Meeting," *The New York Times,* June 24, 1980, p. A7, col. 2.

INDEX